Conversations in Tehran

CONVERSATIONS IN TEHRAN

Jean-Daniel Lafond & Fred A. Reed

Talonbooks

Vancouver

Talonbooks
P.O. Box 2076, Vancouver, British Columbia, Canada V6B 3S3
www.talonbooks.com

Typeset in Adobe Caslon and printed and bound in Canada.
Printed on 100% post-consumer recycled paper.

First Printing: 2006

The publisher gratefully acknowledges the financial support of the Canada Council
for the Arts; the Government of Canada through the Book Publishing Industry
Development Program; and the Province of British Columbia through the British
Columbia Arts Council for our publishing activities.

Library and Archives Canada Cataloguing in Publication

Lafond, Jean-Daniel, 1944–
    Conversations in Tehran / Jean-Daniel Lafond & Fred A. Reed.

Includes bibliographical references.
ISBN-13: 978-0-88922-550-3
ISBN-10: 0-88922-550-8

    1. Iran—Politics and government—1997–. 2. Iran—History—1997–.
I. Reed, Fred A., 1939– II. Title.

DS318.9.L34 2006   955.05'44   C2006-904156-3

Contents

He who clings to darkness
fears the wave,
and the mighty whirlpool's roar.

He who would join us on our journey,
must dare to leave
the reassuring sands of shore.

—Ha'afez, *The Divan* (1368)

Preface

Fear of the Wave

HE WHO CLINGS *to darkness fears the wave, and the mighty whirlpool's roar.*
These words from Iran's greatest poet, Ha'afez, end my film *Salam Iran,*
a Persian Letter,[1] as the setting sun turns the sky of Shiraz ablaze.

Seated on a hillside above the city, my thoughts turned to the journey
that had led me from Montreal to the heart of today's Iran. It had been
my second extended visit to the Islamic Republic. Finally, the month of
filming that had brought me and my crew from Tehran to Shiraz by way
of Arak and Khorramabad was over. It had taken me four years to lay the
groundwork for the film. But in truth, my first travels to Iran had begun
fifteen years earlier, without ever leaving Montreal. Those first
encounters I owed to Fred Reed, to his friendship, to his passion for the
Orient, and to his singular attachment to Islam and to Persian culture.

The Iranian Revolution of 1979 and its political program, founded
upon a combination of constitutional principles and religious morality,
had powerfully affected me. The Islamic Republic had portrayed itself
to the Muslim countries of the then–third world as an exemplar. It had
not taken long for the scales to fall from my eyes. I began to realize how
difficult it would be to reshape Iranian society based on a program that
relied on the charisma of a single man, Ayatollah Ruhollah Khomeini,
on the submission of the people to him, and on the cult of martyrdom.
From 1989 onward, it seemed as though Khomeini's successors had
hastened the country's downward spiral into the dark realm of violence
and oppression, crushing freedoms as they went. What could only be
described as a caste had grown up around President Ali Akbar Hashemi
Rafsanjani. As this caste concentrated power in its hands, the decline
and ultimately the breakdown of the revolution seemed inevitable. But

---

1. Jean-Daniel Lafond, *Salam Iran, une lettre persane* (Québec: InformAction and Télé-
Québec, 2002), digital video; research by Fred A. Reed.

even though Iran had turned its back on the revolution, Fred Reed refused to turn his back on Iran. Full of emotion, he described Khomeini's funeral, which he had attended in the blazing heat of June 1989, in the midst of a surging tide of humanity. For all his reservations, Fred had maintained what could only be described as deep respect for the man he referred to, with a tinge of affection in his voice, as "the late Imam." As for me, I'd always kept my distance from the historic figures that can monopolize revolutions, even as they relegate to the shadows— and often shove aside without compunction—whomever may have opposed them, whatever other dominant personalities may have embodied the converging currents that generate great social upheavals. A visit to the Museum of the Revolution in Tehran—as would a visit to its Cuban counterpart—was to furnish an eloquent illustration of how history can be recomposed in the name of victorious orthodoxy, and to the glory of the revolutionary icon, be he the Supreme Guide Khomeini or the Lider Maximo, Fidel Castro.

The museum is situated in what used to be a brewery in the western part of Tehran. There, the visitor is led step by step through the events that culminated in the overthrow of the shah and his replacement by the regime of the mullahs: a blemish-free vision of "official" history. If the same visitor were to credit the edifying images and dioramas, he could not help but conclude that a single personality—that of Imam Khomeini acting in perfect symbiosis with the people—personified the revolution.

But the historical reality of that revolution we know was quite different. Curiously forgotten, and conspicuous by their absence, are three of its leading personalities: Dr. Ali Shariati, Ayatollah Mahmoud Taleqani, and Ayatollah Hossein-Ali Montazeri, head of the opposition today. We knew that during the mass demonstrations of 1978–1979 that led to the shah's precipitous departure, the crowd also carried their portraits. Yet not a trace of them is to be found; the throngs surging through the streets of Tehran are shown carrying only one photograph, that of Imam Khomeini. Why has Iran's "official history" forgotten them?

Fred returned to Iran again and again. After a subsequent visit, he described the immense mausoleum being built atop the Imam's grave, at the edge of the desert south of Tehran, close to the cemetery of Behesht-e Zahra where thousands of martyrs of the Iran-Iraq war lie buried. In the wake of another trip he spoke indignantly of the ascendancy of President Rafsanjani and of the overnight wealth of the petrodollar clan. Fred went on to denounce the rising political violence, the witch-hunt of intellectuals, and the imprisonment and murder of dissidents in a series of articles and in his book *Persian Postcards*.[2] In spite of it all, he kept returning to Tehran, each time with the same conviction: that the revolutionary ideal could not be so easily obliterated; that the betrayal of Islamic Iran's founding ideals and the bitter struggle to return to them was perhaps the price of freedom.

Then, one day in 1997, Fred came back full of enthusiasm, and with a challenge to my gathering pessimism about Iran. A new wind of hope had sprung up, he told me, with a tone of vindication in his voice. Seemingly against all odds, Mohammad Khatami had just been elected president on a reform platform. Excitedly, Fred spoke of "another revolution," a "second revolution," a "quiet revolution" led by a pacifist reform movement. Bringing to mind Herodotus, I replied, "I do not refuse to believe what I am told ... nor do I entirely believe it."[3] By now, Fred was all but daring me to come and see for myself. Together, we left for Iran, where we stayed for a month. I was now convinced that I could make a film. Discreetly, using a small digital camera, I began to shoot. One year later I returned with a technical crew to begin filming what would become *Salam Iran, a Persian Letter*. The film premiered in Montreal in 2002, and is now circulating surreptitiously in Iran. In January and February 2004, Fred and I returned to Tehran to launch the conversations that make up this book. Like Montesquieu, I was convinced that "there are certain truths of which it is not sufficient to persuade, but that must be conveyed."[4]

Jean-Daniel Lafond

* * *

2. *La Presse* (Montréal), 1990–1996; *Persian Postcards: Iran After Khomeini* (Vancouver: Talonbooks, 1994).

3. Herodotus, *Histories* (c. 450 B.C.).

4. Montesquieu, *Persian Letters* (1721).

Fear of the Other

The year was 1984: my first journey to Iran. The venerable Iran Air Boeing that had carried me from Athens to Tehran touched down like a feather after coming in to land over a city in darkness.

The country was at war, a war that was being fought simultaneously on several fronts. The Iranian army, backed up by thousands of young volunteers, was engaged in the south against the armed forces of Iraq. Supported and equipped by a Western coalition headed by the United States, and aided by Great Britain, France, Germany, and the former Soviet Union, Saddam Hussein had already begun to use chemical weapons on the battlefield. At the same time, a violent conflict was raging in Iran's major cities, where the fighters of the People's Mujahedin[5] faced off against the Revolutionary Guards in a bloody contest of bombs and assassinations, expeditive trials, and repression. And all the while, a third conflict was unfolding. It sought to transform Shi'a Islam—the motive force of the revolution—into a principle of governance for the country as a whole.

I went to Iran for the simplest of reasons: I wanted to witness firsthand the events that were reshaping an ancient land. I had a hunch that the Western media had concluded too rapidly that the new regime was merely a reincarnation of medieval obscurantism. Its unchallenged leader, Ayatollah Ruhollah Khomeini, had been reduced overnight to a caricature, a figure at once enraptured and dangerous. As if that were not enough, we were warned that the Islamic Revolution would soon sweep the Muslim world, overturn the status quo in the Middle East, and— horror of horrors!—threaten Western energy supplies.

What I found was quite different. Since then, I have redoubled my efforts to understand, to step beyond the clichés and the commonplaces: in twenty-two years I returned to Iran twenty-eight times to track and to chronicle a constantly evolving situation. I made friends among Iranians: intellectuals as well as simple citizens, fervent supporters of the revolution and its bitterest opponents. My intention was to immerse

5. Mujahedin Khalk Organization (MKO), an Islamic Marxist opposition group founded in 1963 against the Pahlavi dictatorship. Closely allied with the first elected president of the Islamic Republic, Abolhassan Bani-Sadr, the MKO in June 1981 launched armed resistance to the dominant faction led by Ayatollah Khomeini. After more than a year of violent civil strife, the movement was defeated and brutally repressed. Exiled in Iraq, thousands of its members served under Saddam Hussein in the Iran-Iraq war, earning it the opprobrium of a vast majority of Iranians.

myself in Iran's reality, then to bear witness to what I heard and saw. As I understood it, my task was not to confirm my Westerner's prejudices but to fathom an upheaval that had boiled up from the depths of a society emerging from twenty-six years of dictatorship, and from a tradition of absolutism two millennia old.

Even in the revolution's earliest days, silently, invisibly, the men and women who would become the thinkers and strategists of the reform movement were honing their arguments. They sought not to abolish but to transform non-violently the system they themselves had helped establish. Early on, they had concluded that the Islamic Revolution had reached the end of the line. They would attempt to change it from within. Iran, they believed, could and must pursue its experiment in democracy without relinquishing its own beliefs, without turning its back on its own history, and on the independence it had bought so dearly.

As I came to know Iran, I was drawn to its traditions. As I discovered its poetry and music, its food, its customs and beliefs, I began to understand that my involvement was by no means as simple as it appeared at first glance. The tools I wielded, as a man of the dominant global culture, were unequal to the task of grasping a fundamentally different reality. I had entered the periphery of a world that laid claim to its own specific codes and references, its unspoken assumptions and its deep-rooted traditions. Now, I found myself tip-toeing into a rich and multifaceted civilization deeply immersed in its twenty-five hundred years of history, fourteen hundred of which bore the seal of Islam. Each of my journeys to Iran was galvanizing; I encountered the foreignness of an "other" whose very existence called my deepest-held prejudices into question. As I probed Iran, this singular "other"—the Iranian, the Shi'ite, the Muslim—had begun to probe me and my motives. I had come as an observer, but now I was being observed, sometimes with irony, sometimes with a critical, even hostile eye, and yet often with sympathy.

During these years, I spoke regularly about Iran with Jean-Daniel Lafond, whose work as a filmmaker and whose intellectual discipline, artistic integrity, and ethical principles I had come to know well. I encouraged him to make a film there, in the certainty that he could transform into images the complex reality of a culture so radically different from our own, of an adventure so compellingly human. This was the genesis of *Salam Iran: a Persian Letter*, and eventually also of this book, the fruit of our convergent visions of Iran.

Perhaps it was unavoidable. In Iran, I had begun to take interest in the role of religion in society. As I did so, I became increasingly sensitive to the breadth and depth of Islam, and to how deeply rooted it was in human hearts. I came to understand better the feelings of injury brought about by the militant expansion of the West in the name of "democracy," and of the attractiveness of this same democracy measured against failings of a political system that proclaimed itself religious.

In the course of subsequent journeys to Turkey and Syria this sensitivity grew more acute. For both countries were arenas of conflict, yet places of reconciliation and cohabitation of cultures, religions, and ideas.

Through the Iranian prism, I came to realize that the Western civilization we claim as our own, for all its greatness, could not pretend to encompass the entire world, could not impose upon all others its own thirst for the absolute, its own dream of becoming the world. The charges against it were far too numerous: colonial expansion, slavery, world wars, and today's American drive for imperial domination.

By American reasoning, we should be fearful of the "other." But in fact, it is we in the West who inspire fear in others. The dialogue of civilizations in which Iran's President Mohammad Khatami invited us to participate now lies shattered amidst the rubble created by the Global War on Terror. But had the West truly been prepared to participate in such a dialogue? Could it ever have agreed to a discussion with the "other" on equal terms?

The dialogue of civilizations President Khatami proposed has laid down a challenge to the West. As it comes into closer contact with Iran—and in a broader sense, with Islam—it must find ways to control its own absolutist impulses. Ultimately, these "Conversations in Tehran" are predicated on the modest, yet near-inconceivable, hope that the West might one day lend an ear to such an appeal, might actually engage in such a dialogue.

Fred A. Reed

Introduction

TEHRAN, FEBRUARY 2004. Under an ashen sky, a chill wind swept the sidewalks, driving clouds of fine dust before it. A whiff of rain was in the air. Once more we found ourselves in Iran, the country we had left on a sunny June morning three years before. The filming of *Salam Iran, a Persian Letter* was behind us. Iran's future lay before us. It had seemed so full of promise then: a second revolution was all but inevitable even though no one dared predict where it might lead. Unlike our society, where past and future have been absorbed by the present, Iran was awash with bold ideas, new solutions, experiments that might or might not succeed, but were unfailingly striking.

Historically a locus of cultural conflict between the Islamic East and the West, Iran under President Mohammad Khatami had been struggling to transform itself into a place of encounter and reconciliation, a forum for civilizational dialogue. It was this second revolution that we had returned to Tehran to chart, and which would go down to defeat in the parliamentary elections of February 2004.

The day after our arrival, like all visiting journalists we paid the obligatory call on the Press Office of the Ministry of Islamic Guidance. Having duly completed the required formalities and presented our respectful greetings, we set out on our own, returning the day before departure to offer our equally respectful farewells.

There are two ways for a foreigner to gain insight into Iran. The first is to spend large sums of money to purchase one's sources of information, and even to appropriate their words. This method, favored by the major media networks, can easily engender the kind of "professional bias" seen on CNN, whose reports have more often than not strengthened the hand of the mullahs who hold power in Tehran, not to mention their counterparts in Washington, those two mirror opposites who so often appear to see eye to eye.

The second method is to build slowly, patiently on a basis of confidence and friendship, to develop close personal ties, to enter into social and family relationships. This had always been our approach, and thanks to it, we were able in short order to arrange the meetings that give this book its shape and form.

* * *

President Khatami had perfectly foreseen the daunting impact of his program when he published a book entitled *Fear of the Wave*.[6] His hope and intent was to convince his fellow Iranians to meet head-on and to navigate the whirlpool that would soon engulf their country. The title's explicit reference to Ha'afez, the visionary poet of Shiraz, was hardly fortuitous. It was meant to reassure and, at the same time, to provoke his compatriots. *The Divan*, his masterwork, is one of the cornerstones of Iranian culture, holding pride of place alongside the Qur'an in most Iranian homes. People from all walks of life read it, quote from it, and recite it with reverence and pride. By invoking one of Iran's national poets, perhaps the one closest to today's sensibilities, a man who had lived in a similar, strife-torn age, President Khatami sought to convey a precise message: the interpretation of Scripture, heretofore the sole source of legitimacy in the eyes of the clerical regime, must give way to a more intimate, personal, and mystical approach to the relationship between religion, life, and society.

Mr. Khatami's message was not in the least at odds with the guiding principles of Shi'a Islam, the driving force of the Iranian Revolution. Yet, in subtle ways, it aspired to bring about a shift, both in breadth and scope, in those principles. What if, we wondered, *fear of the wave* had a real, as well as a metaphorical meaning? Were that the case, it could well embody the passage from a state based on divine right to a democratic state on the Western model, with all its accompanying dangers of neo-liberalism. Would Mohammad Khatami dare to push his program beyond metaphor? Would the ultimate outcome reconcile the politician's brave words with the poet's dream?

These two questions lay at the heart of *Salam Iran, a Persian Letter*. In it, we concluded that life in Iran lay anchored in the moment, that the past had been rejected, and that the future seemed truly frightening. But above all, we had concluded that the revolution was well and truly dead.

Was it possible, we wondered, behind the downfall of the Iranian Revolution of 1979, to intuit the outlines of another revolution? The

---

6. Seyyed Mohammad Khatami, *Hope and Challenge: The Iranian President Speaks*, trans. Alidad Mafinezam (Binghamton: IGCS, 1997).

answer was far from certain, and when, in a final attempt, we asked the philosopher Abdolkarim Soroush to enlighten us, he said, "Go to Shiraz; you'll find the answer there, at the tomb of Ha'afez. In Iran, if it's insight you seek, better ask poets than politicians.

"I think, today, in the whole world, like in the third world, we are going through a singular historical period. We are experiencing conditions like those Ha'afez wrote about in his poem. To break through the wave, you need courage. To stay mired in tradition is to live in darkness; to open yourself to the modern world is to confront this terrifying wave."[7]

* * *

The men and women we encountered in Tehran represent a broad cross-section of Iran's intellectual elite. The stories they tell draw a compelling picture of Iran at a particular moment in its contemporary history—and of the unfulfilled promises, dreams, and challenges that loom before it. Several of our partners in conversation are fully involved in the country's political life, in the corridors of power or as members of the civic resistance to the Islamic regime; others are analysts or thinkers who dare to speak out; still others, feminists and grass-roots activists in a region where both can be high-risk occupations. Some have received death threats; others have been arrested and tortured.

On a broader scale, modern-day relations between the West and the Islamic Orient are fraught with danger and turmoil as perhaps never before in their long history of cohabitation and clash. It should come as no surprise that Iran's attempts to grapple on its own terms with the legacy of geography, history, and the hard realities of geopolitics place it squarely in the storm center of conflicts, both latent and actual.

The Tehran we came to know through our encounters is the social, cultural, and political focal point of opposition to a pseudo-theocratic system that has never been able to overcome its own self-created contradictions; of stubborn resistance to a regime that has demonstrated its inability to transform the doctrines of Islam into the lodestone of everyday existence, of social life and economic life.

This had been the intention of the Shi'a clerics who seized power in Iran following the overthrow of the shah. Having emerged as the only political

7. Abdolkarim Soroush, in *Salam Iran, A Persian Letter* (2002).

counterweight to Mohammad-Reza Pahlavi, whose dictatorship had silenced all opposition, the religious establishment successfully transformed the deep mistrust of human authority inherent in Shi'ism into a powerful movement that brought down the ephemeral "King of kings."

But the clerics had not been alone. Others, inspired by the Constitutional Movement of 1906, dreamed of a modern, independent country, open to the world. In 1951, Prime Minister Mohammad Mossadeq transformed the dream into reality by nationalizing the Anglo-Iranian Oil Company. But the dream rapidly soured, and then turned to nightmare when a *coup d'état* engineered by Kermit Roosevelt of the CIA and his counterpart in the British Intelligence Service, Colonel Christopher Montague Woodhouse, overthrew the Mossadeq government two years later. Accused of rebellion against an imperial decree, Mossadeq was sentenced to three years in prison, and spent the rest of his life under house arrest.[8]

The coexistence, collaboration, and often-violent confrontation of these two ideological currents—the religious and the secular—were to give political life in the young Islamic Republic its unique shape. They also provide perhaps the most satisfactory explanation for the seemingly paradoxical, contradictory workings of the Iranian political system. On the one hand, Iran is ostensibly a republic. The monarchy has been overthrown, replaced by a parliament elected every four years by universal suffrage; a putative system of checks and balances prevails, overseen by a nominally independent judiciary whose head is nonetheless appointed by the Supreme Guide. On the other hand, Iran is an *Islamic* republic, conceived in the image of the community founded by the Prophet Muhammed when he emigrated from Mecca to Medina in 622 to begin the Islamic era. As if that were not enough, Iranians must also contend with the startling innovation in Shi'ite tradition, devised by Ayatollah Ruhollah Khomeini, that gives a single man, the Supreme Guide, near-absolute powers based on the principle of the *Velayat-e faqih*, the rule of the jurist-consult.[9] And, to further complicate

---

8. Jean-Pierre Digard, Bernard Hourcade, and Yann Richard, *L'Iran au XXe siécle* (Paris: Fayard, 1996), 101–20.

9. *Velayat-e faqih*: an innovation of Ayatollah Ruholah Khomeini, which postulates that the divine law of Islam had been transferred to the Prophet during his lifetime, and thereafter to his legatees, the Imams—"It is unreasonable to believe, argues Khomeini, that God had left mankind to its own devices after the Occultation of the Twelfth Imam. The difference between the just jurist-consult and the Imam is no greater than between the Imam and the Prophet" (Yann Richard, *L'Islam chiite* [Paris: Fayard, 1991], 110).

matters, certain members of the clergy believe that Khomeini's innovation not only has no basis in the Qur'an and the other sources of Islamic doctrine, but that it draws its inspiration from the Iranian monarchical tradition.

It is a hybrid, one-of-a-kind regime, designed to perpetuate the power of the religious establishment over society. But it is also a regime that must tolerate within it other voices, other forces. These may not be completely secularist, but they are bitingly critical of the mullahs' attempts to obtain a stranglehold on power. Seen from the West, it is tempting to view Iran's religious state as a theocratic monolith. In reality, the state cannot function except by a constant balancing act between factions that believe "Islamic values" to be the only criterion, and others for which religious solutions are far from the sole panacea for the country's political and economic woes.

Not surprisingly, we quickly began the work of unravelling the semantic complexities of Iranian politics, began to "read" its shades of meaning. Thus, in this book, the words "regime" and "government" cannot be understood as synonymous. It had early on become quite apparent that in its dealings with the regime, President Mohammad Khatami's reformist government—Iran's executive branch—had come to resemble nothing so much as an outsized NGO (non-governmental organization). What could it hope to achieve, after all, against a regime based on the absolute power of the Supreme Guide who stands alone as head of state, and who draws his legitimacy from that peculiar institution unique to the Islamic Republic, the *Velayat-e faqih*? But even this institution was grounded in yet another paradox: Mr. Ali Khamene'i, who succeeded Imam Khomeini as Supreme Guide, was awarded his absolute power by the majority vote of Iran's democratically elected parliament!

Readers should be aware, then, that the term "regime" is used throughout this book to refer to the true seat of power: the hard core of the Shi'a clerical establishment; Iran's great traditional families, including those of certain influential ayatollahs; the security and intelligence services; and the Revolutionary Guards, the paramilitary force established in 1980 to protect the nascent Islamic Republic. This power structure finds its official expression in the two bodies created to supervise the key institutions of the dual-headed state: the Council of Guardians, that rules on the conformity with Islamic criteria of all parliamentary legislation, and the Council of Experts, which oversees the work of the Supreme Guide—and whose members are appointed by him.

In these pages, we use the term "conservatives" as it is used in Iran, to refer to those Iranians who share this view of how the state should be organized, and support the predominant role of religion in society.

Their chief opponents, the "reformists," are the no less legitimate heirs of the revolution's strong nationalist and secular streak. Early on, they had diagnosed the malfunction and, worse, the failure of the absolutist model, and set out to transform the Iranian political landscape. Instead of calling for the violent overthrow of the regime, they chose to attempt change from within, to reshape by patient argument the dominant mindset. In their attempt to do so, they underestimated the power of the conservatives. Almost overnight, their brave new movement had fallen apart.

All the while, since 1979, the United States has worked diligently to cast Iran as a "rogue state." Not even the election of Mohammad Khatami at the head of a reform government in 1997 brought about more than a slight shift in American attitudes. When, in 2003, with the full approval of the Supreme Guide, the Khatami government submitted to Washington an offer designed to settle all outstanding differences, it was rejected out of hand.

American policy toward Iran sees "regime change" as the only option. And when Washington says regime change, it really means destruction of the regime. In 2006, American intransigence was to fortify—if not justify—the outspoken stance of Iran's newly elected conservative president, Mahmoud Ahmadinejad, on Iran's nuclear energy program, and on the Palestinian conflict. Long targeted, and threatened, by the Zionist state, Iran has developed its own perspective on Middle Eastern geopolitics. In challenging the legitimacy of Israel, it has substantially increased its popularity among broad cross-sections of the Arabo-Islamic world.

The aim of these conversations is neither to approve nor disapprove of what Iran says or does, but to trace the ebb and flow of ideas across the immense and fragile space of the Middle East, and of Iran as a discrete component of it. Iran has become particularly vulnerable to seismic shocks, both natural and man-made. In this book we have attempted to understand what we have seen and heard, far from the shopworn clichés and commonplaces that so often masquerade as informed comment in our docile media. Political life in Iran marches to its own drumbeat. Threatened by nuclear attack in the wake of George W. Bush's "Axis of Evil" speech, Iran, as an independent country, is arguably taking whatever action it considers as necessary to defend itself and to protect its interests.

We decline, in short, to measure Iranian society against the yardstick of American foreign policy imperatives. Instead, we hold it to account against its own contradictions, its unkept promises, its own failings.

* * *

Welcome then to Tehran, a city where modernity often finds a violent, even virulent outlet; a city that at the same time harbors a religious tradition that has survived the assaults of the modern age intact. Could there possibly be a more propitious place for these conversations with our Iranian friends and acquaintances, for a free and unfettered exchange of words and ideas?

Ours has been a geographical journey, an excursion into the society around us, and a voyage into the imagination. We sought out—and often accidentally encountered—assertive, powerful voices. Each one staked its own claim to legitimacy; and as we were formulating our questions, each one was probing us for answers.

My past is indistinguishable from the present—
it is my constant reference; I breathe new life into it—
and from the present that is also my future....
Now, between the two, I hang suspended, awaiting an End
that is always a new Beginning.

—Daryush Shayegan, *Le regard mutilé* (1996)

Iran: The Other Revolution

TEHRAN IS A FASCINATING PLACE. No sooner have we arrived than we feel its curious attraction. After breakfast, we venture out onto the sidewalks for a brisk stroll. We're anxious to relocate the old familiar streets, to feel the ebb and flow of the crowd, to listen to the music of the language. There is something alluring, irresistible about the city. A few hours later we return to our hotel exhausted, coughing and sputtering, half-choked by exhaust fumes. Tehran may be irresistible, but we'd forgotten just how disagreeable it could be.

To search for traces of Iran's millennia-long history by strolling the sidewalks of Tehran is to compound illusion with bitter disappointment. Iran's capital is a new town, a megalopolis under permanent construction, girded by expressways; a commercial powerhouse, a city on the make, where modernity is breaking out all over. There was a time—"before"— when major thoroughfares were named for the illustrious figures of Iran's twenty-five-hundred-year-old dynastic history. Of Cyrus and Darius not a trace remains. Today, place names hew to strictly religious standards. A busy downtown square is named for Imam Hossein, the martyr of Karbala; the main east-west expressway bears the name of an anti-constitutionalist clergyman; one of the principal cross-town boulevards that of the founder of the Islamic Republic, Imam Khomeini.

A century ago, Tehran was the theater of a stillborn constitutional revolution. Its memory lingers on in the speeches of reformist politicians, but it has been expunged from the city's urban fabric. Reza Khan, the usurper who founded the Pahlavi Dynasty in 1925, ordered built a lengthy and majestic boulevard stretching from the railway station to the feet of the mountains. Modestly he named it Pahlavi Avenue. Today, its beauty imperiled by constant traffic jams, it is known as Vali-é Asr, the Lord of the Age, in reference to the Twelfth Imam of Shi'a eschatology.[10]

---

10. Born in 869 (255 A.H.), Abol-Qasem Muhammed, the twelfth and last Imam of the lineage of the holy Shi'ite Imams, disappeared miraculously at age eight. Thereafter he communicated with the visible world through the intermediary of four representatives. With his death, in 941, begins what in Shi'a doctrine is called the Major Occultation, which will come to an end at the End of Time, making him similar to Jesus in Christian doctrine. The Imam is thus alive, but invisible. (See Yann Richard, *L'Islam chiite*, 69–161.)

Today's stifling cloud of pollution often obscures, as it does the mountains that tower over the city, the high hopes—and the aspirations for freedom—raised by the Islamic Revolution of 1979. The overthrow of Shah Mohammad-Reza Pahlavi created a shock felt around the world, particularly in the West. An Iran finally at liberty to choose its own political system, free of outside influence and without domestic repression, might well become, in ways utterly unexpected, a threat to the established world order. Today, the regional system established and maintained by the Great Powers since World War I through the agency of client regimes and petro-monarchies totters on the brink of collapse. The oil shock created by OPEC in the 1970s had provided a small taste of what could happen to the West's complacent grip on the levers of global economic and political power.

The stakes were high: if Iran were to succeed in setting up a government inspired both by Islamic values and by the West's self-proclaimed democratic principles, it would transform the image of a religion associated, rightly or wrongly, with an obsession with the past, with narrow-mindedness, and with the rejection of both present and future. Were that to happen, it would have become possible to speak of another revolution, with consequences extending far beyond Iran's borders.

But the Islamic Revolution has not so far been able to deliver on its promises. Social inequality and political repression have been the dominant aspects of its twenty-five years in power. But neither its failure, nor the immense sacrifice of Iran's youth during the war with Saddam Hussein's Iraq, nor even the heavy-handed approach of the country's hard-liners have been able to extinguish the dreams of the country's democratic forces.

Unexpectedly, the Islamic regime—which we define as the overarching confluence of state and religious institutions, and informal power centers that rule Iran in the name, though not the letter, of religion—itself has proven to be a source of surprises. The clerical establishment, often seen as a monolithic party whose identifying mark is the turban, has fostered the emergence of clearly identifiable sub-groups that reflect the internal dynamics and disputatiousness of Shi'ism in Iran. The most interesting, and the strongest of these groups to date, has been the reform movement that sprang up around President Khatami, known as the "Second of Khordad—*Dovvom-e Khordad*—Movement," in reference to the Iranian solar calendar date of his election in May 1997.

The democratic dream is still alive. But it has been unable to overcome a fundamental challenge: how to avoid the appropriation of Iran's

Tehran was ours to explore. (*Salam Iran*, courtesy of InformAction Films)

immense oil income by a tiny fragment of the population, principally for the benefit of the religious class that holds power. The result has not simply been the failure of an economic policy—not unlike the experience in the West—but also of the application, surprisingly continued by the reformist government, of a strategy to transfer wealth, including oil income, to a handful of insiders from the majority of the population.

After seven years in power, Mohammad Khatami had proved incapable of fulfilling the promises implicit and explicit in his program, particularly in terms of rights and freedoms, and social justice. As the end of his term approached, Mr. Khatami seemed more and more yesterday's man. At the same time, it was far too early to talk of a "third wave" that would break with the clergy, and with Mr. Khatami's refinement and elegance. For the moment, the only "third wave" on offer holds out little more to Iranians than the restoration of the monarchy presumably following an American intervention.

More than twenty-five years ago, an overwhelming majority took to the streets to demand not only an end to the imperial regime, but also that Islam become the guiding principle of the state. Some sought a broader, more generous interpretation of the sources, directly influenced by the Western experience of representative government; others, a narrower, more restrictive understanding, with a complex structure of putatively religious prohibitions and restrictions. It was not long before many of those who fought to make the moderate version of the revolutionary ideal a reality were pushed aside. Many were persecuted, imprisoned or, worse still, executed. Tens of thousands who might have brought this dream alive volunteered to fight in the 1980–1988 war against Iraq instead. Many died there as martyrs; others returned, feeling embittered and betrayed.

Still others, war veterans of the same generation, believed they had identified the reasons for the eclipse of their ideals. Their prescription would be a radical one: a return to religious values. As patient as they were methodical, they would wait in the shadows for power to fall into their hands.

Before returning to Iran in January 2004, we believed that Supreme Guide Ali Khamene'i's repeated admonitions against "liberalism" had not been able to muffle popular aspirations for a more open society. For us, the decline of the traditionalists was irreversible; we were certain that, despite appearances, the road to reform still lay open.

In the light of the conversations that make up this book, and of what we saw, felt—and the experiences we shared—in the course of one month in Tehran, our earlier and rather optimistic convictions seemed suddenly far from certain. If anything, they had become untenable. The flourishing public debate about Iran's political future had come to a halt; the opening we believed we had detected on the far horizon had now been closed off.

What we had interpreted as the earliest signs of the decline of the conservative faction had, in reality, masked the predictable fall from grace of the reformists. The movement, which had seemed destined for a brighter tomorrow, had crumpled under a fierce, unrelenting, and well-planned campaign of repression orchestrated by the traditionalists. But this campaign, no matter how well planned, no matter how brutally executed, could not have succeeded had the reformists, and Mr. Khatami himself, not also fallen victim to their own inability to translate the ideal of reform into down-to-earth political and economic measures. Their generous promises remained far removed from the day-to-day problems faced by the majority of Iranians.

The Living and the Dead

IT WAS SPRING 2000. We had travelled to Iran to begin filming *Salam Iran*. That year, Iran's solar new year coincided with the Islamic lunar month of Muharram, when Shi'a Muslims commemorate the martyrdom, fourteen centuries before, of Imam Hossein, grandson of the Prophet and third in the lineage of the Twelve Holy Imams. The tourist guidebooks are unanimous: avoid this month of mourning and processions at all costs. The country will be paralyzed.

We ignored the advice. Instead, we saw an opportunity to explore both the visible and the hidden contradictions of a revolution that was now a quarter-century old; a revolutionary upheaval that 60 percent of Iran's current population had not witnessed.

Tehran was ours to explore, from the crowded narrow lanes to the major thoroughfares closed to automobile traffic. We shared the sidewalks and the pavement with processions of black-clad flagellants beating their chests in rhythm, whipping their backs in carefully choreographed movements that oscillated between the seductive and the violent. We stepped into the *hosseiniyeh*, the immense inner spaces reserved for the commemoration of Ashura and Tasua, on the ninth and tenth days of Muharram. Those are the days when thousands of the faithful relive, in tears that seem to flow from the depths of time, the sacrifice of Imam Hossein, who in 680 C.E. refused to submit to Caliph Yazid at Karbala, on the banks of the Euphrates. There, at Yazid's command, the upstarts, the Imam, and his small band of faithful followers and family members were massacred. Among the survivors was the Imam's son, Ali Zeyn al-Abedin. The head of the man who would become known as the Prince of Martyrs was carried by his surviving sister Zeynab to Damascus, where it was buried in the western wall of the Great Umayyad Mosque. Like the crypt in which the head by legend lies, Zeynab's tomb in the suburbs of the Syrian capital is today a prized destination for Iranian pilgrims.

In Iran, the regime does not control the Ashura commemorations, even though it has always attempted to exploit them to its advantage.

Ashura commemorations in Tehran in front of the Hosseiniyeh-e Ershad.
(*Salam Iran*, courtesy of InformAction Films)

The night processions we witnessed were striking; the participants were as numerous as they were animated. Young men were bent double under the weight of their *alams*, the enormous effigies that represent Hossein's forces in battle array. Still others beat their chests and backs as they marched, almost dancing, to the piercing, rhythmic lament of the martyrdom narrative. Although the police were on hand, the strong sense of internal discipline among the religious mourners made their presence unnecessary. The young men who formed the bulk of the demonstrators were all volunteers, their motivation a fierce dedication to tradition.

As we watched each group attempting to surpass its rivals by the quality and the audacity of its performance, and in the force of its self-flagellation, we suspected that Ashura also offered an unequaled opportunity to impress the young ladies who lined the sidewalks. Their stolen glances and furtive smiles only confirmed our suspicions—and provided a happy counterpoint to the somber commemorative ceremonies. For all intents and purposes, the processions were street festivals, impossible to restrict.

Shah Mohammad-Reza Pahlavi learned to his cost that there was a revolutionary side to Ashura, a latent power that could bring down an incautious tyrant. The memory of martyrdom, the cult of mourning, and the spirit of insubordination coalesced as the driving forces in the uprising that overthrew the monarchy in 1979, and became powerful ideological weapons wielded by the religious leadership in the war against Iraq that followed so closely on the heels of the revolution.

That Obscure Object

IT WAS THE NIGHT OF ASHURA, near the Tekiyyeh Dowlat, a sprawling *hosseiniyeh* just north of the Bazaar. Thick crowds thronged the streets, which had been closed off for the occasion. A police presence was hardly necessary in this part of Tehran, with its tradition of piety and Islamic militancy. But on the sidewalks our film crew did not go unnoticed. With us was Ali Arabmazar, a long-time friend who was then deputy minister of finance. As a public figure, his face was well known to the authorities and to the organizers. Nor was he a stranger to the place: as a boy his father would bring him here, to the heart of the Bazaar district, to take part in the Ashura ceremonies.

When a uniformed officer asked us for our papers and filming permit, Mr. Arabmazar rapidly put him at ease, and opened the door to the *hosseiniyeh*, from which the cadences of chanting echoed up and down the streets.

We stepped inside. For the next two hours we listened transfixed to the litany of a blind reciter reading his Braille text with his fingertips while all around us, more than a thousand men beat their chests, as though the martyrdom of Imam Hossein were theirs as well. We felt far removed from the power of their rhythmic blows, and yet gripped, drawn in by the thump and whoosh of open hands rising then falling upon human torsos while lungs expelled pent-up air in unison, and piercing voices intoned over and over again the blind man's litany.

The intensity of our experience, alongside the chanting congregation of mourners, was a fair match for the questions that flooded into our minds. What did Ashura, this radical commemoration of mourning, mean today for the reform movement that emerged with the election of President Khatami? How could a movement that styled itself as open to the modern world, as dedicated to the transformation of society, possibly be compatible with an anniversary that, for the foreign visitor, seemed shrouded in darkness, at best a folkloric throwback, at worst, a dangerous return to the past? A few days later, quite unexpectedly and in defiance

The thump and whoosh of open hands rising then falling upon human torsos while lungs expelled pent-up air in unison ... (*Salam Iran*, courtesy of InformAction Films)

of protocol, a woman—Massoumeh Ebtekar, vice-president of the Islamic Republic, and head of the Department of Environment—gave us our answer.

Ms. Ebtekar embodies many of the contradictions of the revolution, and the branching paths followed by the revolutionary generation of which she is a part. That same generation, today deeply involved in the reform movement, sought to take over the state by peaceful means, in the name of equality and justice. In November 1979, eighteen-year-old Massoumeh Ebtekar was one of the leaders of the group of Islamic students who had stormed the U.S. Embassy in Tehran and gone on to occupy it for 444 days. In doing so, she and her young cohorts had unwittingly paved the way for the takeover by the mullahs of the state apparatus.

The day after the embassy capture, Mehdi Bazargan, the prime minister appointed by Imam Khomeini, tendered his resignation. The clerical party rapidly formed a new government, seizing the power it was not to relinquish.

By the time the fifty-six American hostages had been released, nothing remained of the apparent control over the course of events that the students had exercised in the beginning. The hostage incident, as it came to be known in the West, had combined improvisation with the brashness of the young men and women who, during those days of unbridled activism, sought to depict themselves as being just as revolutionary as their fraternal rivals from the left-wing student groups. But their poor preparation made them vulnerable to being rapidly co-opted by the power structure. On orders from Imam Khomeini, the question of what to do with the hostages was handed over to parliament where Ali Akbar Hashemi Rafsanjani, the speaker, quickly took control and, ultimately, brought it to a profitable conclusion.

The dispute was finally settled in a secret deal between Rafsanjani's men, including Mehdi Karoubi, who would be Majlis (parliament) speaker under President Khatami, and clandestine operatives of the American Republican Party. The hostages were released on the day of Ronald Reagan's inauguration ceremony—a fitting culmination to the October Surprise, whose long-term repercussions have tainted Irano-American relations to this day.

When we met her in a conference room on the ninth floor of the Environment Department building on downtown Villa Street, Massoumeh Ebtekar was in mourning. Her father, with whom she had been very close, had died a few days before. During the bitter years of the Pahlavi dictatorship he had emigrated with his family to the United States where his daughter Massoumeh attended primary school and acquired the perfect English she still speaks today. It was this command of colloquial English that was to make her the ideal spokesperson for the students during the embassy occupation.

Her father, a man of wide-ranging intellectual pursuits, had introduced his precocious daughter to Dr. Ali Shariati, the influential contemporary Islamic thinker and radical philosopher who identified with the third world liberation movements of the 1960s and '70s. Shariati, who was a charismatic speaker, used his writings and public lectures to bring a significant segment of Iranian youth to understand martyrdom as liberation, what he termed the "Red Shi'ism" of freely accepted sacrifice, in opposition to "Black Shi'ism," with its cult of tears, breast-beating, and resignation.

The interpretation of Ashura we were to hear from Massoumeh Ebtekar that day was a heady blend of emotion intensified by her own mourning, of her personal history and political path, and of the influence of Ali Shariati. We soon appreciated that her words had a double meaning, that she was updating the exemplary conflict between Hossein and Yazid to modern times, cast as the battle of reformist President Khatami against the authoritarian figure of Supreme Guide Ali Khamene'i, the personification of arbitrary power.

"Ashura is about justice, about freedom and human dignity. It is an event that has a beautiful, luminous side, and another side, a dark side.

"If Ashura has its dark, somber side, that is because it reminds us that justice has been historically sacrificed by those who seek only egoism, sensual pleasure, and power.

"This is not simply a judgment we make about the past. Today, in postmodern times, in the era of globalization, we believe there is something about it that touches our hearts, whether we're Westerners or Easterners. Today we live in a world that is dominated by power, political and economic power. Our world is governed not by charity, not by reason, and not by the search for righteousness or justice. Those who have economic power are not prepared to sacrifice the economy to the search for a better world. And even the people who claim to do it quickly forget their promises when they must take action.

"We're living in an age of suffering. Whether you're European, American, Asiatic, Iranian, or African … whoever you are, you feel the suffering; human values are being sacrificed, human dignity above all.

"On the battlefield where Imam Hossein has gone to die, he calls out to the enemy, 'Even if you have no religion, no beliefs, keep your human dignity, be free, be free of all the chains that enslave you to egoism; even in the most degrading circumstances. Be free!' That is his message, and it is a universal one.

"This means that there are certain values that must be preserved. And if we lose them, whatever our scientific or material progress, if we lose the very things that make a human being, then we regress. It's truly unfortunate that in today's world, in the universities and among intellectuals, we seem to have come to a consensus that human reason is based only upon appearances. And the medias reinforce this attitude. What gives Ashura its dark side is that humanity is sacrificed to appearances; this is why we mourn; this is why we weep."

Where's the Meat?

WE INTERRUPTED MASSOUMEH EBTEKAR to describe an incident that had taken place during our filming, a few days before. We had found ourselves in a narrow street in the village of Evin, in the northern part of the city not far from Tehran's main prison. A crowd had gathered to watch an Ashura procession that would end with the slaughter of a sacrificial animal. Most of those present were families with children in tow; they'd crowded around a pick-up truck that had just delivered the sacrifice, a heifer determined to do whatever it could to escape death. As we looked on, cameras running, what should have been a routine ritual slaughter turned into bloody, high drama.

Suddenly, the heifer surged forward. It was all the four men holding the ropes could do to restrain it, as the butcher's knife flashed through the air seeking the jugular. With a twist of its head, the animal escaped the fatal thrust. The knife blow fell wide of the mark, plunging into its chest; blood spurted onto the pavement. With another toss of the head the heifer threw the butcher's assistants off balance. They dropped the rope and the animal charged into the crowd. The butcher managed to stop it, and slashed out again, once, twice. Finally, he found the jugular, and the blood gushed out. The heifer stumbled from side to side as the crowd recoiled. Then it sank to its knees and collapsed on its flank in a sea of blood that the spectators stepped over or sloshed through in their haste to get clear.

A young man that had been looking on since we'd begun to film came up to us. He was a student at Tehran University, he told us. He was so sorry, but he was speaking French for the first time.

"I would like to ask, what will you do with these pictures? You will use them against us, maybe? To show how Iranians are barbaric and bloodthirsty, like in the film *Not Without My Daughter*?"

Tormented by the thought, he seemed torn between calling his friends over to insist that we stop filming, and the urge to explain what we had just seen, to avoid any misunderstanding. We invited him to speak to the camera. He accepted our invitation.

With a twist of its head, the animal escaped the fatal thrust. (*Salam Iran*, courtesy of InformAction Films)

"What you see here is part of a wider ceremony, a 'total ceremony.' It is not just about killing an animal, not at all. You have to consider the whole ceremony; for me, it is much happier, more complete. We do not kill for the pleasure of killing; what you see is a sacrifice, and a way of sharing. This animal was killed just as lambs are sacrificed. Then they are cooked in a big communal kitchen where everybody can come and eat. Ashura is a time of sharing. Everyone, rich or poor, can share in the common meal; anyone can come and get food for his family, his friends, and his neighbors. You're welcome to come too. Yes, it's for everyone. There's something sacred about this sacrifice; it's an invitation to all, believers and non-believers, to share in the feast that we all celebrate together."

As the sun was setting we left Evin. In downtown Tehran, the Ashura processions would continue uninterrupted well into the night, punctuated by the slaughter of lambs. Their blood ran down the shiny black asphalt in bright vermilion rivulets, finally flowing into the *joubs*, the open-air storm-sewers that line the city's main streets and back alleys. Not far from the *hosseiniyeh* where we had attended the ceremony led by the blind chanter, a man in a black shirt and pantaloons beckoned us, "Come on in! Come and see!" We stepped into a vacant warehouse that had been transformed into a field kitchen. To the sounds of the music and chanting that retold the martyrdom of Imam Hossein, sacrificial lambs and heifers were delivered to a platoon of butchers that split the carcasses, chopped and sliced the meat into pieces that a brigade of cooks prepared and tossed into bubbling stew-pots, alongside cauldrons of fragrant, steaming rice. At the far end of the chain, laughing and singing, another group of men stuffed rice and stew into portion-size plastic containers; further on, still others handed them to the thousands of faithful lined up patiently on the sidewalk. Everywhere in the city, everywhere across the country, at home or on a patch of sidewalk, for one night at least, everyone ate to their heart's content.

It was an invitation we couldn't refuse—nor resist. Off to the side of the temporary kitchen, we found a place to sit down. There, beneath the washed-out light of a fluorescent tube we wolfed down our share of the flesh of sacrifice. The meat melted in our mouths, but our pleasure was tempered by what we had seen earlier that day. We could not forget the heifer's last struggle against the butcher's clumsy assault. What would we do—what would we say—with the haunting scenes we had filmed?

We were not alone. The spectacular, brutal unedited scene of the slaughter that appeared in the film shocked audiences, and stimulated vigorous debates both in the West and in Iran.

"It's disgusting. You had no business showing that; there are so many beautiful things to see in Iran!" a publisher of academic books in Tehran burst out after a screening. Our friend, who belonged to the broad, ill-defined category of "religious intellectuals," was shocked by a reality that he would have preferred not to see. Like many of his colleagues, he had never left Iran except for the occasional business trip, but his children were studying abroad. Perhaps we should not have been surprised: we knew that our critic belonged to the circle of those who attend official symposia broadcast live on state-controlled television, alongside the usual cohort of semi-somnolent clerics whose love for culture remains, to put it politely, limited to the values produced and promoted by the regime.

The slaughter scene had been more than he could take.

"If you publish a book on the splendors of Iran, will you show photographs of ugly things? How much better it would have been to choose more typical scenes!"

Massoumeh Ebtekar would have none of it.

"You must show everything, even at the risk of misunderstanding.

"What you heard is part of the misunderstanding of Ashura, which exists first and foremost in approaching it from the outside: all your critic can see is the sacrifice of the animal, the violent movements; but you have to see the whole picture to grasp its meaning and its deep significance."

But how is it possible to integrate the meaning of Ashura into your political activity and vision today?

"In my work, Imam Hossein is the light that guides me, by his sacrifice, and that of his companions, in the name of a higher cause, of universal humanity. For me, his lesson is perfectly pertinent—and inspiring. When we must sacrifice something in order to carry on, to remain faithful to our principles, so that we do not betray the deepest meaning of these principles, Imam Hossein shows us the way.

"Take a practical example: the Islamic Revolution. For everyone here in Iran, the analogy with Imam Hossein was clear to see. The tyrannical dictatorship of the shah was comparable to Yazid's, and the people's uprising was like that of Imam Hossein and his companions. They were fighting for justice, democracy, for their rights and dignity, for their independence. Against them was a dictator who had all the power, and the support of a foreign superpower, the United States. The analogy was perfectly clear then: it was necessary to sacrifice our lives, to accept martyrdom.

"Martyrdom has probably never really been understood in the West. I've had to answer many questions about the meaning of the term. Do the people who seek it not care for life? Does it mean that when a mother encourages her son to go off to the battlefront that she is not truly a mother?

"These are reasonable questions, and we have to try to understand them. Your audience, in the Western cultural tradition, has a perfect right to ask these questions, because the philosophy that underlies our traditions is totally unlike contemporary attitudes towards life, death, and sacrifice. Still, I believe that there is a lesson for us all in the life of Imam Hossein, in his death for a sacred cause, and through his philosophy of self-sacrifice.

"There can be no doubt that this was the main reason for the success of the Islamic Revolution in Iran. There was no fear, no fear of death. People fear nothing when they believe they are fighting for the Almighty. That is life's ultimate purpose. There is nothing beyond it.

"That same lesson applies to the revolution, and to everyday life whenever we must decide, whenever we must choose which path to follow.

"You can see it at work in difficult situations. Look at the eight years of war, when Iraq attacked Iran with everything it could. We were the weaker party. The whole world supported Iraq. Iran was bombarded as though it were an aggressor, a terrorist state. But Iran didn't commit the aggression. Our revolution was young, there was no way we could attack another country.

Massoumeh Ebtekar: "Today we're facing a political challenge." (*Salam Iran*, courtesy of InformAction Films)

"What protected Iran? What protected the Islamic Revolution, in spite of economic blockade, in spite of internal pressures? Why did people stand up and resist? It was the spirit of Imam Hossein; that was what sent young people off to the front as volunteers. And yet, they had the same aspirations as young people all over the world. They wanted a good education, a pleasant life, a wife, everything a young person could hope for from life. Instead, they went off to war, voluntarily, even youngsters of fourteen who were too young to fight. They falsified their birth certificates. Why? What drew them? What did they see there that attracted them? The lesson of Ashura, and the martyrdom of Imam Hossein. Over and over again history repeats itself. That is why we must wear mourning, and sacrifice ourselves for human dignity."

We had to admit it: the notion of sacrifice for human dignity has disappeared from the horizon in Western civilization today. Westerners find martyrdom repulsive, and see in it little more than blindness and despair. They cannot recognize the affirmation of individual free will behind what appears to be merely the glorification of death; for most, it is a perverse terrorist tactic that transforms individuals into down-market cruise missiles and docile human bombs.

In Iran, an entire generation sacrificed its youth, and in many cases its life, to the revolution, for the assurance of better days for the survivors, and for the promise of paradise for themselves. Today, those who did survive are far from happy; and many are resentful. We encountered embittered veterans, men who made no effort to conceal their feelings of betrayal; we met former prisoners of war who wondered aloud why they had spent a decade in Iraqi prison camps and now faced the scorn of cock-of-the-walk opportunists who had slid themselves into their empty place in society; we spoke with demobilized militiamen who were only waiting for the day when they could take revenge for the murderous lies that sent them off to combat.

"It's true. The younger generation, all those who sacrificed themselves during the revolution and during the war, have high expectations. They have a sense of idealism that has to be channeled, on the one hand, into the continuation of the revolution; on the other, that same idealism has to be properly guided to ensure the survival of the Islamic Republic of Iran. Their values must be fully interpreted and integrated into our society, otherwise they will be nothing more than theories with no practical application, with no place in today's world. We believe that religion, and the philosophy of Imam Hossein, the very objectives and values upon which the Islamic Revolution was founded, can be applied to this situation, that it can respond to people's needs.

"Today we're facing a political challenge. You can see it in the confrontation between the reformists, who want greater openness, and the conservatives, who want to maintain the status quo. On the one hand, you have a society struggling to move ahead and to develop the qualities of the Islamic Revolution; and on the other hand, you have a conservative society that is quite skeptical of the reform process, and is afraid that its dynamism might destroy the principles of the revolution. The conservatives have their fears, and the younger generation has its expectations. This is the game now being played out. But the internal dialogue must continue; it's impossible to turn back now.

"I think it will work. It's a difficult process, and it may be a painful one, but it is part of Islam, and in conformity with Imam Khomeini's interpretation and understanding. As Supreme Guide of the revolution and founder of the Islamic Republic, he understood that we needed that dynamic spirit, that need to open up new perspectives, new horizons for the revolution, and to develop the basic elements of democracy for the people.

"This is not what certain conservatives believe today. The Imam never looked upon the people as a tool. He believed in the people's power to decide for themselves. This is why the people turned to him, and why the revolution succeeded. He believed in the dignity of the people, in their right to decide, to determine their own future. That was why he gave the people an identity, a sense of responsibility for their own decisions, their own judgments. This feeling is still strong in Iranian society."

Today, that feeling is tinged with bitterness. Many Iranians feel they have been betrayed, or abandoned by the systematic blocking of the system carried out since the election of Mohammad Khatami in 1997 by the powerful conservative faction. The Khatami government proclaimed the principles of dialogue and non-violence, and made no secret of its intention to apply them at home and abroad. But these principles could only be put into practice if the rules of the game were changed.

"That is exactly why President Khatami continually expresses his respect for the law. He insists that, in the final analysis, the rule of law must prevail; that in Iran, it must be the last word. In all cases, legality must be the final consideration. We have to proceed according to law, and not consider the law as a means of exercising power, or of promoting a partisan point of view.

"It's a difficult process, especially in a country that has had an autocratic system for so many centuries, a country where people never had the right to decide anything, nor to participate in discussions that affect their future.

"For sure, self-confidence is back; but we have a long, hard road ahead of us. We continue to believe in dialogue even if, formally speaking, it doesn't exist. Dialogue must be established. The different groups and political parties are all moving in this direction.

"President Khatami himself is a believer in dialogue. I think he has a very dignified, elegant approach, even when he negotiates with the opposition—with his adversaries, but because of the way he's treated you'd think he was an enemy—he says, 'I defend the right of my opposition to be where it is, to say what it says, and to vote.' He really believes it. He is an excellent example of how Iranian society should operate. Here, we're carrying out a unique experiment, trying to establish a religious system, with all the different ways that religion can play a role today in politics, and in economic and social life.

"And alongside it, we have democratic institutions that are serious about fulfilling their roles, and that are looking for their share of influence. The political system in Iran is very complex. It's a challenge. But many Iranians believe that it will work out in the end. All this has a price; it's already cost us dear.

"But we've reached a critical point; we must take a decision based on dignity and freedom, or on active violence. It's the same question that Imam Hossein faced. Could he forget justice and dignity in order to remain faithful to non-violence? He fought in war, and went into battle against a well-trained army. It was a question of principle. It was no longer a question of saving his skin, or that of his companions, but to save the fundamental principles of humanity. You know, there are values you can live or die for. If it's important to live well, it's just as important to die well.

"The lesson of Imam Hossein will surely be useful to us in these circumstances."

As we left Massoumeh Ebtekar's office, we were certain that she had spoken to us not only of her principles, but also of the very real possibility that the reform process would fail, that violence and intimidation would overtake dialogue. What modern-day Yazid, armed to the teeth, lay in wait for what Hossein? Surrounded, thirsting, for what principles would he yield up his life today?

Labyrinths

TEHRAN HAS ITS SHARE of emblematic places, charged with memories that have frequently been concealed, and often reduced to silence. The Islamic Revolution—a tremor as unexpected in its particulars as it had generally been long awaited—took shape in the singular geography of the densely populated working-class districts of the south of the city. There, networks of alleyways form a compact labyrinth, joining houses with their tiny enclosed gardens. Further north, crowds mill about the entrances to the Bazaar. To the east, an entire district of warehouses marches to the infernal din of trucks loading and unloading, of the metallic screech of overloaded push-carts pulled or pushed by grunting, sweating porters. To the west, tiny workshops spill over onto the sidewalks. The air stinks of sulfur, whistles with the hiss of welding torches, echoes with the roar of motors as they spew a cocktail of oil and gasoline fumes into the polluted air. The streets resemble nothing so much as an open-air manufacturing facility from hell. Tehran's real soul is here, in the winding streets of its southern districts where the idle stroller can lose himself in the crowd, far from the expressways and the cosseted villas of the northern suburbs and their sleekly groomed inhabitants.

Here, the men wear dark-colored clothing, black shirts and trousers that symbolize the mourning of Ashura. The *chadors* that envelop the women from head to toe are just as black, touched with a dusting of gray-ochre deposited by the desert wind.

* * *

It's a warm spring morning in downtown Tehran. The sky is cloudless, but already veiled by a milky-gray haze of pollution. Breathing is becoming difficult. Even to cross the street is a test of will, an ordeal fraught with peril. Pirouetting like bullfighters, we dodge oncoming cars and darting, swarming motorcycles. The sidewalks are thick with people:

schoolboys in hot pursuit of one another weave through the crowd; university students pausing to argue, boys and girls in distinct groups; all around us ambulant vendors, loquacious housewives, impatient delivery-men jockey for position.

As we make our way from Baharestan Square to the Sepahsalar Mosque, and then venture into the commercial district of Sarcheshmeh, we are moving across three of the most symbolically laden places in contemporary Iranian history. Once the focal point of the struggle for democracy, Baharestan Square conjures up the Western influence that found its expression in the Constitutional Revolution. For it was here, in the old parliament building that still dominates the square, that Iran's first democratic constitution, the first adopted by an Eastern country, was proclaimed on December 30, 1906. But the constitutional order it inaugurated was not to last. Soon afterward, to protect the borders of their respective empires, England and Russia would conclude a partition agreement that sliced the country into two zones of influence.[11] This blatant interference in Iran's internal affairs created tensions between those favorable to the European model of governance, and the defenders of traditional forms more in keeping, they claimed, with the nation's past. The ultimate victim would be Iranian constitutionalism, which breathed its last breath in the early hours of February 21, 1921 when Reza Khan, a near-illiterate officer but a natural leader of men, seized power in a military coup.

Only a few minutes' walk from the square stands the Sepahsalar Mosque. From its high pulpit—the *minbar*—a succession of preachers and ayatollahs faithful to the monarchy lashed out at the constitutionalists and attacked their arguments. One of their most illustrious spokesmen, Sheikh Fazlollah Nouri, was to die a martyr's death by hanging at the hands of his democratic opponents. Today, the mosque is quiet, an oasis of calm in the bustling heart of the modern city.

Further south, the Sarcheshmeh district holds its share of surprises. As we make our way down the street choked with automobiles, delivery vehicles, motorcycles, and porters steering their top-heavy push-carts through the multitude, a man hails and beckons us. In fragmentary but serviceable English he points to a tall, arched doorway that leads to a large warehouse.

11. *L'Iran au XXe siècle*, 38.

Then, before we know it, the man has taken us aside—perhaps "buttonholed" would be the better term—and guided us into his kingdom. His name is Mr. Mohammad, a wholesaler of dried fruits by trade. But under the guise of showing us his wares, offering us tea and Bam dates, he would reveal to us a singular aspect of the Iranian national character.

In his early sixties, stocky, muscular, with abundant black hair and a sparkle in his eyes, Mr. Mohammad projects an image of energy, self-confidence, and strength. Not surprisingly, for he soon informs us that he is a practitioner of the *Zourhane*. Literally translated as "house of power," this age-old corporal and spiritual discipline combines physical training with music and religious ritual. Initiates manipulate heavy dumbbells in the shape of bowling pins, each weighing ten kilograms. That morning, in a corner of his warehouse, Mr. Mohammad quickly arranges a small training area, pushing aside crates of dried fruit, barrels of olives, and sacks of aromatic spices. With a piece of heavy cardboard filling in for a mat, he picks up his heavy "bowling pins" by the handles and lifts them above his head as though they were sheaves of straw. Then, with wrist-strength alone, he twirls them at arm's length, describing a series of arcs in the air with a breathtaking mixture of grace and power.

The display of strength and concentration suddenly causes the crates of dates to disappear, the bags of rice and dried beans to vanish, the din of the street to fall still. The old warehouse, with its sculpted columns, illuminated by a high window like a painting of an Italian Renaissance interior, is metamorphosed into a place that breathes with spirituality.

A few glasses of tea later, we've begun to feel quite at home. Tea, in Iran, possesses that unique quality of loosening tongues, and facilitating communication. Not to mention that Bam dates are the finest in the world, and that Mr. Mohammad's generosity seems without limits.

"Do come back to see me again," he insists, handing us a box of dates for the road.

A few days later we return, this time to learn more about his social function as *Zourhane* master in a neighborhood where he seems universally known and respected. The master, we learn, is a grass-roots legal system unto himself, the protector and defender of the weak, and guardian of the downtrodden. He is surrounded by a climate of confidence, of self-reliance, and above all, of dialogue that we can grasp as soon as we step out of his warehouse and onto the street.

In fact, the *Zourhane* master takes for his model Imam Ali,[12] whose portrait hangs in the center of the main wall of the warehouse.

The same portrait of Imam Ali, the embodiment of Shi'ism, can be found in every *Zourhane*: a lion seated peaceably at his feet symbolizes the nation. The lion has lost none of his strength, and is prepared to fight for religion with all its might should ever the need arise.

With Mr. Mohammad as our guide, we explore the neighborhood southward, its streets and alleyways, its tiny shops and shady corners, penetrating as far as Imamzadeh Yahya, a minuscule shrine dedicated to Saint John the Baptist, surrounded by bicentennarian plane trees as old as the city itself.

This is everyman's Tehran, far from the mansions of the north that ostentatiously flaunt their landscaped grounds and private swimming pools high up in the foothills. Here, we are surrounded by the visible world of the narrow laneways in their branching, ramifying complexity, and the invisible world of small gardens hidden behind high ochre walls.

Sarcheshmeh is like them: a secretive place that was one of the hotbeds of the revolution against the shah. Twenty-five years ago, its inhabitants marched out empty-handed into Jaleh Square to demonstrate against the imperial army. Hundreds, if not thousands, were to die. It was, to use Imam Khomeini's favorite expression, "the triumph of blood over the sword."

Eighteen years later, in 1997, the inhabitants of Sarcheshmeh voted overwhelmingly for the democratic reformist Mohammad Khatami. Feelings ran high throughout the district when the shadowy authorities that wield real power closed *Salam*, the only daily newspaper that dared to say aloud what people thought.

In 2000, they again voted for reform candidates to parliament. But the third time around, in the 2003 municipal elections, they stayed home, turning their back on the reformists whose ineffectual tenure at city hall had ended in a morass of discord, corruption, and cronyism. It was a first sign of discontent. An unknown face would henceforth be sitting in the mayor's chair. His name was Mahmoud Ahmadinejad. No one could have foretold that two years later he would be elected Iran's president.

It was here, in Sarcheshmeh, that disappointment with the inability of the reformists to deliver on their promises of a more open, democratic

12. Ali ibn Abi-Talib, cousin and son-in-law of the Prophet Muhammed, fourth Caliph of Islam. Considered by the Shi'a as the legitimate succcessor; first Imam of the Shi'ite "Holy Family." See Yann Richard, *L'Islam chiite*.

society and an improved economy first appeared. Discontent was to grow stronger as the self-proclaimed reformists, for all their lofty pronouncements, proved themselves incapable of solving the day-to-day problems of the population.

Their discontent would be reconfirmed in the Majlis elections of 2004. The reformists had called upon their supporters to stay at home in protest against the massive rejection of their candidates by the all-powerful Council of Guardians. In Sarcheshmeh, few heeded the call. For the reform movement's erstwhile supporters, impatience had been replaced by a combination of cynicism, frustration, and demands for action—whatever it might be.

Weighing Words

WHAT CAN A WORD LIKE "REPUBLIC" mean when a popularly elected president must submit to the arbitrary dictates of the Supreme Guide chosen by a faction of the clergy? What, at first glance, seemed to us an exercise in irrationality reflects, in fact, the complex structure of the Iranian state, which is both republican and religious.

Still, we frequently have the feeling that the meaning of words eludes us, that definitions vary from one conversation to another, depending on whom we're talking to. How are we to understand what is happening in a country where the dead seem more alive than the living, where the past is more present than the present, where the invisible overshadows the visible? One May morning in 2001, in our suite at the Vanak Hotel, we were listening to Radio-Canada International on a portable short-wave radio. It's a paradox: if we want to keep up with current events in Iran, we must rely on foreign radio stations. The sound is being transmitted from Montreal, but we're only a few blocks away from the reporter whose voice we hear: Siavosh Ghazi, Radio-Canada correspondent in Iran, reporting on the regime's latest clamp-down on the press:

> On March 18, just before the Iranian New Year holiday, judicial authorities ordered four more newspapers closed. A few days later Ismael Sheikh, one of the leaders of the student movement, was arrested. It appears likely that there will be more arrests of members of the reform movement and the liberal opposition.

An hour later, we meet Siavosh Ghazi in front of a street corner newsstand just around the corner from his home, in north Tehran.

"I buy all the papers, anywhere from twenty to twenty-five. I've got to stop at a couple of newsstands to find them all. More than a dozen dailies have been shut down in the last year, along with between fifteen and twenty weekly and monthly publications. Some of them have been replaced, but there are currently more conservative than reformist newspapers. The papers that have been shut down have been replaced by conservative publications, which are not as widely read as the reform papers. According to the Press Law, the justice department cannot keep a newspaper closed for longer than six months. But most of them have been closed for more than a year. This shows the strength of the conservatives within what we call the power structure. Their power does not lie in society, where they're in the minority, but inside the regime, which they control from top to bottom. Which means they can afford to ban newspapers without any regard for majority opinion, or for the law.

"We have to add that, behind the newspaper closings, there are journalists in prison. Right now, there are more than a dozen. Some of them have been tried and convicted. Others are awaiting judgment; they've been in jail for one, two, or even five months. What many Iranian journalists say is that this is the price we have to pay to democratize Iran. For the people who are behind bars, it's a very high price, but it's a price we have to pay if things are going to change. We've got to pass through this period of transition so that people learn to accept a free press, so that all political opinions can be freely expressed. The vocabulary of violence that some high-ranking clergymen have been using for the last four years has created an atmosphere of justification for violent acts, even for assassinations. Just recently, Said Hajjarian was attacked by a group of young people who believed he was acting against Islam."

In Iran, the regime invokes defense of Islam to justify its worst abuses. It insists that the revelation of secret police involvement in the murders of dissident intellectuals and the disappearance of opposition political figures had nothing to do with the shutdown of several reform newspapers, that in fact these newspapers had violated religious regulations and offended the religious sensitivities of certain citizens— usually the same offended citizens. Islam, it seems, can be counted upon for yeoman service in the defense of the regime.

It is hardly surprising that the extraordinary outburst of free expression that followed Mohammad Khatami's election has yielded, seven years later, to an atmosphere of fear and suspicion. From fanciful accusations through intimidation, beatings, and "exemplary" murders, no method can be ruled out in the campaign to silence those who talk too much. Lest there be any misunderstanding, the Supreme Guide himself, Ali Khamene'i, weighed in on the side of repression when he accused the reformist press of being "a base for the enemy in Iran."

As a result, Iran has almost overtaken Turkey in the sad race for the restriction of press freedom in the Middle East, though it lags well behind China and Cuba for the number of journalists incarcerated.[13] Evin Prison could almost lay claim to being the country's most prestigious newsroom. Two of Iran's most intrepid writers were behind bars: Akbar Ganji, "guilty" of exposing the secret mechanisms that made it possible for a small group of influential men to consolidate their "behind the curtain" power of life or death over those brave enough to challenge their stranglehold on the instruments of the state; and Abbas Abdi, one of the student leaders during the American Embassy takeover, "guilty" of having published a public-opinion poll showing that more than 75 percent of Iranians desired renewed relations with the United States.[14]

The death—under suspicious circumstances—of an Iranian Canadian photojournalist in 2003 added one more name to the long list of murders, kidnappings, condemnations, and torture of intellectuals and journalists. Fifty-four-year-old Zahra Kazemi was arrested by members of the Revolutionary Guard intelligence services in front of the prison where a peaceful demonstration organized by families of the incarcerated was taking place. Accused of spying, she was beaten, and died three days later from a skull fracture caused by a blunt instrument. Some observers believed they recognized the signature of Said Mortazavi, the Tehran public prosecutor and judge who had handed down guilty verdicts to several journalists. It is known that Mr. Mortazavi was present at Ms. Kazemi's interrogation.

What was her crime? She was in possession of a press card issued by the Press Office of the Ministry of Culture and Islamic Guidance, whose director came under fire for coming to the journalist's defense. Assuming that she was taking photographs in an area where photography was forbidden, Ms. Kazemi hardly represented a threat; no state secrets were on display; only Iranians who had gathered to denounce the abuse of power and to demand respect for human rights: nothing that could possibly justify a death sentence with neither judgment nor appeal.

Despite insistence by the Canadian government on an open hearing, the investigation promised by the authorities has several times been

---

13. Committee to Protect Journalists, *Attacks on the Press* (New York, March 2004). According to the New York–based organization, two journalists were killed in Iran in 2003, and three were serving prison terms, compared with Turkey, where five remained behind bars. The country where the practice of journalism is the most dangerous, with the exception of Iraq where twenty-three journalists were killed, is the Philippines, where five journalists were killed, followed by Colombia.

14. Both Ganji and Abdi have subsequently been released after serving their sentences.

postponed. Ms. Kazemi's son's efforts to repatriate his mother's dead body have proven futile. Funeral services were hastily organized; Zahra Kazemi was buried in Shiraz, where her mother still lives. There is good reason to believe that the inquest will never take place.

In Iran, the regime has treated the death of Ms. Kazemi as a minor incident comparable to cases of police excess in Montreal or Vancouver. For the power structure, it is clear that the death of Zahra Kazemi was little more than an unfortunate accident; at worst, it may have been the work of a handful of notorious "rogue elements" who are frequently cited as perpetrators of crimes against anyone suspected of standing in the way of the power structure.

The incident, whether a case of police misconduct or the work of "rogue elements," was consistent with the internal logic of the Iranian system. Its near-absolute power has fostered a culture of impunity. The perpetrators of criminal acts disguised as accidents seem always to be the same people: single-minded men who can be easily convinced that they are acting in a just cause. In fact, they are simply carrying out decisions made higher up, applying *fatwas*—religious rulings—drafted in secret. Their function is that of strong-arm men for a regime that occasionally, from behind the curtain, shows its true face. If, in the murder of Zahra Kazemi, that face had been temporarily shrouded, it could be clearly seen in the attack that nearly cost Said Hajjarian his life—and decapitated the reform movement.

A Marked Man

SAID HAJJARIAN WAS SEATED UPRIGHT in his wheelchair, his forearms resting on the armrests, his head held motionless by a surgical collar. Behind him, a mechanized rehabilitation apparatus took up the better part of the office that had been transformed into a full-fledged rehabilitation facility. Off to the side, partially hidden behind a screen, stood a hospital bed. Fluorescent tubes cast an icy light. Directly behind the wheelchair, a physiotherapist supervised his patient's every movement with infinite patience, like a mother helping a child to take its first steps, encouraging with his looks and gestures the man for whom every movement was a new, and uncertain, beginning.

In a weak but warm voice, enunciating slowly, painstakingly, Said Hajjarian bid us welcome and, at the same time, attempted to draw himself upright in his wheelchair. Every word was an effort, a victory over silence. He begged us to excuse him for not receiving us as he would have liked. Even though he had suffered crippling wounds, and barely escaped death, his sensitivity to the rules of politeness, which Iranians call *ta'arof*, had not deserted him. And as he spoke, his hands moved up and down in jerky movements, as though his half-paralyzed fingers were making one final attempt to grasp an object just beyond his reach. But Hajjarian's eyes, behind heavy horn-rimmed glasses, conveyed a sense of vitality totally at odds with the inertia of his slouching body—the bullet that struck him had failed to destroy the pugnacity of the colossus he had once been.

Who wanted Said Hajjarian dead? Iranians consider this singular survivor—the "miraculous one," as he was described by the press in the days following the murder attempt—as the architect of Mohammad Khatami's election in 1997, and the strategic intelligence behind the overwhelming victory of the reform coalition in the parliamentary elections of 2000. His was also the theoretical mind behind a new concept of relations between the state and its citizens, one that had seemed inconceivable in the Islamic Republic.

Said Hajjarian had become a marked man. (*Salam Iran*, courtesy of InformAction Films)

Few doubted that Said Hajjarian had become a marked man. A man who had broken ranks, more than once.

His path had been a long one, at once uncommon and yet typical among followers of Imam Khomeini. After the revolution, he launched his career as a radical Islamist. He climbed the ladder rapidly: as a founding member of the Revolutionary Guards, he organized its intelligence network, and then served a term as deputy minister of information.

Leaving government service, he enrolled in a course of study in *fiqh*, the classic Islamic jurisprudence curriculum, as interpreted in Iran by Shi'a religious scholars, and began to distance himself from the conservative elite that held power. Almost overnight he became the voice and chief strategist of a social and political reawakening, the "brains" of the nascent reform movement. Not surprisingly, Said Hajjarian's political development became a cause for suspicion and, among the hard-liners who ruled the country from behind the curtain, a motive for revenge. On March 12, 2000, he paid the price.

That morning, Said Hajjarian was on his way to Tehran City Hall. He had not noticed the motorcycle that was following his car and stopped a few paces behind him. He took no heed of the young man who handed him an envelope on the sidewalk. Beneath the envelope was a pistol equipped with a silencer. The security guards in front of the building saw nothing, heard nothing. The shot was fired at point-blank range. The bullet grazed the base of his brain, lodging in his neck next to the spinal column.

A few days later, state television broadcast a picture of the would-be assassin, a certain Said Asqar. But the petty hired hit man had no motive for attempting to kill Said Hajjarian. No one fell for the story. Asqar had pulled the trigger, but someone else had given the order. The evidence was overwhelming: Asqar had used a service revolver and a powerful motorcycle, strictly limited to the police and the security services. At his trial Asqar boasted that if he had wanted to kill Hajjarian, he would have aimed higher. It was a warning, he said.

Asqar was nothing more than a hired killer, an executioner. Such a man could not have acted alone. The order had to have come from higher up, backed by a *fatwa*, the only authority for killing or grievously wounding someone considered to be outside the bounds of faith. To warrant death, Said Hajjarian had to have ceased to exist as a member of the community of believers. His was an "Islamic" version of outlaw status, of excommunication. But unlike the hoary Western practice, the process of designation and the identity of the designated person remained state secrets to be revealed only upon carrying out the "sentence."

What had been his crime? Seeking an answer, we rapidly reviewed what we had heard in a town where rumors spread more rapidly than verifiable information, and where fear of possible consequences was entirely justified. There in front of us, in his wheelchair, sat Said Hajjarian, eloquent proof of the consequences of words and deeds threatening to the regime.

The attempt on Hajjarian's life was part of a strategy of violence, clearly designed to suppress any form of opposition to the clerical state. It was not long before people began drawing connections to a series of murders perpetrated a few years earlier with the intent of creating an atmosphere of terror. In November 1998, five dissident intellectuals, members of a tiny political party tolerated by the Islamic regime, were found with their throats cut in their Tehran homes. The discovery of their mutilated bodies touched off shock waves, not only among political circles but also among the citizenry at large.

An investigation commissioned by President Khatami revealed that the murders had been the work of "rogue elements" belonging to the security police. Suspects were arrested, tried, and condemned to ludicrously short prison terms. Public opinion would have none of it, especially since all the "guilty parties" were released shortly thereafter, with one exception: a certain Said Eslami (also known as Said Emami). Eslami's life would later end on the floor of the prison bathhouse, where he was found dead after swallowing a depilatory substance. To no one's surprise, suicide was the verdict. Once again, public opinion would have none of it.

Said Eslami had been a high-ranking intelligence operative; a man of strange and intense religious views. He had been videotaped as he addressed a political meeting in the city of Hamedan, where he boasted of the punishment he would inflict on "the accursed unbelievers" who dared defy the indisputable doctrine of the state, sacred dogma in a regime that styles itself as religious. He was quite open about his intention to eliminate them; to do so was his duty, and a source of pride.

These were the facts as revealed by *Salam*, the newspaper that for many years had been the only voice of resistance to total control of information by the clerics. *Salam*'s relative immunity had, paradoxically, been guaranteed by the fact that its publisher was himself a leading Shi'a clergyman. The revelations had the effect of a political bombshell. Iranians, unsurprisingly, had long since learned to believe the opposite of the official media story. But this time, *Salam* had the real story, and played it front page, sparing no details. Above all, it named names and connected the dots: unprecedented ever since the religious faction had consolidated its power in 1982. *Salam*'s revelations not only affirmed the independence of the press, they drew a powerful response from a public that had all but lost faith in the 1979 revolution. They were also a part of the reformist strategy to open up Iranian society devised by Said Hajjarian.

Events unfolded rapidly: in July 1999 *Salam* was banned, then closed; its publisher, Ayatollah Mousavi Khoeiniha, was brought before a special clerical tribunal. Reaction from the street was instantaneous. The day after the closure was announced, students came out by the thousands to protest. The hard-line clerical faction fought back, using plain-clothes thugs from the hyper-fundamentalist Ansar-e Hezbollah (Companions of the Party of God), who attacked the students, invaded and trashed their dormitories. When it was all over, one student had been killed and dozens wounded.

For more than a week Tehraners watched—and sometimes joined in—as demonstrators clashed with police. Only a huge counter-demonstration organized by the regime was able to turn the tide: order was gradually restored. The Islamic Republic had been shaken to the core as never before in its twenty-year existence.

Said Hajjarian had intuited that the press could become a key force in the battle to reform and democratize Iranian society. It would now become his principal ally. Taking matters into his own hands, he became publisher of an independent daily, and recruited Akbar Ganji, a sharp-witted journalist with a reputation for pugnacity, to join the fight. The two men founded *Sobh-e Emrouz* (This Morning), which took over where *Salam* had left off.

A series of hard-hitting articles appeared over Ganji's byline, throwing the heretofore anonymous heavyweights of the clerical establishment on the defensive. He reopened the infamous "serial murders" scandal of 1998, tracing the orders to kill to the very top. The investigation carried him well beyond Said Eslami/Emami, the hothead from Hamedan. Ganji dared to disclose the name of the man that gave the order: Ali Fallahian, a mid-ranking cleric and minister of information, whom he described as the "gray eminence" of the regime.

But Ganji was determined to go farther still. He proved that behind Ali Fallahian hid the man he called the "red eminence" (red for blood), the former president and strongman of the regime, Ali Akbar Hashemi Rafsanjani. This particular bit of information, which completed the chain of responsibility for the sordid murders of 1998, could only have come from Said Hajjarian, the former head of the intelligence services and ex–deputy information minister.

For the regime's darkest and most powerful figures, Said Hajjarian had just signed his death warrant. The man who had once been their confidant had now become a dangerous foe, a marked man.

"The people who shot me are victims themselves, men who were manipulated. The brains behind the attack wanted to terrorize the reform movement. I can't tell you their names, but if you read the papers, you'll understand who they are."

That very morning, perhaps by coincidence, the Tehran papers headlined a statement by Ayatollah Qazzali, one of the regime's most notorious hard-liners. If religion is in danger, he said, believers must be prepared to die, or even to kill, to protect it. In a country where clerical control over the inner workings of the state in intelligence matters borders on the absolute, the ayatollah's statement could be seen as a thinly veiled incitement to murder—a call that the Supreme Guide himself, Mr. Ali Khamene'i, was not to disavow.

Later we were to learn that one year before the attack, Said Hajjarian had accused another leading ayatollah, Mohammad Mesbah-Yazdi (nicknamed *temsah*, "crocodile" in Farsi) of promoting violence and anarchy by stating that Muslims had no need for authorization to suppress "apostates." The day after he was shot down, several Tehran dailies reprinted Hajjarian's remarks.

Did they shoot you because you had more compromising information to reveal, or because they saw you as the strategist of a movement that threatened them?

"I'm certainly not the movement's only strategist, and not its only theoretician. They wanted to kill me because of my ideas, not because I had any information about them. I don't have any such thing. Don't take me for a movie star. I was very active in the Islamic Participation Front, and that's all there was to it."

Said Hajjarian was no movie star; but he had been a dedicated activist whose change of heart closely resembles that of a generation of young revolutionaries. Most had been students of Ali Shariati, the philosopher and religious ideologue who, by sheer force of character, brought Iranian youth to accept an interpretation of Islam far removed from the arid, pedantic reading of the traditionalist mullahs. Among his best-known protégés were the students who stormed the U.S. Embassy in 1979.

Those were the days when, day and night, massive demonstrations in support of the occupiers streamed past the embassy gates. The country's universities would soon close their doors, swept up in a "cultural revolution" that aspired to rid higher-level education of the Western model and replace it with courses that conformed to religious principles. At the same time, the students "following the Imam's line" organized their own courses within the embassy walls, inviting guest lecturers of their own choosing.

One of them was named Said Hajjarian, then a student who had not taken part in the capture of the U.S. Embassy personnel.

Massoumeh Ebtekar describes him in her account of the embassy takeover: "Even as a student, Hajjarian had developed an uncanny ability to analyze and foresee events. His lectures were very popular, and were one of the highlights of our impromptu study program."[15]

While the capture of the embassy had not launched Hajjarian's career, his lectures to the students quickly consolidated his reputation as an analyst. Soon after, he joined the agency that was to become the new regime's intelligence service, and went on to become one of its main organizers. His mission was to set up an efficient organization capable of protecting the nascent Islamic regime from its foreign and domestic enemies—ruthlessly if need be. Neither the task nor the outcome was always a pleasant one. Civil war was raging; interrogation of suspects

---

15. Massoumeh Ebtekar, as told to Fred A. Reed, *Takeover in Tehran* (Vancouver: Talonbooks, 2000), 205.

could be forceful. Could Said Hajjarian have ever suspected that the very intelligence service he had helped to create would produce the professional killers used against him two decades later?

Hajjarian carried out his assignment to the letter; his penetrating intelligence and organizational abilities attracted attention and recognition. A bright future seemed to lie before him; he caught the eye of Ali Akbar Hashemi Rafsanjani, the man at the center of the regime's secret structure of repression. Mr. Rafsanjani, who had been elected president in 1989, promised Iranians that he would rebuild their devastated country, after eight years of war against Iraq.

An exhausted population believed him, even as many Iranians suspected that he might have prolonged the war with Iraq, allowing him and his political cronies to amass fortunes. Said Hajjarian was appointed to head a research institute connected directly with the president's inner circle. Among his colleagues were such up-and-coming personalities as Abbas Abdi, Mousavi Khoeiniha, and Mohsen Kadivar, a brilliant young clergyman from the Qom seminary who was to become his close confidant. But living and working in the shadow of power had planted the seeds of doubt in Said Hajjarian's mind.

"While I was working at the research center, I drew up a project for political reform, which Mr. Rafsanjani refused to accept. I had come to the conclusion that economic reform was doomed to failure if it were not accompanied by political and social reform. We couldn't keep on ruling the country as an 'enlightened dictatorship.' I began to express my opposition to such methods. Perhaps this authoritarian, bureaucratic model can be applied in Latin America, or China. But here, it would simply reproduce the shah's dictatorship. Iranians have been seeking political liberty for more than one hundred yeas now. People want to have a say, to participate in the administration of their affairs. Iran can no longer be governed with dictatorial methods."

When he realized the then-president's intention to return to a past that Iranians had rejected, Hajjarian took his proposal to Mohammad Khatami. The former minister of culture had just agreed, under pressure from his friends, to run for president. The man who would soon lead the government immediately took it up.

"And that was when I drew up a plan for political reform."

It would have been difficult to imagine a sharper break with the past. Hajjarian had emerged from the core of the regime; he had been a part of the inner structure of the state, had kept the company of the men who had betrayed the aspirations of the Iranian people. He therefore had plunged headlong into the study of religious jurisprudence, had certified the failure of his efforts to shape the course of events from within—he had understood that one dictatorship had replaced another.

"We couldn't eliminate a political culture rooted in twenty-five hundred years of absolute despotism. You can't change everything overnight. We have to try to bridge the gap between tradition and modernity. But if we want to tackle unemployment and political instability, political reform is the only way to go about it. The kind of sustainable development we want for our country is not compatible with a climate of repression."

We parted company on a note that sounded like a political rallying cry. The attack had been devastating; Said Hajjarian had survived a cripple, his powers radically diminished. But we sensed in him a desire to keep fighting that went far beyond the severe wound that had almost killed him. It was as if he knew that in targeting him, his would-be assassins were striking a blow at the reform movement. The attack was intended to destroy hope, to silence opposition, and in the final analysis, to proclaim that a bullet in the neck lay in wait for anyone who dared challenge the regime.

A year later, in April 2001, we visited Said Hajjarian once more. This time, he received us standing erect, leaning on a walker and supported on either side by his physiotherapist and his driver. Since the attack, he had become the living symbol of the reform movement. For a moment, his broad smile made us think that the man and the movement were making similar progress. But we were soon to discover that while Mr. Hajjarian's physical rehabilitation had been painfully slow, the reform government seemed totally immobilized.

Knowing by now Said Hajjarian's exquisite sense of irony, his smile might well have conveyed the same thoughts. But we left the matter unmentioned. Our conversation had focused instead on "the dialogue of civilizations and cultures" that had become the guiding principle of President Khatami's foreign policy.

"Tolerance underlies the very nature of dialogue. If you keep your hands in your pockets and then suddenly kill someone with the pistol you've kept hidden there, that's where dialogue ends. Look at the arguments in Samuel Huntingdon's *Clash of Civilizations*, where he analyzes civilizational conflict. According to Huntingdon, each civilization has its bloody extremities; he enumerates, if I'm not mistaken, eight or nine civilizations that possess this kind of extremity. Conflict between them is the norm, and when it breaks out, no dialogue is possible."

Quite so. Mr. Khatami's initiative may have relieved American pressure on Iran, giving the country the opportunity to catch its breath and to rebuild ties with its neighbors. But isn't there just as great a need for dialogue among Iranians?

"There is a process of dialogue at work in our country. But there are also people who would prefer violent means instead of tolerance; but without tolerance, there can be no meaningful dialogue.

"In Iran, there are sharp divisions between social groups, between different ethnic groups, between the nation and the government. To maintain our unity, we must encourage and promote the culture of dialogue among ourselves. Iran is the heir to a civilization, that of Persia, that coexisted with other civilizations. This is the example we must follow if we want to recreate a dialogue between Iranian civilization and other civilizations.

"Ever since I began my recovery, my main concern has been to find the best way to reinforce the culture of tolerance between our country and other countries, in our international relations."

The man motionless before us in his chair had suddenly come to life, as if fueled by an inner flame. Stopping him was clearly out of the question, even though his physiotherapist had warned us that he was prone to rapid exhaustion.

"Look at me! I'm a victim of violence. After the attack all Iran, from Tehran to the most remote village, came together to pray for my health. A reaction of this magnitude tells you that people don't want any more violence. Representatives of all the political trends, in spite of their differences, came to visit me in hospital.

"That showed that our people react very strongly to violence, and reject it by nature. Take the revolution. If you compare the Islamic Revolution with other revolutions, you'll see that there was not excessive violence. There were some small guerilla groups that wanted to use it, but the Guide, Ayatollah Khomeini, called for patience. He encouraged them not to use weapons, and to put flowers in their gun-barrels.

"Our country's new middle class knows it has everything to lose by violence. Negotiation has become a part of dialogue. All this means that we have to create our own model. We have to draw on others' experiences, but we must find our own path."

As he bid us goodbye that evening, an exhausted Said Hajjarian told us, speaking as though each word were an end in itself, "Now that I have a second life, I am devoting it to democracy, to dialogue, and to strengthening civil society. God has given me this second life."

Silence. He looked at us with a smile and then, with great effort, rose to his feet, steadying himself on his physiotherapist's arm, then taking a few halting steps before coming to a stop, breathing heavily, "I hope the next time you come I can stand up to greet you. Didn't philosophers used to dialogue as they strolled together?"

We could not remain indifferent to this elemental force—a mighty oak that refused to fall, that had become a symbol of struggle and resistance. Said Hajjarian's personality was a match for his career path, that of the revolutionary facing the classic dilemma of all revolutions: to preserve its achievements by repressing criticism and challenge, or to accept the dynamics of history and evolving thought by adapting the model to new realities. Hajjarian had begun his journey at the shadowy core of the regime before turning against it, then becoming its victim—if not a martyr to the cause he had come to serve.

* * *

Since our last conversation two years had elapsed. Whether by coincidence or fate, the reform movement could not break the vice grip of a tightly structured ruling establishment that was far more coherent in the defense of its privileges than the reformists had been in promoting their own program.

Worse yet, Mohammad Khatami, despite—or perhaps because of—his personal integrity, had proven a mediocre politician, unable to carry through his ambitious program for opening up Iranian society. The clerical caste's iron-fisted control had been tighter than anyone could have imagined. Firmly ensconced in positions of authority, in full control of the revolutionary apparatus, skillfully manipulating religious slogans, the mullahs and their allies clearly had no intention of abandoning the field.

Some members of Iran's fiery younger generation had looked forward to outside intervention to settle accounts with the clerical establishment. Now their illusions lay shattered by the American invasion of Iraq. At the same time, the armed threat along Iran's borders provided the mullacracy with an ironclad argument for hanging on to power.

With the election of Mahmoud Ahmadinejad as mayor in 2003, Said Hajjarian lost his political base in the Tehran municipal administration. Things were going from bad to worse for the reformists. Metaphors shouldn't be abused, but we wondered: had the bullet that struck Said Hajjarian not also brought down the movement that he had labored so hard to create?

The Voices of Silence

THE REFORMIST PRESS burst upon Iranian society in the aftermath of Mohammad Khatami's surprise election on May 2, 1997. Dozens of new dailies, magazines, and specialized publications appeared, seemingly overnight, on Tehran's street-corner newsstands.

Financed on a shoestring, published out of storefront offices or private apartments, they took a news-hungry city by storm. Iranians had long relied for information on a mixture of hearsay and disbelief in everything the official media claimed as fact. Citizens snapped up broadsheets like *Jama'eh* (Society) or *Sobh-e Emrouz*, which, for the first time in Iran, spared no one. Major front-page stories by daring, well-informed journalists like Akbar Ganji touched off shock waves in a polity where information had been the monopoly of the regime.

The motto of the reform movement, inspired by Said Hajjarian, became: "A free citizen is a well-informed citizen." For the first two years that followed the presidential election, Iran's press was in a state of continuous ferment, quickly emerging as the driving force for reform. New daily newspapers challenged the regime on its own ground, bringing to light the sordid details of political scandals, lashing out at a culture of murder, imprisonment, disappearance, and torture. There had been nothing like it since the earliest days of the revolution. Journalists like Masha'ollah Shamsolvaezin, one of Iran's keenest analytical minds, emerged as public personalities, calling for ever greater openness, seeming at times to taunt the regime. Some had gone so far that cooler heads among the reformists began to advise caution, as if to say, People appreciate us, but they may not necessarily follow us. It was only a matter of time before the regime launched a well-planned counter-offensive.

The closing of *Salam* was to bring the euphoria to an abrupt end; now the reformists would be confronting the hard-core of the conservatives' power-base. *Salam*'s revelations about the 1998 serial killings were more than the regime was prepared to tolerate: a capital offense, which could not go unpunished. The ruling elite could live with revelations of corruption, of shady dealing and influence peddling common to any political system. It could not accept a frontal attack on its basic premises.

It was a pivotal moment.

To reassert control, a new law governing the press was sent to parliament for debate. Its conditions were draconian, providing the judiciary with powerful tools for enforcing silence. On the eve of the first reading of the law, *Salam* struck again. In a press conference, journalist Abbas Abdi brandished a photocopy of a hand-written draft of the law: the author, he stated, was Said Eslami/Emami, the mastermind behind the serial killings.

The following day, *Salam* was shut down for good.

The closing had the effect of a bomb at the heart of the power structure. It was clear that the regime could silence a newspaper that dared to claim that not only were killers at large in society, but that they were now drafting legislation to protect themselves. Suddenly, the entire country was confronted with the cold truth.

The impact was immediate. Within days, new reform dailies appeared. But many of them lacked *Salam*'s high standards and sense of professionalism. Journalistic quality began to drift, and information presented often seemed closer to rumor than confirmed fact. Turnover was rapid: one paper would vanish, to be replaced by others that hardly had time to establish themselves before disappearing from the newsstands. The crackdown broadened: whatever was too critical, whatever went beyond an increasingly moveable red line, was ordered closed.

One of the first items on the newly elected reform parliament's agenda, in 2001, was to revise the Press Law. But, a few hours before debate was scheduled to begin, the speaker of the house, Mehdi Karoubi, was handed a directive from the office of the Supreme Guide. His instructions were clear: for the good of the nation, and of Islam, it was preferable that no debate should take place; the law was not to be modified. In the legislative chamber, consternation gave way to silence.

Despite its strong pro-reform majority, for all its determination and good will, the legislature had been reduced to impotence. Its fate was sealed; true power lay elsewhere. Mr. Khamene'i's intervention had signed the death warrant of parliament as a sovereign institution that claimed to speak for the people. The Supreme Guide had reminded anyone who cared to listen that he represented another, more powerful institution.

Three years later, when the Council of Guardians, the group of elderly jurisprudents who evaluate legislation for conformity with Islamic principles, decided to exclude a significant number of reform candidates from the 2004 parliamentary elections, the die was cast. The Majlis had become a mute, phantom institution; its failure to amend the Press Law had confirmed its marginality; its lack of combativeness was now clear for all to see. It was as though Iranians knew that they could expect nothing more from this shell of a democratic institution reduced to silence by the Guide's fiat.

The Messenger

IRAN'S PRESS IS A STUDY IN CONTRASTS. Reformist publications lead a nomadic existence, with no fixed address, and with no guarantee of survival from one day to the next. But the "official" press is solidly entrenched, housed in huge complexes that date from the shah's regime, and have hardly changed since the Islamic Revolution. The head offices of the Kayhan Group occupy a full city block in the south-central sector of Tehran, near Imam Khomeini Square. *Kayhan* had once been the pride of Iranian journalism, and the flagship of the largest press group in the Middle East. Today things have changed. The once-proud establishment looks seedy and down-at-the-heel; advertising revenues have plummeted. Readers stay away from a newspaper that depends on handouts from the Supreme Guide's office.

In Tehran, two journalistic worlds exist side by side. The largest by far is that of the city's Persian language dailies, which must respond to public demand and to the political constraints of the national market. Divided roughly between reformists and conservatives, it is a hotly competitive environment—and one that is closely watched by the regime. Alongside it, in miniature, is the much smaller world of English-language dailies. Though far less visible, English dailies can be found in almost all newsstands. Their readership consists principally of foreigners residing in the capital, businessmen, embassy personnel, visiting journalists, and the odd tourist—as well as those Iranians who read English. This is where readers can find editorial comment and international news that is less restricted, more open than in most of their Persian counterparts. Today, there are four: *Iran Daily*, published by IRNA, the semi-official news agency;[16] *Iran Times*, mouthpiece of the Foreign Ministry; *Tehran Times*, published by former president Hashemi Rafsanjani; and *Kayhan International*, the oldest.

For several years, *Kayhan International* represented an anomaly: an independent voice in the dreary landscape of Iranian journalism.

16. Islamic Republic News Agency, politically pro-reform.

Hossein Raghfar, a bright young economist with a sharp pen, had been *Kayhan International's* editor for six years, between 1985 and 1990, recruiting a corps of equally bright, committed writers. Those were the days when *Kayhan International* published well-researched, in-depth analyses of government economic policy and international affairs. Given its low circulation, it would be less likely to rock the boat—and to incur the wrath of the powers-that-be.

Hard on the heels of Hashemi Rafsanjani's election as president, Mr. Raghfar resigned. His replacement was Hamid Najafi, a veteran journalist and strong supporter of the regime. A long-time contributor to *Kayhan*, Mr. Najafi enjoyed a reputation as a satirist whose weekly column featured the misadventures of a court-jester figure known as Simple Jamshid—Jimmy to his regular readers—whose utter ingenuousness allowed him to speak the unspeakable.

But the election of Mohammad Khatami and the rise of the reform movement, along with the flowering of a freer, more critical press, deprived Mr. Najafi of his best targets—in addition to shaking up the Iranian press.

The Kayhan Group emerged as the official voice of the Supreme Guide's office, which would in turn wield decisive ideological and financial influence over its publications. Hamid Najafi has stayed on as editor-in-chief of *Kayhan International*, where he receives us in a small, dusty cubicle. High bookcases hold olive-green leather-bound file volumes covering the newspaper's last twenty-four years; those on the top shelves are warped from a chronically leaky ceiling.

A semi-opaque film of tobacco smoke residue coats the glass walls separating Mr. Najafi's cubicle from the newsroom. We hear none of the hum and bustle of the typical newsroom, neither the clatter of typewriters nor the click of computer keys. While *Kayhan International's* page layout is now done electronically, its journalists still write out their stories in longhand.

It is late January 2004. The Council of Guardians, which controls the electoral process, has just announced its refusal to accept the credentials of more than half of the eight thousand reform candidates in the upcoming parliamentary elections. Tensions are running high among the political elite. In response to a challenge from excluded candidates, the Supreme Guide ruled that the Council was to be obeyed. Those who dared to take issue were opposing the founding principles of the Islamic regime. How much editorial latitude did our host have in commenting on Mr. Khamene'i's ruling? The answer is terse.

"You'll permit me to remain non-committal on this issue; I hope you'll understand," he says, with a touch of irony.

Does your non-committal position influence your editorial freedom?

"No one can tell me what to write; but sometimes I'm asked to publish or to translate an article. We're free not to do so, of course; and often we do not."

Mr. Najafi skirts the question with a smile that seems to say, Ask me no questions and I'll tell you no lies. In his expression, there is something of the victim's hangdog look. We attempt another question.

As a professional journalist and now, editor, what do you make of the newspaper closings that have taken place since 1999?

"When the Islamic Revolution overthrew the former regime, the United States and its allies concluded that they would try to nip it in the bud, or to overthrow it if it somehow managed to survive. They failed. They tried to use their influence among certain parts of the population by purchasing people's beliefs. That's why, all of a sudden, we see so many opposition newspapers.

"As a journalist with more than twenty years' experience, I know how difficult it is to publish a daily newspaper, especially from a financial standpoint. These papers that are popping up like mushrooms can't survive on their own. How can you explain twelve or sixteen daily newspapers, appearing all at once?

"Of course, I'm simply raising a question. The overthrow of the Pahlavi regime was a bitter defeat for the United States, you know; ever since then they've been doing everything they can to re-establish their hegemony over Iran. What we're seeing now is the continuation of this effort in the cultural field. For me, this is the explanation for the rise of the independent press.

"Some journalists, people like Hajjarian, Abdi, and Ganji, have totally reversed their positions. I think they were upset with the failure of the preceding governments; they were looking for a change."

As a veteran journalist, don't you feel a sense of indignation when a high-profile writer like Akbar Ganji is languishing in jail?

"I do. But the way foreign intelligence agencies—the CIA, the British Intelligence Service—operate is so refined and so subtle that even journalists like Ganji don't know where the money that pays them is coming from. It's all done very professionally."

You're talking about "dirty" financing, but you didn't answer our question. What exactly is Ganji's crime? Why is he in prison?

"His crime? He openly challenged the sacred principles of the regime. Why is a university professor like Hisham Aqajari in prison? Because, during a meeting of devout Muslims, he criticized some aspects of the fundamentals of Islamic belief."

So, there are limits, but what are they?

"You cannot spread doubts among young people about the Holy Qur'an as the Word of God, even in the most subtle way. You cannot raise doubts about the life of the Prophet, or about the lives of the Imams. Aqajari insinuated that if such an Imam existed, but is not among us, what is he good for? I'm telling you this by way of example; that was what he said in Hamedan."

Wasn't Ganji's real offense to have criticized openly former president Rafsanjani? As far as we know, he hasn't questioned the bases of Islamic belief.[17]

"It's all politics. Look, Ganji shouldn't have taken on Mr. Rafsanjani in the first place. We're talking about one of today's most influential political personalities. Let's look at it this way: when a family wants to throw a party it doesn't matter who pays the bill. Everyone wants his fair share of the fun. If the head of the family is clever, he will make sure no one is left out. But if someone is left out, that person won't go home and wait for his turn to come; he'll be looking for a more active role. If you want to understand the case of Ganji, Abdi, and others, you have to see things from that standpoint."

It's easy to understand their frustration. But does that mean they should be thrown in jail, eliminated by force?

"I think they're frustrated. But I also don't think they should have been pushed aside the way they were. The authorities have made an error. They should not have expelled them forcibly from the group."

But how democratic is it to intimidate reformists, to tell them to watch their words, to keep their mouths shut? When you have power, don't you think it's a bit too easy to slip from admonition to threat?

"But the reformists haven't been shunted aside. They've been in parliament for four years. They haven't been true to their constituents. During the drought, farmers were having serious problems with the banks, but all the reformists could think about was political infighting. Nothing was done to help ease the farmers' burden. While people are

17. In 2004, the Supreme Court of the Islamic Republic overthrew the death verdict against Hisham Aqajari brought down by a court in the city of Hamedan.

starving, you have members of parliament who can only talk politics. What a farce! And they wasted four years playing games like that, not attending to their voters' needs at all."

But isn't reform a political program that's based on the principle of a democratic debate, one that the conservatives have refused to participate in?

"Reform has failed because of the mistaken approach of the reformists. They should have devoted their energies to improving the living conditions of the masses. But they did nothing. Nothing but idle chatter and theoretical debate!"

In these circumstances, what are the prospects for the reform movement?

"Reform's prospects are a part of Muslim society; they're grounded in the ideology of Shi'ism; they're a component of our tradition, of our jurisprudence. This spirit of ongoing, dynamic research is a characteristic of the Shi'ite tradition as opposed to the Sunni tradition, which hasn't evolved for centuries.

"But I'm not convinced that this group of reformists is sincere. That's what hurts."

But weren't the reformists right in wanting to remake society, especially when society has democratically expressed its will?

"They moved too fast. For more than two thousand years, kings and emperors have lorded it over Iranian society. Before the arrival of Shi'ism, it was under the thumb of caliphs who couldn't have cared less about freedom of expression. The people knew the caliph had no legitimacy, and that was the reason why he did everything in his power to restrict freedom of expression. It was the same under the shah and under the sultans: people didn't have the right to speak out.

"The reformists were in too much of a hurry. That is one of the reasons for their failure. In Shi'a ideology the people have the right to express themselves, and to criticize their rulers. If the ruler is unjust, we cannot remain silent. We believe that the tyrant, as well as those who have allowed the tyrant to commit injustice, will be judged in the hereafter."

We get the impression that religion has taken the place of politics. Couldn't this be a danger for Islam?

"In certain circumstances, perhaps. But the drafters of the constitution took great pains to make sure no such thing could happen. This is where the Council of Guardians comes in: to make sure that politics do not replace ideology. But the danger existed then, it exists today, and it will still exist tomorrow."

The assassination attempts, the murders, the jail terms: are all these things being done in the name of politics, or in the name of religion?

"They're being done in the name of religion, and they're very wrong. It's unjustifiable to try to kill Hajjarian in the name of religion. The people who attacked him claimed they did it because he had become an apostate.[18] But then the question arises: who are you to decide whether so-and-so has become an apostate? Are you experts, or are you street thugs? What is the source of your authority?"

You know better than we do that in an Islamic society, when such acts take place, someone has made the decision. You cannot kill without authorization, without a *fatwa*. Who decides?

"Certainly someone decides, but we don't know who. Because the killers we're talking about are gangsters, street thugs. This kind of behavior is against religion. It's unacceptable in a religious society, under an Islamic government. It has to stop immediately; it's detrimental to the system."

It is difficult for us to grasp the nature of religious power. Isn't religion making use of politics to consolidate its power over society? If you politicize religion, aren't you taking the risk of destroying it, or at least discrediting it?

"You're looking at things with your Westerners' eyes. In Islam, politics and religion are one. The Prophet is God's Messenger, and at the same time, the leader of society. Ali is the Prophet's successor, and a political leader. Today, the Supreme Guide is both the leader and the substitute for the Twelfth Imam: two in one."

It's a curious paradox. Even though his power is absolute, the Guide's power is limited by the constitution. If he should fail to carry out his duties, the Council of Experts can dismiss him. That would seem to indicate that his power derives less from God than from the will of the people as expressed indirectly by the Council of Experts. Are we looking at a system of religious domination, or at a political system that uses religion as an instrument of power?

As we take our leave of Mr. Najafi, the question remains unanswered. It is the ultimate red line, the line that cannot be crossed without calling into question the Guide's power and legitimacy. Anyone who steps over that line enters into the forbidden zone, the core of power in the Islamic Republic of Iran.

---

18. One who renounces his faith.

The Heart of Darkness

HAMID NAJAFI WAS A MESSENGER. We intended to get to the bottom of things, and he knew it. A few minutes were enough for him to arrange an appointment for us with the head of Kayhan Group, whose business card reads: "Hossein Shariatmadari, Representative of the Supreme Guide, President, Kayhan Press Group."

Who better could help us enter, as an Iranian friend put it,[19] into "the heart of darkness"? It might be impossible to meet Ali Khamene'i himself, but we could question his representative, his spokesman—the voice of the Guide once removed, the media expert hand-picked by the regime to muzzle, if not silence altogether, the voice of the reform movement that had sprung up in 1997.

To curb the impact of reform, the conservative power elite would develop a sophisticated strategy, employing both brute force and ideological manipulation. Asserting control over the Kayhan Group would be a key element of this strategy. In 1998, the Supreme Guide appointed Hossein Shariatmadari, one of the leading spokesmen of the regime's conservative wing, as publisher and editor-in-chief.

Mr. Shariatmadari is a man who has paid his dues. As a front-line fighter in the struggle against the monarchy, he experienced the horrors of the shah's prisons, where he was brutally tortured. He went on to play a significant role in the revolution, and became one of the regime's most dedicated—and unconditional—defenders. The Guide's choice proved a perfect match to the new circumstances. Mr. Shariatmadari would become the man of the hour, the man who would prove the truism that torture victims can be the best torturers. His appointment indicates that it would be an error to underestimate the regime's political strength, its intelligence, and its cold determination to weather all attacks.

With a smile, he shows us into his spacious office on the top floor of the Kayhan complex. Mr. Shariatmadari is chatty, self-assured, and courteous—and anxious to correct our mistaken impressions. Yes, he

---

19. A connoisseur of Joseph Conrad.

knows Westerners well, he assures us; he knows how they classify political realities in the Islamic world; as a result they caricature the complex relationship between conservatives and reformists by labeling them right and left, respectively. But Iran is neither the United States nor Europe. The Iranian political landscape is different.

"On the one hand, you have people who believe in Islamic values and the Islamic Revolution, and on the other, you have people opposed to it. There are only a handful of such people, but they create division and undermine the country's unity. Their propaganda has turned friends into enemies."

Mr. Shariatmadari believes that the "outside enemy" is the source of conflict in Iran, and not local causes.

"According to our information there is a close resemblance between what is being said here, and what the foreign radios and newspapers are saying. When we hear such opinions here at home, we quite logically conclude that the people expressing them are being manipulated, if not directly controlled, by the foreign enemies of the Islamic Revolution."

What evidence does he have to support such a claim? The argument is a circular one: the reformists' slogans and those used by the foreign press and radio are similar, and that is proof enough, and not at all a matter of simple coincidence.

"Of course, it's the job of the authorities to shed light on all of this, and to make their conclusions known."

Mr. Shariatmadari remains convinced that certain groups, disguised as reformists, are using the current election campaign to promote their true purpose, which is to overthrow the regime. They had better think again.

"What they forget is that any law adopted by the Majlis must also be approved by the Council of Guardians."

As editor and publisher of *Kayhan*, he knows whereof he speaks: the Council of Guardians is the watchdog of the regime. As if to prove his contention, in January 2004, as we were meeting, the Council had just disqualified nearly four thousand parliamentary candidates with only the most cursory examination. Any attempt to reverse its decision would be seen as defiance of the regime itself.

Just who are the "foreign enemies" that are scheming to bring down the Islamic regime? Mr. Shariatmadari describes them as the capitalists who fled Iran after the revolution, the people who made a fortune during the Iran-Iraq war, and worse.

"There are people living right here, in Iran, and who maintain illicit relations with foreign powers, or who belong to illegal groups."

Mr. Shariatmadari's hatred for the Western powers that backed the shah while they turned a blind eye to the monarch's reign of terror is deep and abiding. The torture inflicted on him cost him a kidney. It is not difficult to understand his deep mistrust of anything Western, his conviction that opposition is nothing less than treason, that criticism masks a strategy of Western-fomented destruction of the regime. His intention, in unmasking the "true nature" of the reform movement, is clear: to stymie the advance of the reformists by all possible means.

But there is more to Mr. Shariatmadari than the hard-line CEO of the Kayhan Group and the Supreme Guide's representative. He has also won a reputation as a specialist in interrogation for the Information Ministry, the government department in charge of internal security. Who could forget that ministry agents had been implicated in the violent assassination of opposition intellectuals in 1998?

Well-informed sources claimed that, during the months leading up to those crimes, which were designed to create an atmosphere of terror, Mr. Shariatmadari had received several visits from Said Eslami/Emami, suspected of being the mastermind behind the murders committed in the name of Islam.

Akbar Ganji, who at the time had first identified Hossein Shariatmadari as part of the intelligence apparatus, was later to recall: "When we published the story, he defended himself, saying that he was 'dialoguing' with the accused! What a joke! You can have dialogue among free citizens, not between the torturer and his victim!"

Mr. Ganji has been behind bars for more than three years; Said Hajjarian has barely survived the attempt on his life; more than fifty newspapers and magazines have been shut down. The reform movement that seemed poised to transform the Iranian political scene has been slowed to a crawl, while the power of the regime has grown with every passing day.

Tea, two platters of fresh fruit and sweetmeats now appear before us on Mr. Shariatmadari's opulent oval conference table.

Between sips, we remind our host that we have already been in Tehran for three weeks now; that we have closely followed the rejection of the reform candidates by the Council of Guardians, and the resignation of several ministers of the Khatami government. We feel that we are witnessing a political and social crisis. Does he have the same sense of crisis, and if so, how does he interpret it?

"It's not a crisis of the usual kind. We've been dealing with similar situations since the beginning of the revolution. Almost immediately after victory, the United States, the European Union, and several regional countries claimed that the revolution was a threat to their interests and started to cause problems for us. We had to fight terrorist groups, wage an imposed war for eight years. Europe and America have both admitted to supporting Iraq in its war against us. We had the war of the oil tankers; they bombed our cities and towns, used chemical weapons against us, set up an economic embargo. But throughout those years, we managed to live normal, ordinary lives.

"Let me give you an example of how we look at these issues today. Even as we speak, the qualifications of some candidates in the upcoming parliamentary election have been rejected. The Council of Guardians has based its rejection on the law. The work of the Council is quite unlike that of any similar agencies in other countries. For example, the United States Supreme Court was under no obligation to explain why it decided to validate the election of George Bush rather than that of Al Gore, even though the vote-counting process had not yet ended.

"But in Iran, the Council of Guardians must make certain that candidates' qualifications conform fully to the law. If their qualifications have been rejected, it is simply because they were not in full conformity with the constitution and with regulations. So, what is the problem?

"You may have noticed that some of the current members of parliament whose candidacies were rejected have started a hunger strike. But people are not supporting them. The political world is concerned, but not the general public. But you can only have a real 'crisis' if the general public is involved. I say there is no crisis; but I don't claim there is not a problem."

But on the one hand you have an elected chamber, with a strong popular mandate; and on the other hand, a small group of officials who claim to be the only people capable of interpreting the law. Isn't that a sizeable contradiction? How do you intend to resolve it?

"If we compare the situation with the previous parliament, the number of candidates whose qualifications have been approved is greater. The ones who have been rejected belong to two factions, the left and the right. You can judge by whether or not people turn out to vote; then you'll see, plenty of people will be casting their ballots. This is why I say that there is a problem, but not a crisis."

What's the distance between problem and crisis? The reformists claim that they are the only ones being disqualified.

"If there are more rejected reformists than conservatives, it's because they simply don't have the qualifications. It's a matter of legality. Don't worry about it. The Council of Guardians has twenty days to review its decision."

We are certainly aware of the procedure. But it seems to us as though the conservatives are hiding behind a particular interpretation of the constitution, not to mention disregarding public opinion. The reformists say "let the people choose." The conservatives eliminate their opponents by claiming them to be unqualified. What's democratic about that?

"These are imaginary definitions. 'Reformists' and 'conservatives' are figments of the West's imagination. According to the most widely accepted definition of conservatism, people's opinions are unstable. That makes the conservatives opportunists; people ready to do anything that profits them in the short term. As they're prepared to compromise even at the international level, they really form a sub-category of liberals.

"So please tell me how can a Muslim, whose aims and whose intentions are quite constant, possibly be a conservative? To equate Muslims with conservatism is to take George W. Bush for a democrat. This is my answer!

"If some candidates have been excluded from the elections, it's because they've done something illegal. The Council's decision has demonstrated that the reformists have no popular support; that's exactly why the fundamentalists would like them to participate in the elections.

"The Council couldn't care less what people think. It works according to law."

The time has come for the crucial question: What is the basis of political legitimacy in Iran? The answer could not have been clearer.

"Islamic regulations. These regulations are enshrined in our constitution, and the constitution establishes what we can and cannot do."

Do you believe that the reform movement has tried to change the Islamic nature of the constitution?

"Some of them may think that way, but not all. The qualifications of many reform MPs were approved; only a few were rejected."

We are not pleading the case of one particular party over another; we want to understand. Hadn't the behavior of these MPs, and the legislation they submitted to parliament, been the real cause for their rejection? For example, the reformists had proposed legislation that would increase the president's powers, and restrict those of the Council of Guardians; the laws were passed. Wasn't that reason enough to eliminate them from the next parliament?

"Under our constitution, the Council must approve all laws adopted by parliament. If a law violates constitutional regulations, the Council will reject it and must officially explain why. So, if a law runs counter to the constitution, why wouldn't the Council of Guardians disallow it? It's all perfectly legal. But there has never been any question of MPs being rejected on account of the laws they've adopted."

Three years ago, when parliament wanted to debate the Press Law, the Council of Guardians never even made a ruling. The Supreme Guide himself intervened to stop it. How can a society function democratically when you have a parliament elected on the basis of universal suffrage on the one hand, and a Guide who has decisive power over parliament, and can neutralize it, on the other?

"That kind of situation can arise occasionally, when a law raises the kind of issues that the Council cannot resolve. These kinds of issues are referred directly to the Guide. It's true that such a situation is possible; the constitution provides for it. But there have been many instances of laws favorable to the reformists that the Guide has approved. Four years ago, the Council was opposed to the Tehran municipal election. It wanted to review the qualifications of a number of elected city councilors, all reformists. The Council attempted to do so, but the Guide ruled that it was unnecessary.

"And when Tehran's former mayor Mr. Karbaschi was condemned to a jail term, the Guide intervened, ruling that it was preferable that he pay a fine rather than go to prison. Let's look more closely at the Press Law: when parliament adopts a law, that law must be applied for a six-month period before it can be modified. But less than six months after the law was adopted, several MPs wanted to change it. The Guide ruled that it would be counter-productive for parliament to change such a recent law, a law that hadn't been tested. He simply suggested living with the current law for a certain time, and if problems arose, then it could be modified. Some of the MPs who wanted to change the law probably felt that it could not be applied as written."

Did Mr. Shariatmadari notice the paradox—and the problems— created by such an unequal balance of forces? Iran has a parliamentary democratic system that claims to represent the people's will; yet the Guide wields absolute authority. Where does the people's will leave off? Where does the Guide's power begin?

"The complexity is natural enough. To understand what is happening today, we have to look closely at how things are done in a country whose political infrastructure is based on Islam and upon Islamic regulations. But first of all, we have to recognize that democracy, by any definition, presupposes limitations, a kind of 'red line' that cannot be crossed. No democratic regime, no government can operate without a red line. All of that is quite normal, and generally accepted.

"According to Jean-Paul Sartre, in his *Social Contract*, all individuals living in a civilized society are free. But if each individual behaves only on the basis of his individual will and takes no account of anyone else, there will be contradictions and conflict. Society must establish laws and regulations, which limit what can and cannot be done.

"As a government in the Islamic world, we are the only ones who can truly decide what system should apply in our country. We are also the only country where the authors of the constitution were chosen by elections, and the only country in the world whose constitution was approved by plebiscite. So we have the right to define our red lines, don't we?"

Mr. Shariatmadari's tone leaves little room for discussion. But our silence does not signify total assent. We attempt to bring politely to his attention that the author of *The Social Contract* is Jean-Jacques Rousseau and not Jean-Paul Sartre. He brushes this secondary detail aside with a condescending smile, and continues his peroration.

"It's all set forth in our constitution, which also determines the specific tasks of the Guide and the conditions in which he is appointed. The Council of Experts, which is elected by the people, chooses the Guide. The Council's duty is to supervise and to monitor the Guide, to renew his mandate or to relieve him of his functions. In any event, we see no contradiction between the Guide and the constitution.

"What could be more normal? After all, our Guide possesses a deep knowledge of the infrastructure of our religion. That is why he was chosen, and elected as Supreme Guide in the first place. As for the Council of Experts, it supervises everything he does. Our red lines are those of our Islamic religious beliefs."

If we are to go by his description of the Islamic Republic, the line between democracy and theocracy seems a fine one indeed. He responds with a burst of eloquence.

"Well, I have a question for you!

"Roger Garaudy was put on trial in France; but what exactly was he accused of? Based on his research and investigation, all of which is backed up by documents, he asserts that the information put out about the Holocaust is erroneous.

"In the land that is the symbol of liberty, Roger Garaudy was accused, tried, and condemned. When he asked the prosecutors why they doubted the objectivity of his academic research, the justice minister replied that there are limits that cannot be exceeded. Everyone must respect them.

Monsieur Faurisson has been called before the courts fifteen times for the same reasons. And now, President Jacques Chirac wants to pass a law that would ban women wearing headscarves from public places, on the pretext that the headscarf is a religious symbol. So how is it that in the same country, Catholic nuns dress in the same way, and keep their heads covered in the universities and in public places? For me, that's a big contradiction. Of course, we're not like the British parliament, that wants to authorize marriage between homosexuals!"

Hossein Shariatmadari knows English well enough to understand our questions, but he insists on going through our translator. We quickly realize that he uses the time taken up by the translation to formulate evasive answers to troublesome questions. He perfectly understands our reaction to his praise of Roger Garaudy, the Holocaust negationist, whom he would transform into a martyr on the altar of free speech. Garaudy, we remind him, was tried before a civil court representing the people; not by the regime. The same court found him guilty of producing false documents and hate propaganda. But we are wasting time in arguing. We are talking with the official representative of the Supreme Guide, after all. Questioning the verities is not part of his job description.

"We have our own laws and regulations; the Guide cannot contravene them. In fact, it is his duty to respect them to the letter."

Each society lays down its own limits, and they must be respected: that much we agree upon. The purpose of our visit is to try to understand Iranian society. Mr. Shariatmadari's words of explanation are not particularly helpful. We attempt another approach: in 1989, under Mr. Rafsanjani's presidency, the Iranian parliament revised the constitution to give the Guide absolute power. Isn't this a contradiction? How can you pretend the system is democratic when one person possesses the power—in theory—to do anything he wishes?

"I agree with you; but it would take a much more detailed discussion to answer all your questions. The absolute power of the Guide is called *Velayat-e faqih*, or the rule of the jurist-consult. But his is not the absolute authority that we find in despotic countries today."

We don't really grasp the distinction. After all, despotism and tyranny have always attributed divine prerogatives to themselves to prop up their thrones.

"There's no connection. The absolute authority of a dictator is to do whatever he wants, whenever he wants; there are no limits. But when we speak of the absolute power of the Guide, we mean that the Guide is absolutely free to do what he wishes within the limits set out in the constitution. The Guide must be able to exercise his authority with full freedom, and even to deal with contradictions that may arise between Islamic law and certain aspects of government management. To be able to settle these disputes, he needs absolute authority. On the other hand, the exercise of this authority is transparent. Let me give you an example: the Council of Experts is responsible for supervising how the Guide performs his functions and duties. Can the Guide abolish the Council? No, he cannot. This is what makes his authority different from the despotism of an emperor. The distinction is clear. But, that having been said, I must add that we believe that the Guide should have the last word in all decisions; that is our religious belief.

"There is another factor that we haven't yet touched upon in this conversation. I am obliged to tell you that everybody believes that we have an obligation to obey the person who holds the position of Guide. Why? Because of the supernatural, spiritual quality of the position itself. For us, the Twelfth Imam, the Mahdi, peace be upon him, is the one who supervises everything, who looks after everything. This is the crucial distinction between secularist and Islamic regimes. If such a provision did not exist, there would never have been a revolution."

Mr. Shariatmadari is not an easy man to interrupt. As head of the Kayhan Group, editor and publisher of *Kayhan*, and representative of the Supreme Guide, he commands all available information, all questions, and all answers; there is little room left over for debate, and even less for contradictory opinion. His near-monopoly of speech, his certainty that his are the weapons of truth, if not truth itself, conjure up the image of a fearsome dialectician, of a man who hides behind his "journalistic immunity" to utter words that can kill.

He is even less prepared to reconsider his position on *The Social Contract* when we point to the contradictions inherent in the Islamic Republic. In Rousseau's definition, the social contract consists of assigning individual liberty to political power, but without relinquishing the liberty of the people, who continue to exercise democratic control over the government. How are we to describe the Islamic Republic, where power is concentrated in the hands of a single man? Can this be democracy? Can we speak of a social contract when all power emanates from the sole authority of a Supreme Guide?

We try our luck one last time, with a question on the contradiction between political and religious power. Our hypothesis is that if politics uses religion to achieve its ends, religion will first be weakened, then destroyed. Mr. Shariatmadari's response is curt, incisive.

"There is no contradiction whatsoever. Every democracy has its red lines, which cannot be crossed. What differentiates these regimes is the exact nature of their red lines. In secular systems, judges and politicians set the limits. But here, in Iran, the limits are laid down by fundamental religious rules and regulations.

"In Islam, unlike other religions, there are rules concerning management of the state. For us, politics and religion are combined and cannot be separated. God never indicates what we must accept or reject, but there is no place for those who do not believe in the religious regulations. When it comes to formulating political programs, there is no room for non-believers. In Iran, that is the limit, that is the red line."

We have clearly reached the limits of our conversation. We venture one final question: When will Iran resume diplomatic relations with the United States. Will it be soon?

"No."

Was that a moment of hesitation we noticed between question and answer?

"Perhaps I did hesitate, but I give the same answer to many people. If the United States persists in behaving like imperialists, there can be no relations with them. Now that the United States has lost respect internationally, how could we possibly resume relations? Imam Khomeini spoke the truth when he described the United States as the 'Great Satan.' Nowadays, if you read the headlines you understand that Bush himself has become a great Satan."

We can't help but smile. Dirty as this particular great Satan's hands are, he claims his power comes from God, just like the Supreme Guide. Like Mr. Khamene'i, Mr. Bush trumpets the power of religion, and its primacy over political decision-making.

He looks hard at us for a moment, before concluding, "By way of answer, I'd like to tell you a little story.

"Long ago, a man who claimed that he was God was captured and brought before the emperor. To frighten him, the ruler related how, the previous year, a man who claimed to be God's prophet had been brought before him. He had ordered him summarily executed. The man looked the emperor in the eye and said, 'You were right to kill him. I don't recall having sent a prophet last year.'"

Like Father, Like Daughter

MAY 2000. Azam Taleqani, venerable veteran of the struggle for women's rights, shows us into her modest office in a densely populated neighborhood in east-central Tehran. The Islamic Women's Institute, which she founded, occupies the first floor of a dusty, poorly lit building concealed behind high walls that stand between the street and a small, paved courtyard. The high wrought-iron gate is closely monitored to keep out undesired visitors. The institute has received its share of threats; Ms. Taleqani's combative spirit does not sit well with the powers that be. The monthly newsletter she publishes has recently been ordered to cease publication.

Azam Taleqani has won a reputation as a fighter, as a woman accustomed to speaking her mind—loudly and clearly. It runs in the family: she is the daughter of the late Ayatollah Mahmoud Taleqani, who died an untimely, much lamented death in 1979. Ayatollah Taleqani, a looming presence in the pre-revolutionary years, a man widely respected for his social concerns and broad-minded outlook, has been all but written out of "official" accounts of the historic upheaval by Ayatollah Khomeini. There are few hints of his role on display in the Museum of the Revolution. In fact, forgotten faces abound: as if everything had been the work of a single man, and of a single political faction: Khomeini and Khomeinism.

Since her father's death Ms. Taleqani has continued to fight for the same ideals of humanism and social justice with unflinching vigor and conviction, focusing her energy and actions toward improving the condition of women, particularly women living in poverty. The institute itself is a bare-bones affair. Its hard-working, devoted staff operates out of two offices, a kitchen, and a large common room that doubles as a library and classroom where it dispenses information, provides instruction, and leads discussion groups. The institute also furnishes legal aid, and helps draw up projects that respond to the needs of women from the poor districts of Tehran and the grubby, dusty satellite towns that ring it.

Short, plumpish, clad in traditional garb that shows only her face and the large, round glasses that magnify her bright, alert eyes, Azem Taleqani could be mistaken for a much-loved grandmother. But behind the impression lurks an exemplary figure of stubborn resistance to the regime. Not for nothing has her monthly magazine *Payyam-e Hajjar* (Hagar's Message) been added to the long list of reform-minded newspapers and periodicals banned by the power structure.

During our conversation, we speak of the political currents that had shaped the Islamic Revolution, and of what remains of them today, in the society that has emerged from it. Imam Khomeini, she reminds us, became the uncontested—and uncontestable—head of the revolution only after eliminating its other leading figures. The revolutionary movement had been complex and multifaceted; the process was far from painless. Her father, the late Ayatollah Taleqani, had been much more than a bit player. He, like Shariati, represented an entire component of the movement that had overthrown the shah and brought about the revolution.

Ali Shariati died, assassinated in London in November 1977. The monarchy steadfastly refused to allow his remains to be interred in the shadow of the Hosseiniyeh-e Ershad, where he had delivered his most celebrated lectures. Today he lies buried in Syria, in a rough cinder-block mausoleum in a suburban Damascus cemetery. Mahmoud Taleqani was a young cleric when he joined the movement in the wake of the Anglo-American *coup d'état* that overthrew Mohammad Mossadeq in 1953. In 1961, he helped found the Iran Freedom Movement. Its liberal nationalist orientation was "tempered by an explicit reference to Islam, to a modern Islam open to democratic values."[20] He maintained contact with the People's Mujahedin, better known as the MKO (Mujahedin Khalk Organization), that had early on abandoned as fruitless any form of parliamentary opposition to the shah's dictatorship.

In 1977, the imperial regime decreed the Tehran Spring, a thaw that reflected then-president Jimmy Carter's international campaign for human rights. Long suppressed, opposition to the dictatorship bubbled to the surface. Mahmoud Taleqani was arrested, tried, and imprisoned on charges of supporting the MKO. Though isolated from his clerical peers, he was extremely popular among broad segments of the population. His long years of prison had transformed him into an ally of

20. *L'Iran au XXe siècle*, 114, 122.

the oppressed, and of the victims of the long struggle against the shah and his pitiless secret police, the SAVAK. In the shah's prisons, Taleqani came to know and respect the members of the non-religious opposition, and to appreciate their courage and their determination. Above all, he came to understand that they shared the same objective: the fall of the monarchy.

But it was Mahmoud Taleqani's intimate ties with the National Front, the organization created by Mohammad Mossadeq, that won him a leading role in the heady months of 1978 and 1979, when the shah's regime collapsed like a house of cards before passing into the hands of the Islamic revolutionaries. He became the first imam[21] designated to lead the public Friday prayer in Tehran, the weekly ceremony that was to become the new regime's rallying point. His growing influence in the young Islamic Republic was such that he won the greatest number of votes in the regime's first parliamentary elections.

But the years of imprisonment had finally undermined the health and vitality of the man who was perhaps the most committed advocate of democracy within the inner circles of the clerical establishment: Mahmoud Taleqani died on September 10, 1979, six months after the fall and flight of Shah Mohammad-Reza Pahlavi.[22]

His death, like Ali Shariati's, was premature. Even today speculation continues about the sudden, unexpected demise, only two years apart, of these two powerful and potentially burdensome personalities. Each, in his own way, had developed a socially oriented approach to governing Iran, drawn from the tradition of constant innovation characteristic of Shi'ism. Their deaths cancelled out any possibility that their liberating vision might become a reality.

The same capacity for innovation, largely absent in the Sunni world, had enabled Imam Khomeini to assume the mantle of sole leader of the revolutionary movement. From there, it was only a step to imposing a governmental model—that of the *Velayat-e faqih*—which would concentrate power in the hands of the Supreme Guide and of a select circle of mullahs. Still, the ideas of the two "forgotten faces" of the Iranian Revolution have resurfaced, taking the form of a powerful thrust for critical innovation embodied by President Khatami and the reform

21. Not to be confused with the title of Imam, i.e., belonging to the lineage of the Holy Imams, a connection Khomeini never explicitly denied.

22. Nikki R. Keddie, *Roots of Revolution: An Interpretive History of Modern Iran* (New Haven: Yale University Press, 1981), 210–11.

movement—up to and including a call for a reduction in the powers of the Guide, and for rules of accountability to be applied to the privileged handful who run the regime. Stormy weather could have been predicted, and was not long in coming. For all her optimism, Azam Taleqani acknowledges that when power feels threatened, it can strike back.

"We knew that there would be problems for the reform movement. The two main currents in society have outstanding differences. Mr. Khatami's slogan is: "Respond politically," which is an appeal for freedom of expression—something that is unacceptable to the conservatives. In a sense, the conservatives are losing ground and they know it. That's why they are creating difficulties."

Do you think there is a danger that the repressive, authoritarian attitude of the clergy will end up discrediting religion, and cause people to reject it?

"There certainly is. Here in Iran, more and more people equate religion with violence; instead of standing for freedom, it has come to stand for servitude. Other people believe in the principles of religion but do not accept violence. They believe that if you want to change people's minds, you must do it through dialogue.

"Today, in our society, there are two main positions: on the one hand you have the traditionalist right-wing, on the other, the left, which supports reform and has a realistic appraisal of religion. We're not too concerned; more and more young people are coming around to this point of view. The reform movement is still weak; it's young, its experience is limited, and after three years, it's all but paralyzed. But we think it should go on, because the movement has left its mark on society; it's had an influence on the way people think. It won't be easy to stop it, or change it; the population simply wouldn't agree."

Just a few weeks ago, before the latest newspaper closures, the regime stated that the banned newspapers were "an enemy base" in Iran. Did that statement come as an insult to you?

"Worse. I was hauled before the courts on seven charges, and condemned to pay a fine. Most of the accusations were laughable; they mentioned Mr. Mossadeq, Dr. Bazargan,[23] Ayatollah Montazeri, the reform movement, the police, and other religions that seem to cause

---

23. Named Iran's first prime minister by Ayatollah Khomeini upon his victorious return to Iran in February, 1979, Dr. Mehdi Bazargan resigned on November 5 of that same year, one day after the capture of the United States Embassy.

problems in Iran. But they said not a word about me. They handed my paper a temporary suspension, without any further explanations.

"I'm not about to give up. Things are changing rapidly. I know we will be facing more trouble. I know too that I won't be here to see the results; but the upcoming generations will.

"There's no reason to be afraid that religion will disappear, because what remains of religion will be its spiritual nature—not a religion that can be made to mean anything at all, according to the needs of power. They claim one thing one day, the exact opposite the next.

"It's true, there are people in jail, and most of them are our people. But we're ready to go to jail; all of us."

Azam Taleqani belongs to the heroic generation of the Islamic Revolution, the same generation that witnessed the religious hierarchy's seizure of the power that an unprecedented mass movement had torn, at a heavy price, from the hands of the royal family. She will not admit that it is a generation betrayed; she does know that the road forward promises to be long and fraught with peril.

Few are more alert to the dangers that lie in wait for the people of Iran, and for the political future of Iranian society. Despite personal threats, despite legal harassment, she refuses to abandon her grass-roots efforts among that society's poorest citizens, its women, all the while fighting for her ideas in the political arena.

The Azam Taleqani we encountered has no illusions. In Iran, when you take on the regime, a prison cell awaits.

Follow Me

JANUARY 2004. Haft-e Tir Square, the sprawling crossroads that is the nerve center of Tehran, never sleeps. From dawn to dusk and beyond, vehicles by the tens of thousands jockey for advantage, while in the middle of the square, commuters and shoppers surge out of the underground subway station, then dart across the lanes of fast-moving traffic in a death-defying choreography of danger, dodging oncoming buses, taxis, trucks, and backfiring, overloaded two-wheelers. At the corners, in a cacophony of blaring horns, swarms of *mosafer-kesh*— collective taxis that carry up to six passengers in ancient rattletrap Paykans—troll for fares, sometimes pulling over to the curb, sometimes stopping in mid-pavement oblivious to the traffic swirling around them.

Haft-e Tir is a monument to transience: here nothing ever stops. Even the stores and offices in the anonymous gray buildings overlooking it change names and owners as rapidly as they turn over their cheap, shoddy merchandise. All is evanescent, as quick to disappear as the fresh breath of morning beneath the billows of pollution.

Five years ago, a second-floor office in one of these faceless buildings was home to the editorial offices of *Sobh-e Emrouz*, the daily published by Said Hajjarian that was to become, for a brief few months until it was closed down, the spearhead of the reform movement. Only a few blocks from there, an identical building housed the bare-bones offices of *Kian*, the reform-minded monthly published by a group of religious intellectuals that served as a showcase, at great risk to itself, for articles by Abdolkarim Soroush.

Not far from this crossroads of the ephemeral, Iran's recently authorized Women's Party has just opened its headquarters. Predictably, the taxi that brought us from the other extremity of the sprawling Tehran downtown core could not find the address. We had been driving in circles for what seemed like hours when the driver finally threw in the towel. This "women's party" can only be a figment of our imagination, he muttered. Whipping out a telephone number, we instructed our skeptical cabbie to stop at the first available street-corner convenience store for a quick call. Yes, the Women's Party did exist; in fact, it was just around the corner. Running on ahead, a charitable shopkeeper guided the doubting taxi to the point of maximum proximity. There, at the edge of the four-lane expressway that funnels traffic from north Tehran down into the square, the driver abandoned us.

On the other side, outside the door to the Women's Party, stood our interpreter Nahid, who had been waiting for us. All we had to do to join her was to cross the northbound lanes of the expressway, negotiate a low steel barrier, then make our way across the two southbound lanes, and thence to our ultimate destination. Easier said than done. In both directions, cars and trucks were moving along bumper-to-bumper, at a speed that totally defied our pedestrian capacities. On the other shore, so to speak, stood Nahid, waving us over. Not even the smile of encouragement that shone gracefully in the oval left by her flowing black *chador* was motivation enough. Vehicles continued to speed past at more than seventy kilometers per hour as if we simply didn't exist. Experience had taught us just how pitiless toward the human biped Tehran drivers could be. Our tardiness may well already have tarnished our reputation, but we weren't about to budge.

At that precise moment, as we stared in astonishment, Nahid stepped out into traffic and nonchalantly made her way across the expressway, one hand outstretched to halt the oncoming cars, motorcycles, and buses, the other elegantly clasping her *chador* beneath her chin. She walked up to us and told us, in a voice as firm as it was calm, "Follow me!"

A passerby would have beheld, on that day and at that hour, two tall, lanky gentlemen of a certain age winding their way through the fierce traffic north of Haft-e Tir Square under the guidance and protection of an imperturbable young woman, to overcome the final obstacle that separated them from the Women's Party.

The party president herself was waiting at the door to greet us. From the window, she must have been observing our curiously pathetic crossing, and witnessed what little heed we had paid to masculine pride. Surely we had accumulated a certain capital of good will even before we met.

Fariba Davoudi-Mohajer is in her late thirties, small in stature, with a round face and a lively, direct expression. Politically close to the reformists, she graduated in political science from Tehran's Free University before going to work as a journalist. We sit down face to face at the long table that almost fills the narrow room. At one end of the table, a man who is barely to open his mouth takes notes. Opposite us, the woman who aspires to make the voices of Iran's women heard in a world where men wield the power, speaks out with the passion and clarity of a militant fully prepared to accept the consequences of her words and her actions.

"I am the founder of the Women's Party. I set it up; I have been elected as its leader. I am also the founder of the Women's League, and am an active member of the Central Council on Women's Rights. Politics is my main activity, but not the only one. It's true that the press can be an excellent political tool, but here in Iran, it is still weak. This is why I established the Women's Party. I didn't want to create a women's union; what I wanted was to work to narrow the gap that exists between men and women in my country.

"I know it's a radical feminist position. We draw attention to all the aspects of inequality between men and women in every sector of society. Our aim is to improve the conditions of women in four main areas: equality of powers, wage equity, equal access of information and education, and social equality.

"When it comes to these four points, women in Iran have traditionally been at a disadvantage. We are not looking for authority over men. In our society this is a delicate question; women simply do not occupy positions of authority in relation to men. We do not want that in any event; what we want is equality with men, and not authority over them.

"We can find the underlying reasons for this situation in the family. Women's alienation is rooted in our cultural traditions, in religious discourse, and particularly in the way religion is interpreted—by men and from a man's point of view. Men have always been the masters of religious definition and interpretation. Religious organizations and foundations have always been in the hands of men. Men wrote our constitution, and have given society the shape it has today.

"It's important to realize that the problems of women have emerged as an issue here just as the Islamic world confronts the West. It is at this precise point that Iranian women have realized how broad the gap is that separates them from men. Forty years ago, this gap had four main components: women's rights, the status of women, women in public life, and women's development.

"I can assure you that one man almost single-handedly widened the gap in our society: a certain Ayatollah Tehrani. Woman's only social role, this gentleman asserted, was to bear and nurse children; maternity was her only destiny. On the four points I just mentioned, he believed that men and women were unequal—to man's benefit, of course.

"When you investigate the religious basis for this kind of attitude, you realize that it draws more on the words attributed to the Prophet than to a close reading of the Qur'an. In our opinion, a great many of these sayings are spurious if not simply false. What passes for religious discourse on women in Iran is based on these *haddith*, and not on the reality of the Qur'an.

"Between the 1940s and the 1970s, and even during the first decade after the revolution, some changes did take place, brought about by four leading religious jurisprudents: Ayatollah Alma Tabatabaï, Ayatollah Morteza Mottahari, Dr. Ali Shariati, and of course, Ayatollah Khomeini. They believed that women were equal in their creative powers, in their participation in society, and in social development. But when it came to women's rights, they differed; in fact, they did not believe women enjoyed equal rights. The debate between traditionalists and self-styled modernists continued after the revolution. The would-be modernists held that, since women are biologically different from men, they have different rights and duties. This is certainly the case in matters of divorce, and of capital punishment as applied to women and men.

"You could say that there are three traditionalist trends: the first is convinced that women have no rights; the second, so-called modern one derived from Imam Khomeini; and the one that is currently the most prominent, sees women through the prism of reason, and not of *haddith*. People who follow this trend believe that women's rights must be updated, but because of the current political situation, its leaders must be very cautious about how they express their ideas. They cannot speak openly, or make detailed information available to the general public. Its best known advocates are Dr. Mehrpour, Mullah Mehridi, and Dr. Jannati."

At the mention of the last of the three names, we started. Was she talking about Ayatollah Ahmad Jannati, head of the Council of Guardians and watchdog of the most baneful orthodoxy? Ms. Davoudi bursts out laughing.

"No, no! It's not the same person. The Ayatollah Jannati I'm talking about lives in Qom, but he is forbidden to teach in the seminaries where new members of the clergy are trained."

Then, back to the subject at hand.

"But the critical question all three of these groups must deal with is that of women. Each one has a distinct approach to the status and condition of women in society. It's essential to point out, too, that this question lies at the heart of Iranian tradition. Women are less involved in social and cultural activities today, and if we compare with the era of the shah, there has been a regression, both in terms of quality and quantity.

"How did it happen? After the revolution, official propaganda focused on the role of women in the family, and as homemakers above all. In fact, no other image was promoted. Just look at the textbooks used in the primary schools. There are two dominant images: that of the mother, and of the homemaker. A woman's life is placed within a domestic context only: she knits, she cooks and does the dishes, but plays no role in society. Language and education are what shape the role of women, and make it possible for her to progress in society … or make it impossible! You can judge for yourself by watching television, in the theater, in the cinema: women are trained to respond to men's wishes and needs. As a result, society defines women's rights to conform to this vision.

"In my opinion, our culture has produced an image of women as weak and inferior beings. Men control every organ of authority in this country, and in the government in particular. They lead society, and make it function. Why? Because women have no economic independence. According to the constitution, men govern a woman's right to employment. If a man does not want his wife to work, and if she insists on working, he can seek a divorce."[24]

But is someone in the government responsible for women's issues?

"There is an agency that examines and reports on whatever progress is being made. But there is still a lot to be done.

"What distinguishes Iran from the West is religion. If a woman wants to go beyond the current situation, she runs up against religion. Which means that women's struggle against this regime demands organization, authority, and money. That's why we've founded the Women's Party. We need it to finish what we've begun.

"During President Khatami's first term much was accomplished, but it always ended up being in conflict with the constitution and with existing laws. And in any case the Council of Guardians blocked everything. Our response was to become more active: we set up more NGOs and other civil society organizations. Women were participating on a personal, volunteer basis, in a wide range of social and cultural activities.

"The Women's Party grew out of this increasing sense of involvement and commitment. For the time being, I don't intend to run candidates in

---

24. Iran's constitution contains no such clause. The practice originates in the regime's repressive interpretation, and of restrictive regulations adopted by the first post-revolutionary parliaments.

parliamentary elections. The way things are today, if we do present candidates the results will be meaningless; nothing will change. Our first job is to train grass-roots activists in the social and cultural fields; later we can field serious candidates—because serious changes to our constitution are in order.

"We aren't demanding more women members of parliament; that wouldn't change anything. In fact, we would be accepting a regime we don't believe in. You see, we're against the structure of the regime itself. After the elections to the sixth Majlis, the reformists formed a majority in parliament. They were convinced they were the winners. But if you ask me, they lost everything. The Council of Guardians annulled every single law they proposed and adopted. People expected a lot from this parliament, but the MPs couldn't live up to their expectations. How could they, when they weren't even able to make their own laws stick?

"If today the reformists denounce the election and resign, they will simply be handing over parliament to the conservatives, who will then have to pass laws to improve the lives of ordinary people. Of necessity, the conservatives will even make a few changes to the constitution. But most people are not going to vote.

"As I see it, participating does not necessarily mean voting. Abstention is also a form of participation. Our constitution is weak and unstable. It would be dangerous to encourage women to place their confidence in such an unsound structure. The future is not clear at all. The people voted for the reformists out of disgust at the conservatives; but the reformists have shown they can do nothing. Where are the results? Nowhere."

Could you be going too far? Your judgment seems extreme. Couldn't there be a third way, between the failure of the reformists and the return of the conservatives to power?

"There is a third solution to our problems, one that would take a long time. But please take note: I am not expressing opposition to the system. I am a part of this system and because that's how things are, I simply identify the flaws in the constitution, in our laws and regulations. And because I belong to it, I want all of the components of the system to work efficiently. That's why I am a part of the system, just like the regime.

"When Habermas[25] visited Iran recently, he was asked at the end of his visit if he could predict any short-term changes. His answer: 'You'll find the answer in women, in women's minds.'

25. German sociologer and philosopher Jürgen Habermas.

"There are men in our party who support women's rights. They believe, as we do, that women should claim their rights and change their status in society. Women's opinion on the fundamental problems facing our society should be attractive to men as well: the problems of our young people, of our minorities, of class differences, of non-religious people, and even of those who are against religion. So, unlike every other political group in our Islamic society, we don't require that our members be Muslims. They are members of Iranian society, without regard for their religious beliefs or social origins. Their only obligation is to work together to solve problems from women's perspective. That is the only way we are going to bridge the gap between men and women. If we don't, the gap will widen.

"Our principal strategy is to inform people by publishing newspapers, by organizing public lectures, by participating in public meetings, and perhaps eventually taking part in elections. First of all, our party must consolidate its base; after all, we've just now organized ourselves. But we're the only party to be supported by Ayatollah Montazeri; we have it in writing."

The support of Ayatollah Hossein-Ali Montazeri has proved a vital encouragement to Ms. Davoudi-Mohajer's newly created party. His endorsement identifies it as belonging to the regime's most intransigent opponents. Montazeri is perhaps the only member of the high clergy to have maintained the respect of the population, a respect he may well owe—ironically—to having been placed under house arrest six years ago by the Supreme Guide. Mr. Montazeri, with characteristic frankness, had repeatedly excoriated the Guide's haughty attitude and princely life style: a habit that was to cost him dearly.

Before taking our leave of the founder of the Women's Party, we are curious to hear her opinion on Zahra Kazemi, the Iranian-born Canadian photojournalist who died at the hands of the secret police, and on Shirin Ebadi, the Nobel Peace Prize winner for 2003. Characteristically, Ms. Davoudi-Mohajer does not beat around the bush.

"What happened to Ms. Kazemi is a disgrace for the regime and for the judiciary system. But it was predictable. In a country where people are thrown into prison illegally, or with only a semblance of legality, you have to expect this kind of thing. We issued a statement on the death of Ms. Kazemi, describing her not as a journalist, not as a woman, but as a human being, a person. Let's assume this person had been condemned to death; even then, they had no right to kill her by fracturing her skull before the date of her legal execution. Let's assume she deserved capital punishment: she should have enjoyed her full rights right up until the last; she should have had a fair trial on the 'espionage' charges brought against her. But none of that took place. The power structure respected nothing, not even the most basic rights of the person as a human being. Let's say she was a thief; even then, the fundamental right of any accused person is not to be 'executed' before being judged.

"Shirin Ebadi's Nobel Prize? It was a great honor for Iranian women, and for Iranian society as a whole. In a speech to the journalists' association, she said, 'The trail I followed is a trail you blazed.' She knew that her prize and her prestige in society were the result of the work of all the organizations and associations that have been struggling for so many years. She also said, 'I did not win this prize alone. Many hands made their contribution.'

"There are many ways for women in Iran to get what they want, particularly those who are organized. Even if we don't have all the necessary facilities for winning our rights, we do not depend on other organizations or political parties. We are independent. We don't want to submit to the power and authority of men or officials. That's why we didn't choose as our leader a woman connected with the government or the administration.

"Our slogan is: 'Move forward slowly but surely.' And since we intend to keep our independence from men, the women in our party have no relationship, either family or marital, with any men in the government.

"We've already encountered serious obstacles, and we're certain to encounter even more. But the very fact of being women helps us. I know it does. I've just been released on bail after two years of a three-year prison term. If I make the slightest false move, they'll throw me back in jail. So I try to use my wits, and make it difficult for them to arrest me. But it's quite clear that anyone who wishes to move in this direction should expect difficulties. For the time being, I am concentrating on training party members. We need strong women so that in case something happens to any of us, the party itself won't be destroyed. Our party can't belong to one single person. These are our short-term objectives.

"Our main objective is to be transparent. We write and say whatever we think. We hide nothing. It's the best way to attract women who are well informed about their rights.

"For the moment, it's not the number of members that counts. What is more important is to bring together women who think freely. Even if the women who join us are housewives, we don't want them to feel isolated, for them to be the 'second sex'; we want them to practice what we teach them about their rights. They won't be second-class beings in their own homes any more. They will raise their children in a spirit of equality between the sexes. We don't intend to organize demonstrations with a hundred thousand participants. We want women to think for themselves.

"Of course we encounter resistance from men, from the power structure. That's why I was sent to prison; that's why I'm still under threat of arrest. For the regime, for 'them,' I'm a 'threat to national security.' According to 'them,' I've 'damaged the reputation of our country'; I was also accused of being 'in league with the student movement' because I gave lectures and wrote articles for student newspapers. It's true: I participated in student demonstrations after the 1997 elections. But in my opinion, the main reason is that I've always supported the reformists. The core of my difference of opinion with the regime is the question of authority. 'They' have the power and the authority. I'm opposed to them. But just as the reformists in parliament are standing up to the conservatives, I'm not alone in my struggle against the regime.

"It's unfortunate; if only the reformist MPs had shown some backbone during the first weeks of the sixth Majlis, we wouldn't be where we are today. They should have reacted when the Guide suppressed debate on the Press Law. If they had come out into the streets, the people would have supported them. No one could understand why they did nothing. They refused to appeal to the population, to the will of the citizens; it was as though they were afraid they didn't have popular support. It was a poor analysis.

"It's a sad day for the reformists, and for President Khatami. Today, the people don't believe in them any more."[26]

26. In September 2004, seven months after our meeting and the electoral victory of the conservatives, Fariba Davoudi-Mohajer temporarily abandoned her political activities after finding a homemade bomb at her front door. The device did not explode, but its message was clear.

Dirt on Their Hands

HARD ON THE HEELS of the U.S. Embassy takeover in 1979, the Islamic authorities launched a "cultural revolution" to rid the universities of the dominant Western models that had held sway under the regime of Mohammad-Reza Pahlavi.

For many of the intellectuals caught up in the surge of enthusiasm for Imam Khomeini that was sweeping Iran, the "purification" of higher education was a patriotic and a religious task, as necessary as it was beneficial. But many who had fought to overthrow the shah before being forced to flee the crackdown that followed the civil war are convinced that these intellectuals betrayed them. They believe that those who made common cause with the new regime would have been better off keeping a critical distance.

Since then, Dr. Abdolkarim Soroush has provided an ideal scapegoat for the victims of the violent excesses of Iran's cultural revolutionaries. As a brilliant young intellectual, Soroush had been one of Imam Khomeini's earliest supporters. Khomeini, in March 1980, had declared, "Our dear students must not follow in the footsteps of the faithless intellectuals in our universities."[27] The prestige and authority of the Imam in the eyes of the revolutionary intellectuals was absolute; he wielded a power that allowed for no dissent.

In the early 1980s, Soroush, who was then a professor and a budding philosopher, was appointed to the committee to overhaul the university curriculum, and to eliminate anything judged to be incompatible with revolutionary ideals. The purges that followed, among both professorial staff and students, were far from pacific; they were to leave deep wounds. Khomeini's "cultural revolution" brought about the death or exile of a large number of young people.

Dr. Soroush's participation in the supervisory committee has raised questions about his role, and his responsibility, for those events. We

---

27. Quoted in Ali Rahnema and Farhad Nomani, *The Secular Miracle: Religion, Politics and Economic Policy in Iran* (London: Zed Books, 1990), 227–28.

wanted to raise the issue with him, to gain an understanding of why he changed his views—and of his critical stance toward the Islamic regime today.

In the late 1970s, a powerful wave of anti-Western feelings swept over Iran in reaction to the forced modernization imposed by the imperial regime. The United States, Iran's protector and patron of the day, had generously underwritten the shah's program.

Frustration and outright rejection of the pro-American regime awakened many students and intellectuals to the ideas of Jalal Al-e Ahmad, the son of a clerical family who had joined the Tudeh (Communist) Party before emerging as an outspoken proponent of anti-Westernism. A short article entitled "West-Sickness," followed by a longer essay called "Loyalty and the Treachery of the Intellectuals," fired the imagination of the upcoming generation.

Al-e Ahmad's concept of "West-Sickness" can be traced to the teachings of Ahmad Fardid, a philosopher who had constructed an entire metaphysical critique of the West.[28] Fardid had been exposed to existentialism and the philosophy of Henri Bergson in France in the years immediately following World War II; he was also to discover, then be captivated by the thoughts of Heidegger. On returning to Iran, he began to teach, lecture, and above all, to recruit followers, intellectuals from diverse backgrounds who defined themselves in terms of a shared opposition to encroachment by the West. Among them were Daryush Shayegan, who would later become one of the Islamic regime's staunchest critics, and his former colleague, Reza Davari, who would become one of its most ardent defenders, and Heidegger's outstanding disciple at the University of Tehran.

Ali Shariati, another French-trained philosopher—and one of Iran's most uncompromising critics of imperialism in all its guises—galvanized a generation of young leftist revolutionaries drawn to his thought and action. His lectures at the Hosseiniyeh-e Ershad in Tehran drew the kind of crowds that had flocked to the speeches of Jean-Paul Sartre at the Paris Mutualité in the heady days of May 1968. Shariati argued for the convergence of Islam and the ideology of the oppressed: "The Islamic Revolution would bring to a head and translate into political action the quest for identity that saw Islam, and not Persian nationalism, as a bulwark against the cultural influence of the West."[29]

28. *L'Iran au XXe siècle*, 354.

29. Ibid., 355.

This was the intellectual and ideological climate into which the thirty-four-year-old Abdolkarim Soroush stepped when he returned to Iran from England in what were to be the death throes of the Pahlavi monarchy. Trained as a pharmacologist, then a historian of science before becoming a philosopher of religion, he quickly sided with the Shi'a clergy, whose myth of omniscience he would later deconstruct. Placing himself under the spiritual tutelage of Imam Khomeini, he was quick to "deal a crushing blow to the Marxist dogmas that then prevailed among Iran's leftist groups."[30] It was an exploit that won him the Imam's recognition, followed by an appointment to the Cultural Revolution Council under the direction of Ahmad Ahmadi, who would later become head of Tehran University's philosophy department. From there, it was a short step to the curriculum reform committee.

Twelve months after beginning its work, Iran's universities reopened their doors. The balance sheet makes for sobering reading: in 1979–80, according to Iranian government statistics, 175,000 students, including 35,000 degree-holders, attended Iran's universities; in 1982–83, the total had fallen to 117,000, of whom 6,000 held degrees. The professorial corps had lost almost half its members, dropping from 16,000 to 9000.[31]

The human impact of Iran's "cultural revolution" was far from glorious. A significant segment of the young generation was to lose more than its illusions about the direction in which the Islamic Revolution was headed. In the university faculties, and in the streets, the revolutionary committees known as *komiteh* waged unrelenting battle against their opponents. The civil war that wracked the country was particularly violent in Tehran. But in the end it was no contest. After winning control of the streets, the regime cracked down with an even heavier, deadlier hand. Ayatollah Montazeri lashed out at the abuses, comparing them with the violence of the "counter-revolutionaries."

A few months after joining the committee, Abdolkarim Soroush tendered his resignation. But is it possible to pardon an intellectual who participated in a witch-hunt that was to claim so many victims, especially among left-leaning students and faculty? Dr. Soroush makes no effort to evade or avoid the question. In fact, as we were soon to see, he has attempted to articulate an answer. All the while, his subsequent activity

30. Ali Paya, *Modern Trends in Shi'i Thought* (London: Centre for the Study of Democracy, University of Westminster, n.d.), 12.

31. See Fred A. Reed, *Persian Postcards: Iran After Khomeini* (Vancouver: Talonbooks, 1994), 123.

and his firm commitment—the elements by which history will judge and eventually understand—stand not only as attenuating factors, but also can be interpreted as his response to his critics. For in the last fifteen years, he has emerged as one of the regime's most radical critics—for which the regime has repaid him in kind.

Today Dr. Soroush, like Daryush Shayegan, belongs to a select group of thinkers who have exploded the relationship between Islam and politics. He has also become one of the fiercest opponents of the ideological straightjacket imposed by the mullahs upon intellectual inquiry in general, and upon Iranian society in particular. The country's young people—as well its intellectuals—with whom he has made continued efforts to maintain close contact, eagerly await his words. Though he is forbidden to speak, though death threats hang over his head, his books—the only way he can communicate with his fellow Iranians—continue to sell briskly.

All this we knew when we set out to meet Dr. Soroush late one spring day. Our meeting place would be the Foundation for Wisdom, the organization set up to publish and distribute his books, located in a decrepit building at the end of a narrow, dark alley adjacent to Tehran University.

Night was beginning to fall.

Our first question could hardly have been more direct: how is it possible to explain that, in the name of Islam and of the revolution, some intellectuals did not speak out against the excesses and abuses of Khomeini's doctrine, at the risk of being accused today of having dirty hands?

"We believed because we wanted to believe. We went along because we wanted to. We paid too little attention to what was being offered. In my opinion, our revolution was a revolution without a theory. It had causes, but it probably did not have a reason. Today, the job of the reform movement is to create a theory of the revolution, and to provide reasons for it. The danger is that the reformists will end up without a theory and, like the revolution, will have no future."

What made the religious takeover possible? The absence of a theory? When Ayatollah Khomeini became the father of the revolution did he not, at the same time, become its theory?

"Yes, it's true that Ayatollah Khomeini himself became the theory of the revolution. Even today people refer to him to solve problems. His charismatic personality became the theory. In a religious world, people

Abdolkarim Soroush: "Why did we keep silent during the early years of the revolution?" (*Salam Iran*, courtesy of InformAction Films)

are the reasons for what they say; in a non-religious world, they are the causes. So it was that Ayatollah Khomeini, who was head of the clergy and Guide of the revolution, was the living proof of his words and his acts. None of his followers ever asked for any further proof! We turned to him to find out what to do, what to think. He had the same prerogatives as the Prophet himself!

"Today, intellectuals are asking themselves—and I am asking myself, Why did we keep silent during the early years of the revolution? Today, the intellectuals blame themselves. Before the revolution, they were critical of power. They paid a heavy price. After the revolution, they became spectators. But even then, I had no illusions. I knew that religious power would not be a good thing. I participated in the hope of giving advice, of calming things down, of having a positive influence. Which is what I did, but I rapidly understood that I was in the wrong place. I was powerless. I left the corridors of power. But power has its attractions, even for intellectuals; many stayed on for their own comfort, for their well-being, or simply for the sake of power. They stayed on, and today they occupy excellent positions. But I know that many of my religious intellectual friends have lost their illusions."

So, you agree: some intellectuals have dirt on their hands?

"Yes, certainly among those with religious leanings, and less so among the non-religious, who depended less on what we can call men of religion. The dividing line between dependence and independence is not easy to establish, you know. Relations between intellectuals and the clergy have always been difficult. Today, the future of religion in this country is in the hands of the religious intellectuals, and of the clergy.

"President Khatami exemplifies this transition. He is what I call a 'pseudo-cleric.' He is a religious man in appearance and by education, but alongside his religious training he also studied philosophy, Hegel in particular."

The revolution is more than twenty years old. Today in Iran we see a deepening distaste for religion. How does this affect you?

"It's true. I have lost my faith in the clergy, but I haven't lost my faith in Islam. I am able to make the distinction. In any case, this fundamental distinction is the basis of my teaching. There are different possible interpretations of Islam. The regime's reading is possible, but it is an unacceptable reading."

Intellectuals need space to give free rein to their ideas, to exercise their freedom of conscience. Do you think either of these things is assured today?

"They are available under President Khatami, yes. But the conservatives don't want anything resembling freedom of thought. It is only now a possibility, and thought is very dangerous when it is exercised freely. The intellectuals, students, and journalists in prison are living proof of that. We are all in danger."

What are the limits within which you can work as a philosopher and teacher?

"I can say whatever I want about politics, about the theory of the rule of the jurist-consult, about the revolution. But I cannot talk about the personality of the Guide. It is impossible to speak freely about him, and about the situation around him. On the other hand, I can communicate my ideas in my books. But my contact with my students and my friends is restricted. I cannot go where I want! I am banned from the universities, and I cannot go out alone. I must always be accompanied, because of the danger. Do you understand?

"What's more, I must be very careful about who I receive here. Some people come to see me as friends, but in reality they are agents. So I must be very cautious, and not answer their questions. In these circumstances, work as a professor is difficult, because you never know whom you are talking to. But even if these conditions make my work more difficult, my duty as a philosopher is to do everything I can to analyze the situation, and to shed light on the reasons for it, on its causes. But it's truly tragic, yes."

The prestige Dr. Soroush enjoys among members of the reform movement, and his influence among the students may not have entirely wiped away the memories of his past, but his words and his arguments are taken seriously, and his courage and commitment are highly regarded. The regime, meanwhile, has understood perfectly the danger he represents, and has repeatedly let him know it.

July 2000 found Abdolkarim Soroush en route to the city of Khorramabad to participate in a commemoration of the student uprising that had shaken Tehran the previous year. He was accompanied by a colleague, Mohsen Kadivar, a clergyman ten years his junior.

This provincial town was the scene of the annual convention of the country's main student organization, Daftar-e Takhim-e Vahdat—the Office for Consolidating Unity. After years as a regime mouthpiece, the OCU had thrown itself passionately into Mohammad Khatami's victorious 1997 presidential campaign. Bearing the brunt of violent repression during the events of July 1999, the organization became radicalized almost overnight. At its public meetings on campus, slogans comparing the Supreme Guide to Pinochet, and his regime to that of the Talibans in Afghanistan, were heard for the first time.

In Khorramabad, a delegation of students was waiting at the airport to welcome their invited speakers. They were not alone. Ansar-e Hezbollah, an organization that had been originally described as a "pressure group" before becoming enforcers for the ultra-conservative faction, was on hand as well. *O Blood of Hossein*, its weekly house organ, propagates an extremist ideology; its leader, a certain Asgaroladi, is regularly quoted in the press. No questions are asked about its finances, nor about its ties with the shadowy power center that alone in Iran can authorize acts of violence.

A dozen or more armed Ansar thugs were waiting in the arrival hall for the distinguished guests to arrive. No sooner did they approach the entrance than the "welcoming committee" unleashed a hail of stones and a torrent of curses and insults. Escorted by airport personnel, Soroush and Kadivar took refuge in the public washroom, where they spent twelve hours before boarding the next flight to Tehran. All the while, throughout the town, squads of club-wielding hooligans roamed the streets, violently attacking anyone who looked like a student. They had already set up checkpoints on the main roads to Khorramabad to intercept buses carrying students from other cities. There, the students were forced to disembark, then beaten. Despite appeals from the OCU's security officials, the police refused to intervene.

For all the seriousness of his judgment of his own acts, and those of his fellow intellectuals during the early years of the revolution, Dr. Soroush continued to insist that the struggle was worthwhile. This time, he had chosen the right side; history would absolve him. The reform movement would prevail. Such was his certainty as we parted company that he saw the day coming when Iran would no longer be attempting to export Islamic revolution to its neighboring countries. On the contrary, it would emerge as a model of religious democracy carried forward by a revitalized civil society. If he could have heard those words, Imam Khomeini would surely have rolled over in his cavernous mausoleum.

Our meeting took place in May 2000; the reformists had the wind in their sails. Little did they realize that their ambitions not only challenged the interests of the regime, but also those of the United States, which had another outcome in mind: to impose "market democracy" in the former colonial world shaped by the Sykes-Picot Agreement and the Cold War.

Headscarf Blues

KHADIJE SAFIRI IS ONE OF IRAN'S leading sociologists, a professor, and vice-rector of al-Zahra University, the elite women-only faculty. But our appointment with her is scheduled for the Tehran University Management Faculty campus, a mixed facility where her husband, Professor Ja'afar-Nejad, is a full professor.

Far from the central campus that overlooks Enqelab (Revolution) Avenue, site of the Friday prayer, traditional gathering place, scene of demonstrations, riots, and police repression, the sub-campus in Tehran's Guisha district is an oasis of calm. Perhaps even a hint of indolence hangs in the air.

Professor Safiri has asked us to meet her in her husband's office where, to our surprise, he would take an active part in the first half of our conversation. In her mid-fifties, she is clad in a *chador* worn over her *manteau*: a combination of black on black whose austerity her blue headscarf cannot entirely dispel.

We are at a considerable remove here from the radical feminism of Fariba Davoudi-Mohajer. The president of the Women's Party had outspokenly decried the decline in women's employment in Iran. Khadije Safiri is a firm believer in statistics, an academic who chooses her words with caution—due perhaps in part to the presence of her husband who, from behind his desk, leaps into the conversation at will, to agree or disagree with his wife. Even more surprising is the equanimity with which this accomplished scholar acquiesces to Mr. Ja'afar-Nejad's running commentary.

Our first question—has employment for women declined?—draws an equivocal answer.

"During the early years after the revolution, women's participation in the labor force dropped. Since then we've seen a modest increase. Our figures for the last fifteen years show an improvement. Generally speaking, women prefer to work in the public sector. My research shows that, overall, there has been progress in women's employment in all sectors. My assessment is that satisfaction ratings are normal."

The telephone rings; Professor Ja'afar-Nejad answers. Something has come up; he must leave the office. He argues for time, then attempts to postpone what is apparently a meeting. Finally, he informs us that he must take his leave. Meanwhile, hot tea is served, and we resume our dialogue with Ms. Safiri who—are we imagining things?—appears slightly more at ease now that her husband has left.

Is there a discrepancy between men's and women's wages?

"In Iran, the base wage is the same for men and women. But men are considered to be the head of the family, so they are paid an additional amount to cover the family maintenance costs they have traditionally borne, which makes comparing wages more complex. When my husband was hired, our salaries were identical; today, he earns more than I do.

"In Iran women's and men's salaries are all calculated the same way, so there is no serious disagreement on this issue. It's not what women's struggle for equality is all about.

"If women find themselves in a position of inferiority, it is due to the rules of our society. Still, in spite of the rules, women take part in elections, they vote, and participate in social life."

Just what are those rules?

"Most of them concern the family structure; the rest, employment. For instance, there are no restrictions on women's representation in parliament. But in our society, men cannot accept that large numbers of women participate in public life. This mentality is the greatest obstacle to women's advancement."

What should be changed, in order of priority?

"First of all, the masculine mentality, and it should be done through laws submitted to and adopted by parliament. We don't expect to accomplish everything overnight; we need time.

"Women in different fields of activity face different problems. Our job is to change ways of thinking. Looking back, we can see that women have become much more active in society."

Is this one of the consequences of feminism, of a more radical women's movement?

"If feminism has had an impact on the way we act, so much the better. But in our country, the situation is not at all like it is in the West; the comparison just doesn't stand up. Our problems are different; our methods must be different. But no matter your definition, the ultimate aim is to win more rights for women. Each in her own way, women are involved in the fight. For example, at al-Zahra University I edit *Women's Studies*, a periodical that publishes articles on the status of women. This is my battlefield, if you like.

"In Iran, we have many NGOs working in a wide variety of situations. Those that are working in the same area get together to talk over their problems. In the country's sociology departments, just to give you an example, the status of women is our main concern."

What about the state? Does it play a role? Is there a minister responsible for the status of women?

"We don't have such a minister, but we do have a Women's Affairs Bureau directly attached to the president's office. Zahra Shoja'i, the head of the bureau, has a voice in Cabinet meetings, but no vote. Massoumeh Ebtekar, who is a vice-president of the Islamic Republic, does have a vote in Cabinet."

Could a woman eventually be president?

"We certainly hope so! Our constitution stipulates that certain positions are reserved for men. But we believe that these provisions derive from the way certain high-ranking males have translated the Arabic sources."

What are the authorities afraid of? Of women—or of traditionalist reactions in society?

"It's a cultural thing. Until very recently, no one has taken women's issues seriously. Nowadays, much more information is available; the groundwork has been laid to promote women's interests more actively. But we still need time. Governments and political programs can change rapidly, but it takes time for cultural changes to reach every level of society."

It looks to us like the reform process has stalled. What will be the next stage? A new upsurge based on the energy of women?

"I don't agree. The reform process has not stalled. When an idea gains momentum, its appearance may change, but it will not stop moving forward. It will find a way around the obstacles in its path, just like water. I hope that the women's movement will reveal another dimension of the reform movement."

Our discussion seems to be trapped in polite commonplaces. We decide to raise the matter of *hijab*, that object of obsession in the West, a reflection of Muslim womanhood seen in a deforming mirror, a visible sign of religious identity ... and now challenged by more and more Iranian women.

What do you think of the obligation to wear the *hijab*? How are we to interpret it? As one of the regulations governing society, or as part of tradition?

At this exact instant Ms. Safiri's academic aloofness seems to desert her. Setting aside the instruments of sociology, she stiffens in her seat.

"Well, to begin with, it's hardly a matter limited to Islam. You encounter it in other religions as well. In Iran, it's a part of our religion, and as an Islamic country, our laws make it obligatory. As a Muslim woman, I haven't the slightest objection to that.

"I may be repeating myself, but we have chosen to live in an Islamic country. So there's nothing unnatural about it. But in future, we must pay much closer attention to the form of the *hijab*. Not to remove it, but to lighten it."

We spend a lot of time in the streets, and in public places; we often find ourselves amid young women who have already started to "lighten" their head-covering, as you put it. They don't appear to have waited for the law to be modified to take matters into their own hands and loosen the knot of the religious dress code.

"What you've observed among young women reflects their taste. In this sense, the change has already taken place. What I hope is that they will take a more moderate approach, so that everyone else will be able to accept it. Some people are offended by their behavior; they see it as a failure to respect the rules and tradition. I am working on other ways for women to cover themselves. Something like a long dress that would be acceptable to everyone. The path of moderation is the one that is most likely to enjoy the widest acceptance."

In Turkey, where religious dress is restricted rather than obligatory, a genuine Islamic fashion has emerged. But there it represents a woman's personal choice, not a legal obligation.

"This is something I discuss with my students. For us, the important thing is to get rid of the black. Black is unacceptable in Islam. This way of dressing [she touches her *chador*] was Iranian long before it became Islamic. If we can manage to introduce lively colors, the colors of happiness, that would change the face of our society."

How would you describe the question of the *hijab*? Isn't it a decision for the individual woman to take, before God and her conscience?

"We're an Islamic nation, and as such we should have an Islamic identity. Which means that it is not an individual question, but a social one. It is an indicator of identity—something to be worn as a member of a group. In Turkey, we're witnessing a new approach to Islam. Why do women insist on taking the veil in France? It's not an individual issue but a growing trend in society."

In France, where the debate over "ostensible signs of religious identification" was in full swing—and being widely discussed in the Iranian press—the prohibition of such signs had become a part of the constitutional order. The measure reflected the democratic process, and not the decision of a Supreme Guide. If Iran could require that all women on Iranian soil wear *hijab*, in accordance with Islamic rules, then why could France not bar it altogether?

"Well, for me, speaking as a woman, *hijab* creates no obstacle to social progress. We're just wasting our time talking about it."

She falls silent for a moment, before concluding brusquely, "*Hijab* opened our society to women. And that's all there is to it. Let's not be misled by appearances."

* * *

Few would deny that the condition of women in Iran has improved since 1991, when the public prosecutor for Tehran under the presidency of Hashemi Rafsanjani, a certain Abolfarz Mousavi Tabrizi, described Iranian women who refused to adopt Islamic dress regulations as "renegades." For a prosecutor, whether or not a cleric, to describe a woman as a "renegade" was not far from pronouncing a death sentence.[32]

Those were the days when public morality squads patrolled the streets in their unmarked white Paykans, taking in or harassing young women whose headscarves allowed too much hair to show. Yet at the same time, larger numbers of devout women had begun their conquest of public space. Suddenly, they were to be found even in the wealthy northern districts of the city, a place where they had never before been accepted. Fariba Adelkhah, a French-trained sociologist, set herself the task of describing and analyzing what she had seen.

"Through their dynamic relation with religion, Muslim women have become full participants in an original form of modernity, a form often poorly understood by Western observers," she wrote.[33]

As Ms. Adelkhah's research over the last decade has shown, "the condition of women" in Iran is constantly evolving. One only need look

32. Fariba Adelkhah, *La révolution sous le voile: femmes islamiques d'Iran*, with a preface by Jean-Paul Digard (Paris: Éditions Karthala, 1991), 7.

33. Ibid., 252 [My translation. —FR].

around in the streets, in the parks, even in some restaurants to certify that the behavior of girls and young women has changed radically over the last seven years, notwithstanding recurring bouts of repression. In January 2004, we experienced what was clearly a period of relaxation—or of "controlled indifference"—by the power structure with regard to women's dress. In 1997, the newly elected Mohammad Khatami could thank women who placed their confidence in him to transform their informal achievements into broadly respected laws and rights that would protect Iranian society as a whole from arbitrary authority.

The promotion of women's equality is among the most ambitious components of the reform program; the results have exceeded the hopes of their most energetic proponents. But true equality has not been achieved. Fariba Davoudi-Mohajer is right in asserting that the Women's Party still has plenty of work to do. But there can be no mistaking that Iranian women have assumed responsibility for their fate; that they have understood the significance of their struggle.

In Tehran's poorer districts, and throughout the country, following on the initiative of numerous non-governmental organizations, women have coalesced around the basic issues of poverty, birth control, health, hunger, and illiteracy. Around these issues a new sense of solidarity has grown up, pushing aside social differences and bringing the well-to-do and the underprivileged—women from Tehran's sprawling satellite cities and poor districts, and from the middle class—together in common cause.

These women have begun to grapple with their common problems through the networks of NGOs that sprouted up like mushrooms during the Khatami years. More often than not isolated and without resources, they have proved tenacious and effective. Their vigorous grass-roots activity has made them an indispensable part of the daily life of Iranian society.

The very existence of these networks is one of the successes of the reform movement—and perhaps its most enduring legacy. Solidly rooted in their communities, Iran's NGOs have become centers of resistance, places where new approaches to social reform are taking root.

New Waves

LUNCHTIME AT THE ARTISTS' FORUM CAFÉ. The room, suffused with late January light, is already humming with the conversation of small groups of young Iranians who have come to eat, drink a glass of tea, or simply chat. We've chosen the café as an ideal venue for our meeting with an activist from the NGO movement that has become one of the driving forces of Iran's emergent civil society, a space where thought and limited forms of social action have escaped the worst of direct state intervention. Our guest, Omid Memarian, is a journalist and director of public relations for *Nandishan*, the Center for Young Alternate Thinkers of Civil Society—an umbrella organization that brings together NGOs engaged in grass-roots social and civic action.

Omid Memarian is thirty years old, well-dressed and clean-shaven in a country where the lack of a beard stands out. He also speaks fluent English. In the course of his work, he travels the country, from one conference, symposium, or round-table to another: a perspective that has made him a sharp-eyed observer of contemporary reality.

"It's taken seven years," he tells us, "for Iranians finally to understand the meaning of the religious democracy promised by President Mohammad Khatami. My generation sees power as a myth propagated by the previous generation. Now, finally, after Khatami, we can see what it all means."

"It used to be difficult for me to order my thoughts. Today, I can barely believe how much I've changed. But that's not all. Society has changed too. Sure, Mr. Khatami missed too many opportunities, but that doesn't mean that major social and political shifts haven't taken place during his term.

"You can see it for yourself in the street: in social relations; in the way people dress—women in particular; in conversation; in life style. Religion is slowly withdrawing from public life and reverting to its true dimensions.

"One of the most striking things about Islamic Iran is that after attempting to export and impose religion, the regime has ended up importing Western culture, particularly that of the United States, in spite of itself.

"That was the last thing they wanted to do. Today, the regime is like Don Quixote; it no longer lives in the real world, but in a dream, an illusion."

His words have the corrosive effect of acid, laying bare a sense of frustration at the parody of power orchestrated by the mullacracy, at the promises of the revolution sacrificed by the ruling caste.

"We're beginning to understand where religion has led us. We can judge the impact it's had on political life, on society. Religion has meant the institutionalization of corruption. What a joke! It's not surprising that today religion has left the hearts and lives of young people. Our youth has become secularist in its outlook, in its way of life, in its hopes. And this is happening in a time of crisis, when the Islamic Republic is in danger."

The root cause of the crisis is clear.

"Religion has no answer to the problems of society. Even the simplest questions, like sexuality, are quickly turned into tensions. Traffic, unemployment, prostitution, whatever you can think of, in fact, it's the same thing."

Omid Memarian's indignation is the polite form of the dark fury that lies just beneath the surface of Iranian youth, sometimes erupting violently, sometimes turning inward into flight from society, toward drug and alcohol addiction. The power elite has done everything it can to use religion to control people's everyday lives, and yet they have nothing to show for it.

"Their policy was to get people back to the mosque; they advertised, broadcast television programs, and more. But none of it answered people's needs. Take the question of sex, which is a natural need. Today, in Iran, on the one hand you have an informal society where normal sexual relations exist. But at the same time, officially, they simply do not exist. We're forced to adopt two personalities, one private, and the other public. You can see it at all levels. They've driven normal life underground."

What was driven underground has been resurfacing, becoming more and more visible over the last five years.

"Prostitution is now a fact of life, and some of the top personalities of the religious hierarchy are its best customers. Iranians can travel to places like Azerbaijan or Dubai for a sex break. For example, three days in Dubai cost you $300. A man can take his girlfriend, or two or three men can go with a girl. The officials all know about it, but no one says a thing. Which means they're not doing their job. It's not even a political issue any more, just a case of administrative incompetence. Our regime cannot respond to the most elementary demands of the people, who just want to get on with their lives."

Omid Memarian's stinging assessment confirms the evidence of our eyes. The regime has lost control of daily life; it can no longer tell minds and bodies how to think, how to act. If it achieved nothing else, the reform movement could take credit for this: an incoming tide that has been fashioned into a wave too powerful to stop. It is as if the regime has understood, and redirected its efforts to preserving its hold on power. Reason, he says, for rejoicing.

"In spite of everything, I'm happy. Because of this crisis, I can speak out. Things are getting out of hand; they're losing control."

And yet, at the same time—one of Iran's great paradoxes—the regime has shown a high degree of flexibility. As Omid Memarian was talking with us, the parliament had been occupied by hunger-striking MPs rejected by the Council of Guardians.

To hang on to power, the regime will make concessions to its political foes. This Omid Memarian tacitly admits, "In the present circumstances, it would be a mistake to see the Supreme Guide as the leader of the conservatives. He is an influential member of a caste that has the capacity to buy up everything, including big chunks of Iran. This is the strength—and the weakness—of the conservative regime."

In a sense, its weakness is more significant than its strength. The regime can tolerate a toothless parliament, incapable of bringing the citizens into the streets. But it cannot accept the student movement, which has a greater potential for mobilizing public opinion, making it as dangerous as a spark among dry tinder. The reaction to student militancy has been fierce: violence and harsh prison sentences are the tools of choice to crush the movement, and suppress student demands.

"Ultra-fundamentalist goons break up student demonstrations; the regime accuses students of being in the pay of foreign powers. Seventy percent of demonstrators at Tehran University have abandoned their political activity. Many of them were beaten; some simply disappeared.

"Even apolitical events can quickly turn into political demonstrations. This is a sign that dissatisfaction is growing. Outbursts of resentment turn into uncontrolled destruction; people run wild. The power structure takes advantage of these situations to infiltrate provocateurs that lead demonstrators into an ambush, where they'll end up being beaten. This tells us that the regime fears demonstrations—but demonstrations are dangerous for the reformists too."

Omid Memarian is more than an informed observer. His career has been closely linked to the growth of the reform movement, even though today he is openly critical of the government, and of President Khatami.

"As NGO representatives, we had a meeting with Mr. Khatami. He is a true democrat, but he knows who the conservatives are, and what they are capable of doing. He warned us, 'Avoid extreme radical actions; move forward but with the greatest precaution, slowly, gradually.' He knows what he's talking about. He knows the conservative political apparatus from the inside, even though today he's on the outside. He's an intellectual, but he's also the son of a *marja*—a title that denotes someone who, in Shi'ism, is considered as a 'source of emulation.'

"The power holders in Iran today are the same people that made the revolution. They have plenty of experience, and they know what could happen if they were to lose control.

"Look, I am not saying that reform has failed. But we have to admit it: the reformists have missed their chance. For certain, the reform party has been a failure, but the movement is still alive and kicking. Women and young people have been radicalized; today, they're far out in front of the reformists."

Omid Memarian does not mince words: the countdown to the end of the regime has begun, and the regime knows it. But like a boxing match, the last round is the most dangerous one.[34]

"People are fed up with the Islamic Republic. You can't even begin to imagine what has been done in its name. But, at the same time, people are not ready to change the regime: so what will happen, and how?

"We're trapped in a blind alley. The reformists are in decline, and public confidence has been eroded. The only possible way out is to establish vigorous civil society organizations. Today, the circumstances are favorable. Our strategy is to gain control of social power, not political power, a bit like in Turkey, with Recep Tayyip Erdogan, who was elected thanks to a strong social movement.

---

34. Our meeting with Omid Memarian took place in January 2004, a few weeks before the victory of the conservatives in parliamentary elections. Nine months later, on October 13, Mr. Memarian was arrested. On the day before his arrest, an editorial by Hossein Shariatmadari in *Kayhan* accused him of "being in the pay of the foreign enemy." He has subsequently been released.

"Our initiative is a true program for society, and not another way of carving out a privileged place for ourselves. Let's take post-war Germany as an example; we too can produce a democratic society. Our experience so far shows that we're on the right track."

Though he respects President Khatami for his moral qualities, Omid Memarian views him as a product of the Islamic Republic, and not as the founder of a new social order.

"Unfortunately, the Council of Guardians is also a product of this society. There's a bit of the Ayatollah in all of us. But we think that can change if we learn how to be active in civil society."

Today, Iranian civil society boasts more than 2,000 non-governmental organizations, 315 of which are focused on women's issues. Each and every one of them claims to be functioning on a democratic basis.

"You can't find anything to compare with it in any other country in our region. Our movement is a lively, vibrant one."

There can be little doubt about the vibrancy of Iran's NGOs, but the pathway to success may be rocky. The movement is restricted to the upper and middle classes; mobilizing "the masses" has proven to be more difficult than anticipated. NGOs lack the necessary tools and capacity for communicating with the least favored strata of the population; radio, television, and much of the press are tightly controlled by the regime. NGOs have no access to them.[35]

NGOs need financial support to continue to function, let alone put down roots. Since 1997, the bulk of support has come from international donors. Funding comes from sources as diverse as the Population Council, the Ford Foundation, the Netherlands government's Development Program and the Australian Agency for International Development. But the origin of these funds does raise legitimate questions about the motivations of the funding agencies—and about the independence of their beneficiaries.

Another program, financed by the UN Development Program's Tehran bureau, was suspended after an investigation by Iran's Interior Ministry. Yet another is funded directly by the Iranian government, which has contributed hundreds of millions of dollars. The government-supported program is still in operation, but it is impossible to get a clear idea of the extent of its involvement and influence. Paradoxically, the authoritarian

---

35. Maryam Hosseinkhah, "A Cold Reaction by the Iranian NGOs to the Global Peace Movement," *Volunteer Actors* (Iranian CSOs Training and Studies Center), April–May 2003, nos. 11 & 12.

regime has thrown its weight, apparently at arm's length, behind several Iranian NGOs, particularly in the community health field—organizations with a strong potential for dissidence.

Though it is impossible to draw objective conclusions, available evidence points to the need for Iran's NGOs to develop clear strategies to rid themselves of the political and financial constraints that limit their independence and freedom of action. If they cannot do so, they will come under the influence of international funding agencies or foreign governmental sources. The stakes are high, given the regime's intention to hang on to power at all costs. The NGO movement's inability to create a distinct personality of its own may well condemn it to the same fate as other Iranian social institutions: modern in appearance but profoundly traditional in the way they operate.[36]

As we read through the documents Omid Memarian has passed on to us, we cannot help wondering about the language used in creating and sustaining links between NGOs. It is a language borrowed from business administration, modeled on "market democracy." Catch phrases such as "stakeholders," "knowledge workers," or "entrepreneurship" pop up too often for comfort, while there is virtually no reference to the role of citizens in society.

There is a danger that Iran's NGOs may simply evolve into transmitters of the neo-liberal mindset, or of the regime's priorities, assuming the two to be fundamentally at odds. And at the other extreme, the organizations that still stand as symbols of the aspiration to democracy and civil society may come into violent collision with the same barriers that brought about the downfall of political reformism. It may well be that the regime, knowing that it has politically neutralized the reform movement, thus eliminating the only adversary that could have threatened its survival, feels it has nothing to fear from an NGO network that threatens neither the established order, nor the dominant economic model. As long as the basic premises that underlie the regime are not called into question, the power structure may well be able to tolerate alternative methods of management or technocratic modernization—but these methods would be as free of risk as they are remote from the daily lives and concerns of Iranian citizens.

In fact, Iran's mullacracy has adjusted quite nicely to neo-liberal doctrine, whose guiding principle is the transfer of responsibility for

---

36. Sohrab Razaghi, "Capacity Building as a Strategy," *Volunteer Actors*, June–July 2003, nos. 14 & 15.

public services to civil society, of social services and wealth redistribution once provided by the state to the private sector and to charitable organizations.

In the days following the catastrophic earthquake in Bam, we were eyewitnesses to the wave of solidarity that swept the country, running far ahead of government relief efforts. Over the years, Iranians have learned to expect little from the state, and to solve their own problems. So great was the human disaster in Bam that anger was relegated to a distant second place. But an increasing number of Iranians have come to understand that the power structure has abandoned them.

In the wake of geological upheaval, the fault lines that run through Iranian society have widened. Increasingly, Iranians are concluding that their interests are not those of the caste in power. A political vacuum has been created, which the country's NGOs have done their utmost to fill with a freshly empowered sense of solidarity. The danger is that these same organizations could end up diluting popular energies that might otherwise bring people into the streets.

Like a Snake

TEN O'CLOCK: we climb the stairs to the third floor of an elegant apartment building overlooking a quiet street in Tehran's uptown Jordan district. We ring the bell, the door swings open, and Bedokht Roshdieh-Ebrahimi waves us in with a smile. "Keep your shoes on," she says, as if to emphasize that hers is a non-traditional household (in Iran, guests usually leave their shoes at the door). We look around the room: the atmosphere is bright and cheery, the decor refined—discerningly chosen contemporary paintings share wall space with handsome pieces of traditional handicraft.

Our hostess introduces herself as an "open-minded" woman, as if to underline the fact that she wears neither *chador* nor headscarf. For Iranians, the catchphrase "open-minded" indicates acceptance of modern life styles, in contrast to traditional values, to the past, to religion as the focus of everyday life. It can also be understood as the dividing line between the reform movement and the conservative status quo.

The idea is hardly striking or original. It is common knowledge that as one heads north in Tehran, climbing higher up the slopes of the foothills, one is more likely to encounter women who have rejected the headscarf, who wear it far enough back on their heads to display a part of their hair, who simply drop it at home, even in the presence of male visitors. "Westernized" behavior of this variety is the rule among women of Iran's upper and middle classes. But Bedokht Roshdieh-Ebrahimi's description of herself as "open-minded" contains a note of irony, perhaps even of discreet provocation. By uttering the words, she confirms the existence of the gap separating "open-minded" secularist women from their "religious" sisters who have the support of the regime, and hold government positions. For her, as we are to learn, the existence of this gap has weakened women of both persuasions, and pointed up the need to bring the two extremes together in joint action, and in shared approaches to the problems of women's social and political status. The decision by women of both persuasions to join forces cannot have pleased the conservative power structure; in fact, it is an implicit, latent threat to that structure. Yet it lies at the heart of Ms. Roshdieh-Ebrahimi's efforts, and those of the women she works with at the grass-roots level. This is precisely what we have come to talk with her about.

"Don't judge women by their appearance," she warns, as if reading our thoughts. "Behind some particularly austere veils, you'll find extremely well-developed ideas. The more open-minded women become, the greater their grasp of the situation; the stronger their solidarity as well."

Ms. Roshdieh-Ebrahimi comes from an intellectual and economic background well connected with world events. She could easily have chosen a quiet, comfortable life, devoted to her two daughters and her husband, a well-to-do businessman. But she did not. Her own experience, and that of her family, has brought home to her a keen awareness of the realities faced by Iranian women—and of their place in society. That awareness became the starting point for a dramatic change in her life: the decision to join other women in their fight for equality. Ever since, she has invested all her time, resources, and her substantial reserves of energy to that end.

"After ten years of trying, I found my path, my way to being a feminist in Iran. It's a path completely different from Europe or North America.

"I came upon some old notebooks that had belonged to my aunt. She must have been Iran's first female journalist. Eighty years ago, she published the first newspaper for women. The headline in her first issue read: 'Women: Men's First Educators.' I believe we could call her a feminist, even back then. After all, she was searching for ways to have her rights recognized. That was what she fought for."

With a gesture, she draws our attention to a large black-and-white portrait, hanging over the fireplace: a man in Western coat and tie, but wearing the traditional fez. His eyes are animated; his expression, searching. In him, we can see her.

"That's my grandfather. He was very active in politics. He also had fourteen children. Of the fourteen, three were very committed women. One set up schools, the second went on to become a journalist, and the third, a militant secularist. One of them wore the *chador*, another a simple headscarf; the last kept her secular convictions until she died. Each one was different, but they respected one another perfectly. I think you can see a truly modern attitude at work, and it should be a lesson: each of us should find her own way, with mutual respect.

"It's not as difficult as it sounds. You ought to know that people from more modest backgrounds, poorer people, are more and more open-minded. They can understand my choices. They are much more flexible than at the beginning of the revolution, and, to be exact, women from this background are more daring, more courageous than men. In our society, men must work from morning to night; the cost of living is very high; most have no insurance. Work brings with it tensions. Nothing can be taken for granted, neither their lives nor their employment situation. A man who expresses his opinions openly fears loss of his job, especially if he works in the public and private-public sectors. Women are less vulnerable. They don't work like men, and they are more courageous about speaking their minds. They say what they think about society, and they demand their rights in public. It used to be that only educated women behaved that way, women who knew how to read and write. Today, even in the poorest areas, women express their opinions and act on them. The regime may not change, but it is beginning to notice that it will have to deal more and more with people power.

"Before the revolution, you'd find 'open-minded' women mostly among the leisured classes. But in the last ten years, the situation has changed totally. Now, women from the underprivileged classes are studying and graduating from university. Education is no longer the privilege of the wealthy. Today, 75 percent of women vote in elections. They are moving into public and political life. What we need to do now is to concentrate our efforts on the unseen part."

For our hostess, the "unseen part" begins where the southern extremity of her district ends. Her discovery was unexpected, to say the least: a sociologist friend based in Montreal spoke to her one day about the research she was doing into the conditions of Afghani women living in Tehran, women whose lives were totally hidden from the rest of the population.

Having time on her hands, Ms. Roshdieh-Ebrahimi agreed to assist her friend as she pursued her project. Almost overnight, she discovered another world, an invisible, near-underground world, complete with its own self-help networks and clandestine schools. Along with it she discovered a world of poverty and hardship. Indignation swiftly followed. Over time, she overcame fears among these downtrodden women that she might be affiliated with a UN agency. But money was not what she had to offer; instead, she brought these deprived women her dedication, her organizational gifts, her own networks of friends, her communication skills.

It was as if by gaining the confidence of these poor, deprived women, she had gained a new sense of self-confidence. Before long she had laid the foundations of an organization to promote education, tolerance, and solidarity among women: its starting point was the creation of a system of micro-libraries for the women of Tehran's poorest neighborhoods. The model would later spread to many Iranian cities and towns. Under the noses of the authorities, in the basement of her elegant apartment building, Ms. Roshdieh-Ebrahimi set up a veritable depot for the collection, selection, and distribution of books.

"It all happened here, at my house. Women would come to pick up books that they would lend out in their libraries. We met in the basement, and organized distribution without raising suspicions. In our society, it's normal for women to meet in the basement to prepare fresh greens for the day's stew! If I went door to door with a business card, distributing books, that would have drawn the attention of the government people.

"The whole thing began when I met the hairdresser from Shahr-e Rey, a suburban town south of Tehran. What an extraordinary woman she is; a woman who got the book bug! One day she made up her mind to set up a library in her home. Not exactly in her living room, mind you, but in her little hairdressing salon! At first, the neighborhood women wanted only religious books. They were worried about what people would say, so they asked for religious books to avoid raising suspicions. Then, when they got approval from the government to open a library, they began to stock other kinds of books, including novels and even poetry. It wasn't long before the hairdresser closed her salon and turned into a full-time librarian. You see, that's how we move forward, wiggling, like a snake.

"There are plenty of women like her, real fighters. They're my inspiration. Four years ago, I wouldn't have dared to do what I'm doing today. It's not because I've suddenly become more courageous, but because I know what society needs.

"Let me give you an example: I go to the parliamentary research library; they don't have a clue about what we're doing in the NGO movement. So I bring them up to date; meanwhile, we learn about the rules and regulations. We're not interested in fighting the government; we want to help it. That way, we avoid conflict."

Three weeks after our conversation with Ms. Roshdieh-Ebrahimi, Iranians went to the polls to elect a new parliament. But from the tone of her remarks, we had already guessed the outcome.

"For the first two years, everything was fine. But after that, people began to turn their backs on President Khatami. Of course, as president, he does not have enough power. There has been one accomplishment: over the last eight years, newspapers have written more about women's rights. People are more at ease with *hijab*. Many small things have changed in a short time; women have a better grasp of their rights. For young women in particular, if there were any attempt to impose new limitations, to turn back the clock, they would not easily accept it. In everyday life, rules and regulations are changing, and improving; if they want to return to the past, people will resist. They're not interested in changing the way they behave. The rules might be regressive, but that doesn't mean people will agree to regress.

"You know, when women gain a bit of power in the home, they don't give it up. A few years ago, the wives or daughters of men in the power structure joined the government as directors or supervisors. They didn't rank very high in the hierarchy, but when they began to look around them, they started thinking about their rights. They realized that their power had an impact on their husbands or fathers. They recruited other women, like me for instance, to help them and give them support. For the last three years, the women who work in government have been meeting on an informal basis with women working in the universities, in NGOs, and so on.

"Women have changed; they're living by today's clock. Men are still stuck in the past. Of course, in our cultural tradition, men must provide for women's needs. But if women are attending university or working, men still won't change the way they behave at home. Change their habits? No way! The man comes home, sits down in his armchair, and waits. I even have problems with my husband! A week ago, my twenty-year-old daughter had a sharp discussion with her father; he was so upset he told me, 'She's your daughter! Look what you're teaching her!'

"I respect my husband. He is very broad-minded, and gives me a lot of support. I thought it over carefully, then I told him, 'Your daughter respects you as her father, but she cannot respect you as a husband, as a man of your generation. I've changed, and I've done all I can so that you can change too. I respect you, I love you, and I really hoped the two of us could change. If you hadn't done it, we would have separated. But in her eyes, you haven't changed enough.'

"In our society, women are running on ahead, while men are still dragging their feet. Because of our cultural traditions and because of their power they won't change."

How do your two daughters feel about the young men of their generation? Do they come up to their expectations?

"Not really; the boys of their generation haven't changed as much as they have. And it's tough for girls to make them over. Perhaps it was easier for me in my life than it is for them in theirs. When they step outside of the family, they can do whatever they want, but once they're in a family setting, they must follow the rules. We've raised our children in an open environment; we urge them to take their place in society, to insist on their rights at the university, in the street, in the shops, at work. But when they try to exercise those same rights in the home, there's no give-and-take: you can't touch the traditional family rules. It's hard to live with. In the Eastern family, it's not an easy matter to change the rules. As open-minded parents, you want to change all the rules in society, all except in your own home!

"In the family, the unwritten laws are very severe; they cannot be modified. Ever since the revolution, the children who have noticed the contradiction between family rules and the rules of society have been left to their own devices. And it's affected them deeply.

"In the streets the law is severe too, but young people can deal with it more effectively than with these invisible laws of ours. Most young people couldn't care less; they get along just fine, much better than we do. We still have our fears. But they're not afraid of anything. Of course you'll hear stories of repression in the streets, but for a country of seventy million, it's nothing."

Not only is Bedokht Roshdieh-Ebrahimi familiar with the new Women's Party, which had been established just one week before our meeting; she shares its outlook. But, she tells us, Fariba Davoudi-Mohajer's initiative reflects the views of a younger generation, one more familiar with the international feminist movement, certainly more radical, and theoretically better-equipped to deal with the challenges it must face.

Our hostess defines herself as a grass-roots activist, closer to the community-based networks set up by women volunteers in the national health-care system. The government had been unable to respond to the need for family planning, for a nation-wide birth control program. These networks were a creative response: a sharp break with past policy that challenged the "fundamentalist" elements within the Islamic Republic's power structure.

Iran's birth rate is now in steep decline, from 7.3 in 1966 to 6.7 in 1986,[37] six years after the Iraqi invasion. The war had impelled the authorities to adopt a high-birth-rate policy linked to defense of the

37. L'Iran au XXe siècle, 33.

homeland. Today, the birth rate stands at 2.6.[38] Alone, the government could never have succeeded. In fact, Iran's birth-rate policy was the power structure's tacit admission that without the participation of women, the program would never have succeeded.

As Ms. Roshdieh-Ebrahimi explains, "It began with a group of twenty women in the south of Tehran. They were all volunteers, uneducated, women from poor families. Three years later, more than nineteen thousand women from one end of the country to the other are active participants in the program, not to mention another fifty thousand part-time volunteers. They don't all know one another, but I know just who they are, and how precious they are.

"When Mr. Hashemi Rafsanjani was president, UNICEF congratulated him on setting up a volunteer health organization of this magnitude. He replied that one day it would become Iran's largest political party. Now wasn't that nice? He couldn't have imagined how right he was! Today, we know that every volunteer is in touch with between fifty and a hundred families, depending on the population density of her area. That means a woman can exert an influence on fifty to a hundred families. When an organization can build up a network like that, and when it can bring people together, it's no longer a question of a single individual voting, but of an individual who can influence at least fifty families.

"To be effective, the project depends on close ties. Neighbors meet one another at the dispensary in their district or village; that's where they can learn the basics: how to take care of their children, learn about family planning at the health clinic, and so on. People trust these volunteers, which means that in the long run people are better informed, talk over their problems more, and are more open to political ideas. Each volunteer is a kind of one-woman NGO. It goes without saying that the volunteer workers talk about more than health-related issues. They've had a political impact that has led to changes in society as a whole, and in the way people think.

"It's a lot like my own story, you know; I see now just how much I've changed, and how much women around me are changing, just like me.

"After the revolution, most women gave up and went home. Many of them lacked experience and education. Those were sad days for women. We thought we'd lost our lives. Well, we were wrong. Obligatory *hijab* was no reason to stay home. We were wasting our time at home, behaving

38. Roksana Bahramitash, "Exporting Democracy to the Axis of Evil," occasional paper of the Centre Simone de Beauvoir, Concordia University, Montreal, 2004.

as if we were prisoners. So we started to get involved; we started to run. We didn't just walk; we ran. And because of this, society really began to change. Go anywhere you like and look closely. Here, in the wealthy districts, there, in the poorer areas, educated women, uneducated women, older women, young girls, they've all begun to move, and they're still moving. These days, our society is like a kettle ready to boil. We can do much more today than we could eight years ago. Just recently we saw how women took action to organize relief efforts for Bam, after the earthquake. When something happens in our society, we can mobilize very quickly, and in a variety of ways. I tell you again: we're like water that's started to boil."

The Metamorphosis of the Hairdresser

WE DIDN'T LEAVE Ms. Roshdieh-Ebrahimi's home until she'd given us the address of the hairdresser who'd become a librarian—and a militant community activist.

Now we are on our way to the municipality of Rey, on the far southern outskirts of Tehran. The taxi ride there is a long haul through traffic jams and the city's everyday inferno of noise and pollution. But our driver, a native of Rey and proud of it, knows all the shortcuts. In less than an hour we have arrived.

Known in antiquity, Rey had long prospered as an autonomous township before Tehran finally swallowed it up. Its low-lying, humble houses give directly onto narrow streets and sidewalks. Entrances look alike; a discreet sign is all that identifies the library where Farzadeh Gohari awaits us.

Tall, broad shoulders accentuated by a light blue *manteau*, a dark blue scarf covering her head, she pulls open the sliding door with a wrenching metallic croak. We step into what had been a tiny hairdressing salon and today serves as a mini-library. Her office, if it could be called that, consists of a table and chair; three other chairs set against the wall are reserved for visitors. Floor-to-ceiling bookshelves packed with books occupy all remaining space. We take a seat, tea is served, and the metal door slides closed with the same ear-splitting creak. The morning sun shines through its frosted glass panes. There we will stay until the end of our conversation with a woman who, as we quickly come to appreciate, prefers not to be interrupted.

Ms. Gohari and her family—like most of the people who live in Tehran's sprawling satellite towns—are not natives of the capital. She was born in the north of Iran, and married an Azeri, a member of the country's large Turkish-speaking minority. The family settled in Rey, a place where homes could be found at reasonable prices, much lower than in the city. The couple has raised their four children here.

"We're not wealthy," she explains. "But today we might have enough money to find another house, but we're staying put, because we like our neighborhood and the people who live here. I've started something, and I believe in it. I want to help other women; I can't just walk out on them."

Ms. Gohari is a born communicator. After years of caring for her neighbors' hairdos, she now tends to their minds and their ideas with the same energy. The distance from the hairdresser she was to the community librarian she has become, has proved to be short—and her customers have followed her in full confidence. She has wielded curling irons and books with equal skill and verve, transforming her authority as a hairdresser into credibility as a librarian. The transformation has been total, and it works. Once in the chair, who could not succumb to Ms. Gohari's appeal?

"I started out about ten years ago. That was when I had my hairdressing salon right here. I had lots of contact with the women in our neighborhood. Here, you'll find all sorts: workers and unemployed people, educated and uneducated people, civil servants, poor people, and middle-class people like me.

"At that time, there was a project for housewives in the works. The idea was to set up a family health network. As a hairdresser I was already established and integrated into the community, so the organization asked me to talk to women about it, and to join in.

"When I went to my first meeting, it made a big impression on me. I'd always believed that women's health was an important issue, and I promised to talk to my neighbors about it. I did just that. After that, we made up our minds to offer home courses to women in the immediate area. The first step was to talk to them about health, about relations with their husbands, about birth control. Then we added sessions on flower arranging, so they could beautify their apartments. The state paid for all those courses."

Ms. Gohari the hairdresser had taken her first steps in the government program designed to raise awareness and provide practical knowledge to housewives. She was soon to take another step, less strongly supported by the power structure: the awakening of social and political consciousness.

"After that, I thought it was time for my neighbors to get out of the house, to take an interest in social problems, and to look for solutions. We set up a small group to deal with local issues. There was no electricity here back then; the streets weren't paved or maintained at all. The state was doing nothing for us. So we held our own elections, and chose a committee of twenty-six women. That's when we decided to turn our attention to cultural matters. When women are trapped in their homes and don't participate in society, there are a lot of things they don't know: how to talk with their husbands, for example; how to talk to their children. So, the first thing we did was to look for solutions to practical problems.

"After that, they elected me president of the committee. We went to the government and other women's organizations and we told them who and what we were. We said, 'Here we are, and this is what we've done.' Just like that!

"One thing led to another; we wanted to find out what women were lacking in terms of access to culture and education. We realized that there were no bookstores in our district. Not surprising: books are expensive, and people here don't have the money to buy them. How do you expect them to read?

"I was still running my hairdressing salon, right here in this room. So I decided to turn it into a library. The state was prepared to help us renovate, but didn't want to contribute to buying books! So to get us started, I contributed 150 books, and our women's group added another 50. We got our start with a collection of 200 books."

She pauses for a moment, and looks around her at the book-choked shelves that cover the walls of the tiny former salon. Then she turns to us with a satisfied smile.

"All the books you see here were donated. Doctors have given us medical books; teachers have passed on books on science and literature. Religion is important in our culture. If God makes good a wish, you should make a donation to the mosque. But in our neighborhood, the people say, 'Oh God, if you fulfill my wish, I will contribute to the library so it can buy books, or I will give them myself.'

"Not to mention Ms. Roshdieh, who has given us so many. Two years ago, she invited me to speak on March 8. I went. But I was unprepared, plus I was afraid of speaking in public. She said to me, 'You've got to speak, because of all you've done for your neighborhood.' That gave me the courage to speak up, and everybody was very interested in what I had to say. And afterward, they all came up and promised me books for the library.

"After that event, I've kept in touch with everybody who wanted to give us a hand. People keep on donating books, and we even got a fax machine. Some of them even gave us money.

"But I still wasn't satisfied. Women in Iran don't know their rights. All they know how to do is cry, cook, and look after their children. Everything else is men's business. So I started to take an interest in women's rights. We invited a lawyer to give us information and advice.

"After her visit, the men in the neighborhood got upset, and said, 'Now there are going to be more divorces and problems. Life was easier beforehand, it was just fine for us; now, there'll be constant quarreling in every family.' But our lawyer kept at it, 'We have to change women's culture, and family culture. Individuals should have equal rights.' We passed on the message to our husbands.

"But that wasn't all. We have a lot of families where the woman is the sole breadwinner; her husband may be dead, or in prison. I've helped out women like this with food, and with money to pay their telephone and electricity bills."

A library can be a big step toward solidarity. Conclusion: there can be no finer tribute to books than to take them literally. What about the government, though? What has it done for you?

"The government? What government? The people are helping the government, not the other way around. What's the point of sitting here and asking the authorities, 'Why don't you do this or that?' We've got to take action ourselves, come up with ideas, take the initiative ourselves and make good on them. Later, when we've proved that it works, we can ask the state to come and give us a hand."

It looks to us like you're involved in militant, political action, getting women involved in changing society. Is that really your aim?

"Look, we're not interested in politics. Changing society isn't our goal. We want to change the way women think, for them to learn their rights and improve their relations with their husbands and their children. We're not against the state, and we're not against the government. We're an NGO and NGOs shouldn't be involved in politics."

It may have been difficult for Ms. Gohari to answer us more directly. The only NGOs tolerated in Iran are those that can demonstrate absolute political neutrality. Offenders are dissolved at the first sign of suspicion. Objectively, it is difficult to link NGOs with political action. Bearing that in mind, it is easy enough to understand the librarian's caution.

"We work with politicians, but they don't control us. We mind our own business. Except that, when there's no other way, I will work with the government. I don't have any choice in the matter: I have to ask for assistance for my fellow citizens."

Today, more than six hundred families have taken out membership in the library, which now boasts a collection of more than six thousand volumes. Most of the readers are women, Mrs. Gohari explains. It also lends out books to the neighborhood school, which has no library. In five years, what was a hairdressing salon has become a neighborhood institution, a bedrock and "salon" of local cultural and political life. And that's not all. The former hairdresser has just launched a micro-business administered entirely by women: a training center for unemployed women that teaches elementary computer skills, sewing, and—not surprisingly—hairdressing.

There is a subterranean shift working its way through Iranian society. It owes much of its vitality to the women's movement: multifaceted, in constant motion, and as irresistible as the metamorphosis of the hairdresser Farzadeh Gohari.

A.K.A. Hassan

FOR YEARS HASSAN ABDULRAHMAN[39] has been one of our most reliable sources of information—and friendship—in Iran. An encounter with Hassan is a highlight of any visit. There are few things he does not know, does not keep close track of, by way of inside stories and penetrating analysis. Not one for idle chatter, Hassan is a man with a keen eye and consuming curiosity; a passionate, outspoken seeker after truth with a build to match his personality: tall, broad-shouldered, with an ironic eye and a sonorous laugh, he speaks Farsi with a heavy accent. Follow him down any street in Tehran and he'll meet a friend. Everyone knows Hassan—and he seems to know just about everyone. You'll encounter him in the dusty alleys of Tehran's satellite towns, and in the corridors of power.

To be fair, African Americans aren't that numerous in Iran. You won't find many on the sidewalks of the capital, especially not those who have been living in Iran for twenty-five years. All of which makes Hassan Abdulrahman unique: a man whose life seems to embody the tormented relationship between the land of his birth and his adopted country.

Friday—the day of public prayer—in north Tehran, early January. The city, normally a raucous hubbub of activity, has fallen blissfully silent. The weather is chilly, the sky overcast, the air free of the usual choking clouds of pollution. The snow-covered mountains that loom over us like a wall are blinding white in the pallid winter sunlight. In a room bare of furniture except for a few chairs and a sofa, Hassan Abdulrahman tells his story. He speaks with detachment, as if our questions were meant for someone else.

What brought you to Iran?

"It happened in 1980. I was caught between the Iranians and the Americans. To be specific, there was a plot against the life of Imam Khomeini. But my presence in Iran is related to the killing of a certain

---

39. Hassan Abdulrahman's story is the subject of Jean-Daniel Lafond's film *American Fugitive* (InformAction Films, 2006).

Ali Akbar Tabatabaï, who was one of the counter-revolutionary leaders. He had been the spokesman, in the United States, of the shah's last prime minister. He was also in close contact with the White House and with U.S. intelligence.

"He had been connected with preparations for the failed *coup d'état* at Nowjeh,[40] the most ambitious military coup attempt after the revolution. Its aim was to decapitate—literally—the government. Khomeini was the main target. I was asked to eliminate Tabatabaï. I agreed to do so, on certain conditions."

He pauses, falling quiet for a moment. We look each other in the eyes. Finally, he breaks the silence.

"Anyway, he died. He was killed."

Another silence.

You killed him, isn't that right?

"Yes, I did it. I killed him."

What made you do it?

"It was easy. The important thing is to know American history, to understand that it is a long-running history of rape, robbery, and murder."

* * *

In November 1950, in a small hospital in North Carolina, a baby boy came into the world. His parents christened him David Theodore. His mother's skin was pale enough for her to "pass" for white in the color-conscious America of the day. Mother and son were assigned to a private room where they awaited the arrival of the proud—and much darker-skinned—father. No sooner did he step into the hospital than he was asked to pick up his wife and newborn son and vacate the premises. Baby David's skin wasn't as black as his father's, but he had, at one day old, experienced American racism for the first time. It would not be his last experience of this kind in the United States of the 1950s and 1960s.

40. The failed Nowjeh *coup d'état* was to take place in early July 1980. More than six hundred officers of the Iranian armed forces, most of whom belonged to the air force, were involved. One hundred suspects were executed. (See Said Amir Arjomand, *The Turban for the Crown: The Islamic Revolution in Iran* [New York: Oxford University Press, 1988], 164.) The Nowjeh coup had been preceded by the Tabas expedition, which was a stinging defeat for the Carter administration and the American special forces. Ayatollah Khomeini attributed the mission's failure to divine intervention in the form of a sandstorm that grounded the American naval helicopters in the Iranian desert.

Hassan Abdulrahman in *American Fugitive*. Photo by Nezam Kiaie, courtesy of InformAction Films.

The story of this baby, David Theodore Belfield, is the story of an African American, in all its anger, its hopes, its commitments, its hair-trigger responses—and its misfortunes. It is a story that has made him the man he is, a story that he can never leave behind, a story that has followed him through long years of exile.

"I grew up in the sixties. I grew up with the murder of Malcolm X, with the murders of Cheney, Schreymer, and Goodman, the young Jewish civil rights activists in the South; with the murder of Emmett Till, with the murder of Martin Luther King. I grew up with the murder of John F. Kennedy, which was—it's clear to me—the work of the American system. It goes without saying that I was no admirer of Mr. Kennedy, I never was. But his own system killed him. The true story remains unknown to this day. All those things, I knew.

"I was a witness to the decapitation of the Black Panther Party, the Cointelpro program.[41] I knew about the atrocities in Viet Nam as they were being committed; I even lost a member of my family there. Myself, I refused to go, for racial and religious reasons. So, I was intimately

---

41. A secret program of kidnapping, murder, and "disappearance" of Black American militants carried out by the FBI.

acquainted with American realities, and all during the 1970s, that awareness never left me. It only got stronger. When I heard of the attempted coup to eliminate the Supreme Leader of the Islamic Republic of Iran, I had no moral hesitations about doing what I did. What I mean to say is, why do some people just stand there when someone whacks them in the head? What gives them the right to kick you in the ass, but you, you can't do the same thing to them?

"Taking action against oppression, fighting against tyranny, is a true religious duty. It means you may also die in action; it's not a free ticket, it can hurt you. For me, these ideas, which are central to Islam, had been absent in the Black movements in the United States. They told us: sit down in the bus, resist passively; if they send dogs to attack you, don't fight back; likewise if they attack you with water cannons or with live bullets. What noble martyrdom!"

Shortly after the assassination of Martin Luther King on April 4, 1968, at age eighteen, David Theodore Belfield enrolled at Howard University, America's most prestigious Black institution. He was to leave after one semester. The treatment of Black people in American society revolted him; the difficulty, if not the impossibility, of escaping the heritage of slavery frustrated him. He began to keep the company of young Muslims, most of them African Americans like himself. Reading the Qur'an was for him a revelation: struck by the pertinence of its teachings on justice, he converted. It was an awakening, a release of energies he had not known he possessed. Islam revealed to him the deeper meaning of his identity as a Black person, and gave meaning to his social and political involvement.

"When you become aware of your tiny identity in this much greater whole, then you can make decisions about what you must or must not do. Of course, most people don't do anything; they avoid looking at the problem and go their way. For whatever reason, that's not what I did. A lot of it, I owe to my conversion to Islam. Islam teaches you to act; it does not teach you to pray in a corner of the mosque by yourself. That's good too, of course, but most of all, you must act."

In the spring of 1975, David Belfield—who by now called himself Davud Salahuddin—was a regular at the Islamic Center in Washington D.C. There he attended a lecture by Saïd Ramadan, who preached an activist approach to Islam. Davud struck up a friendship with the man who was the permanent representative of Egypt's Muslim Brotherhood in Europe, and who had been a close collaborator of the late Dr. Hassan al-Banna, the movement's founder. Saïd Ramadan's motto, "All Muslims are brothers," was to become his own.

By the end of the decade, Iranians were well along in their preparations to rid themselves of Shah Mohammad-Reza Pahlavi. The writings of Ayatollah Khomeini, translated into English, circulated widely in the Black community. Davud Salahuddin was among those who took notice, and joined the circle of revolutionary Iranian students who were then attending American universities. He quickly became an Islamic combatant, and would soon be called upon to carry out a mission at the request of his Iranian friends. It was a dangerous mission, and he knew it. He was to carry it out, in cold blood, after weeks of detailed preparation. On July 22, 1980, in the Washington suburb of Bethesda, Maryland, Davud, disguised as a letter carrier, killed Ali Akbar Tabatabaï with three shots to the chest at point-blank range. He immediately fled the United States by way of Montreal and, after a two-week stopover in Switzerland, he landed in Tehran, where he began to call himself Hassan Abdulrahman.

Before agreeing to act, he had suggested to his principals that they choose another target, preferably Henry Kissinger or Kermit Roosevelt, who had played a key role in the overthrow of Mohammad Mossadeq in 1953, and in the suppression of the Muslim Brotherhood in Egypt the following year. He found no takers.

"My only regret," he admits today, "is that I killed the dog, and not the master."

And when we ask him, "As a Black, and as an American, when you agreed to kill that man, did you do it for the Iranian Revolution, or against the Americans?" his answer is immediate.

"Against the Americans."

And he goes on to explain, "Much has been said about Iranian terrorism in the last twenty-five years, and it certainly exists; there have been many cases of Iranians killing other Iranians, and these deaths were often the work of the state. But during the same twenty-five years, no one has ever told us that Jimmy Carter created Saddam Hussein; no one has ever said a word about the terror that the Americans have spread in this part of the world. The pope says that more than one million Iraqi children have died as a result of American sanctions. One million dead, that sounds suspiciously like genocide, if you compare it with what happened in Cambodia, or in Rwanda. But no one seems to be interested in state terrorism when it's carried out by the Americans, so you get the impression that what's going on in this part of the world is fun and games. No one talks about it."

Hassan is a free man, in word and deed. No one and nothing escapes his candor unscathed, whether it be the image of the late Imam Khomeini, or of the Islamic Revolution. He lashes out at the violence and the anti-democratic excesses of the conservatives, and at the same time, unsparingly scrutinizes the impasse into which President Khatami's reformists have driven themselves. Recent events only seem to confirm the lucidity of his views. And in the meanwhile, the United States has declared "victory" in Iraq, set up an "Axis of Evil," and announced that Iran is now in its sights.

In Iran, anything can happen. Given the circumstances, yesterday's enemy can become tomorrow's friend. In both Washington and Tehran, the same shadowy figures that brought the two countries together in the past today hold power. Several of the authors of the October Surprise, the secret agreement between the Islamic regime and the Republican Party that saw Iran free the U.S. Embassy hostages on the day of Ronald Reagan's inauguration as president, continue to exert influence on American policy. The same men were also key players in the Iran-Contra scandal, in which high-ranking members of the U.S. political establishment cut a deal with Iranian "terrorism" to free American hostages held in Lebanon.[42] On the Iranian side, several influential and prominent mullahs worked closely with their American "counterparts."

Hassan has kept close track of the situation, which is of immediate concern to him. For the last twenty-five years he has been wanted by the FBI and by Interpol. Both know his whereabouts; they also know that they can do nothing if he does not leave Iran; extradition is not an option. But a thaw between the two countries would bring pressures to bear on Hassan, who might end up as a bargaining chip.

"Iran is not an acceptable future for me. That much is certain, and has been for several years now. I never intended to settle in Iran, but the state

---

42. In November 1986, a major political scandal shook the United States: the Reagan administration had, since January of that year, been providing arms to "Israeli representatives" who had in turn sold them to "Iranian representatives," who had purchased them well above the original U.S. price. Via CIA channels, the United States received the payment owing; the difference between the list price and the amount paid was deposited in a Swiss bank account opened by the Nicaraguan "Contra" rebels. The total amount of the transactions has been estimated at between ten and thirty million dollars. Ronald Reagan would later state that he was not aware of the arms deal. In a press conference, he clumsily contradicted himself when accused of trading arms for American hostages.

apparatus, for its own reasons, has forced me to stay, and if I go outside, I must return. To a certain extent, I've become a kind of hostage myself. And to be frank, I've had it up to here. I'm looking for a way to get out of Iran, whether I return to my country, or leave for another one. I don't really know. But I don't think I'll be here for much longer."

Hassan's story is a tragic one. It is the tragedy of a hunted man who cannot escape his life in Iran, of a man condemned to prison in the United States. He knows that he may soon have to choose between bare subsistence as a "free" man in Iran under threat of an eventual resumption of U.S.-Iran relations, or facing justice and jail in the United States. The bluntness of his answer reveals the man.

"At this particular time in my life, the best way for me to re-enter the United States might be through the prison system. If you really want to learn about the realities of Black America, prison may be the best place to be. After all, it's the continuation of the plantation system. Except for athletes and pop singers—I don't mean to denigrate their achievements, of course—Black America, for Black men at least, is either in prison, about to enter prison, or about to be released from prison. I think a lot about the prison system, not because I want to lose my freedom—I don't—but as a form of education. Maybe there's something there that I should see and understand. Maybe there are even groups of people I should meet, and share my experiences with. I've often survived in difficult circumstances, but I've never lived in prison. Maybe all these years spent abroad are nothing but preparation for my return to the Gulag, to the American Gulag. I'd tell my brothers, whatever their color, what's going on in the world outside. They're likely to have a few illusions on that score. Then I'd tell them what they're up against at home, and on that point, they're not likely to have any illusions at all."

What do you expect from American justice?

"Let's be realistic. We're in a Bush administration. I've committed murder. That might get me fifteen or twenty years in prison, and if the prisons are really crowded, I might get away with ten. But considering all the hysteria about Islam and political assassination over there, I'd expect the worst."

Today, more than twenty years after the revolution, have you lost faith in Iran? Do you still feel the same anger toward the United States?

"Sure, I'm still just as angry at the Americans. But I've changed my mind about the Islamic Revolution. I don't see a revolution. I see a society that kicked out the king, but never made a revolution in the way it behaves. Still, you have to be fair. This country makes its first appearance in the world as an empire, twenty-six hundred years ago. Old habits have deep roots.

"You've got to remember that it was only in 1962 that the shah launched his 'White Revolution,' a kind of global project to wipe out feudalism in Iran. I'd tell anyone who wants to understand Iran today this: the first thing you have to understand is Iran's feudal past. If you do, you will understand the relationship between Iranians and power, and the concept of feudalism. And as a result you'll be in a position to decode what's happening today in this country. I know now how the Iranians view authority; it's the result of their feudal past. It has nothing to do with the teachings of Islam. Take for example a concept like the *Velayat-e faqih*. When Imam Khomeini, God bless him, came across this theory of *Velayat-e faqih*, whether he knew it or not, he was transferring the power of the king to the jurist-consult. Today, we've got a guy who pretends to be a jurist-consult, but who didn't have that qualification before they promoted him to the position he occupies now. It's the old story of the emperor all over again. No one can criticize him. All people can do is tell him how wonderful he is. That's what I call feudalism. I don't think I'm wrong; in fact, I think I'm right."

But you've given twenty-five years of your life to the revolution. When you see the results, aren't you discouraged?

"And how! To a certain extent, anybody who knows the history of Iran is bound to be discouraged. Maybe the most discouraged people of all are the reformists. Now they see what's happening to them. The starting point of the reform movement was to apply the constitution, that's all. They called for transparency, for the rule of law. And what did they get for their trouble? They've been greeted by tyranny, and forced to submit. And you know something? Tyranny works!

"But the greatest tragedy is that of the leadership. They simply cannot understand that outside of the reform movement, there is no other alternative. If they can't agree on their goals—and I don't think they can agree—it will only be a matter of time before the whole system of the Islamic Republic vanishes. It's all a matter of demographics. You have a country of sixty-five million people, and 70 percent—I think it's the correct figure—are under thirty. And they're disillusioned with the way things are.

"For the first time in the country's history since it accepted Islam, parents can no longer transmit the traditions to their children. There are two reasons: first, it's impossible to resist the West, and the modern

136

world; you've got to learn how to deal with it, to adapt it to your situation, to keep up with it.

"Along with that, the image of the leaders is hardly a brilliant one. After twenty-five years of direct experience with this power structure, the people have been kept far away from political decision-making: that's one of Iran's main problems, the power structure won't show the books. From a religious point of view, it's completely crazy. The regime wants to control everything, but it doesn't want to be accountable for anything."

For you, is Iran's near future a dark one?

"How could it be anything else? Just think: the Islamic Revolution took place at just about the same time as the great upheavals in communication technologies. And since then, there have been similar revolutions in other fields. In some countries, it was commercial, but Iran hasn't even joined the credit card age! Which means that the country has been cut off from most of the world, especially in technological development. Iranians are sitting in limbo, while the world leaves them behind. The young people know it, but the people in power, because they've got all the power, behave as if there was no problem. It's crazy."

Can there be dialogue with this regime, with this system? If ever the West were to start up a dialogue with the Islamic Orient, with Iran for instance, what kind of dialogue would that be?

"When Mr. Khatami launched his appeal for a dialogue of civilizations, he was in a completely different position than he is today. His call had a universal appeal. But we were caught up in a paradox: in Iran itself there is no dialogue. I think he was touching on something that could have been the key to world peace. But there's an underlying question: just how far are Westerners, beginning with the United States, prepared to accept the idea of a dialogue among civilizations, to begin a true exchange of views? For them, that would mean giving up what is becoming a monopoly of power in the world.

"This dialogue is of the highest importance, but for the American establishment, it's nothing but a minor irritant. But there's still another paradox: the methods used against Mr. Khatami in Iran are the exact opposite of dialogue. And on this issue, it's not a question of us against the 'other,' the foreigner; no, it's between the Iranians themselves. Not only in Iran, but also in the Islamic world, the Iranians cannot manage to talk to one another. So, to imagine that there can be a dialogue with the rest of the world is meaningless. Who are they trying to fool? Mr. Khatami has succeeded in bringing Iran a respectability that the country did not have before. And that's all well and good. But his enemies have taken control of it—and I'm not talking about that [he points to the Supreme Guide], that everybody's talking about. We always come back to the same fundamental problem: here, everyone talks about the dialogue of civilizations because they're obliged to do so, but the fact is that in Iran, it's quite clear: there's no dialogue at all."

As long as journalists, intellectuals, and opposition leaders are in prison, as long as people are being assassinated, dialogue is unlikely. You speak of the Americans and their flagrant lack of will to join a true dialogue with the "other"; you describe them as a force that crushes everything in its path. But couldn't we say the same thing about the conservative power structure in Iran with regard to its opponents?

"Sure. Except that the United States are much more sophisticated in the way they maintain order, and even exploit situations in their own interests, including in Iran. But this isn't a new attitude in Iranian society. The history of the country's political culture shows that the Iranians have never known anything but absolute power, and the power to tyrannize people absolutely. That's been Iranian culture down through the centuries. Or at least since the Iranians recovered their lands under the Safavids. There has never been a place for voices of dissent. When a dissenting voice spoke out, he would lose his head, and that's all there was to it. It's the same thing today. Maybe one of the factors that mitigates the situation a little bit, is that Iran isn't completely cut off from the rest of the world, due to new communication technologies, and also because so many Iranians have lived abroad and returned. Today, more than three million Iranians live outside the country, and keep in touch. When you get right down to it, the Iranians have always known it much better than I do. I don't think I'm exaggerating when I say that a real dialogue among Iranians would be a much greater revolution than 1979."

The dialogue that Hassan Abdulrahman, always the realist, has given up on, still exists between him and his native land. In fact, it has never stopped. In 1996, ABC broadcast an interview with him, filmed in a safe location in Istanbul, in which he admitted to the assassination of Ali Akbar Tabatabaï. Strikingly, Carl Shoffler, the Washington D.C. police officer in charge of the investigation, showed a surprising degree of understanding toward an admitted murderer.

Over the years, Hassan had built up a telephone relationship with him, built on mutual respect, if not a sense of shared views. Shoffler had come to see the intellectual qualities of his companion in conversation;

Hassan's knowledge of history and his analytical abilities fascinated him. The two men had begun to discuss the terms of a possible trial: Hassan had agreed to return to the United States, on condition that he would be allowed to call former president Carter, as well as Henry Kissinger, to testify. Mr. Shoffler died before he could provide an answer.

His dialogue with his homeland was to take a sudden turn in 2002, when the film *Kandahar*, by Iranian director Mohsen Makhmalbaf, was released in the United States. Shot before the events of September 11 were to shine a cold light on Afghanistan and on the ultra-fundamentalist Taliban regime, the film featured a certain Hassan Tantai, in the role of a bush doctor of African American origin lost in the Afghan countryside, searching for God.

In Washington, U.S. president George W. Bush asked for a private screening. The media reflected American sensitivities after the collapse of the World Trade Center: "The White House last night would not be drawn on whether Mr. Bush, not known up until now for his love of Iranian cinema, was aware of the actor's alleged terrorist links."[43]

When the controversy broke, Makhmalbaf stated curtly, "I don't ask the people who agree to play in my films what they were doing before." The U.S. district attorney in charge of the case declared, "We are certain that the man appearing in the film is, without a shadow of a doubt, David Belfield."

The district attorney was right. Hassan Tantai is the pseudonym that Hassan Abdulrahman—alias Davud Salahuddin, born David Belfield— selected for the film credits: his stage name, if you will. It is also a wink— and certainly a tribute as well—to his spiritual forebears: Tanta is the city in Egypt where Hassan al-Banna, founder of the Muslim Brotherhood, was born.

Hassan's dialogue puts him—in spite of himself—at the point where Iran and the United States collide, between the Islamic world and the West, between "good" and "evil," in the bombsights of the "war against terror." It's a dangerous position to be in for someone who insists on speaking the truth about Iran, who calls for a cross-section of high-ranking United States officials to be called to account for their acts at his trial. As threats and perhaps even secret negotiations have replaced the transparency of the stillborn dialogue of civilizations, Hassan's presence may well prove a major irritant, both to Iran and to his native land.

43. *USA Today*, January 3, 2002.

Reform, You Say?

WHEN, IN 1997, a small group of friends called on Seyyed Mohammad Khatami in his office at Iran's National Library, his response to their request was anything but enthusiastic: "You'd like me to run for president?" he asked. "I know better than you do what to expect!" Still, pressure from those closest to him, promises of support, and political argument finally convinced the man who had been Islamic Iran's minister of culture for seven years before resigning in protest, to enter the race.

As the campaign got underway, the outcome seemed a foregone conclusion. Ali Akbar Nateq Nouri, the regime's hand-picked candidate and docile sidekick of the flamboyant Hashemi Rafsanjani—Iran's "prince of builders," the Potemkin-like figure whose specialty was inaugurating non-functioning projects—had even made a quick trip to England to provide political guarantees and drum up investments. The trade-off was that Iran would stick to its neo-liberal economic policies.

It would be difficult to imagine the surprise, and outside of Iran, the incredulity, when Mr. Khatami swept the polls with more than 65 percent of votes cast. In the event, his true majority was higher still. But to avoid excessive embarrassment for its official candidate, the regime lopped a few percentage points off the actual total.

The election confirmed what most Iranians already knew: the population no longer supported the status quo. The democratic verdict had merely expressed the strength of latent discontent and frustration. It came, too, as a warning: Mr. Khatami's election might well act as a safety valve, venting some of the steam built up after years of intense social ferment. The reformist brain trust, led by Said Hajjarian, had made civil and social rights the key element of the Khatami campaign. The reform program rejected both the Chilean and the Chinese approach, and called for a specifically Iranian model that would meld democracy and Islam into a new system that would broaden freedoms while respecting the country's ancient traditions. To observers, the stakes appeared as high as they were dangerous. Events were to bear out this assessment, in spades.

The results of an election are never as clear-cut as the numbers might indicate. Many analysts hastened to conclude that Mr. Khatami owed his victory to the support of women and young people, who saw in him a modernizer. But their conclusions may have been premature, and probably understated the depth and breadth of his movement. Analysis of voting patterns showed that similar percentages voted for candidate Khatami in all demographic and income categories, even among the Revolutionary Guards and the Basijis, the military and paramilitary militias close to the regime and often suspected of being its unconditional supporters.

Not since the revolutionary days of 1979–1980 had Iran witnessed such an outpouring of enthusiasm. Was it a warning that the end of the religious regime was at hand, the symptom of serious internal dysfunction in the conservative political apparatus; or a thinly disguised call for improvements in living standards? Probably a bit of both. But the 1997 election was, above all, a stinging rebuke to the outgoing government of President Rafsanjani, whose policies had led to the collapse of Iranian purchasing power, while scandalously enriching the country's powerful and wealthy, including the Rafsanjani family itself.

Such was the genesis of the reform movement. Like Mohammad Khatami, it had stepped onto the Iranian political scene by stealth, almost like a thief in the night, with uncontestable democratic credentials, but without a party structure. Three years later, candidates claiming to be reformists won an overwhelming majority of seats in parliament, the Majlis. President Khatami's supporters now controlled both the executive and legislative branches of government: they could enact laws and expect to have them applied. Or so it seemed. For the nominally independent judiciary branch, and the shadowy but very real power of the regime were far from their grasp. These key powers remained in the hands of the Supreme Guide, and of the conservative religious establishment. Still, the second victory touched off an upsurge of hope throughout the country, and instilled the reformists with a sense of mission: they would guide the Iranian nation through the breaking wave of modernity, ensure freedom of the press and of expression, and revitalize the limping economy.

Mohammad Khatami summed up his credo, and his political program, in a book entitled *Fear of the Wave*. There must be social and civilizational dialogue, he argued, if Iran was to avoid regression into tradition and move forward to join the modern world. He had issued a challenge to Iranian society—and to the reformists—to face the terrifying wave, as

Abdolkarim Soroush describes it. It was a daring initiative; the reform movement's hopes may have been unrealistic; it may have underrated the obstacles. In 2004, it was to implode in an atmosphere of cynicism and disillusionment.

The collapse of the movement was not entirely of its own making. The regime's counter-offensive, which was launched in July 1999 when *Salam* newspaper was shut down, gained strength with every passing month. Shortly after the parliamentary elections, Said Hajjarian was shot down in broad daylight on the street. Then came the mass closings of newspapers and magazines, the arrest and imprisonment of journalists, and the bloody repression of the student movement. It would not be long before the reform MPs began to realize how narrow their scope of action was, as the real nature of power hit home. As a matter of course, the Council of Guardians, mandated to scrutinize laws proposed by parliament, and to reject those it considers as contravening "Islamic principles," rejected any proposed legislation that might trouble the regime. Its veto is final; only the Supreme Guide, acting as an arbiter, can overturn its decisions. But in reality, the arbiter is a partisan figure, whose decision can only reinforce the Council's.

In total disregard for elementary democratic principles—with a handful of exceptions—the parliamentary initiatives undertaken by the reformists remained unrealized. They had begun with a strong hand, and above all, with broad popular support; but they proved incapable of mobilizing that support and, by their own clumsiness, were ultimately to undermine it.

In 2001, for the first time in Iran's history, citizens were called upon to elect their own municipal councils. Without obstruction, without restriction from the religious authorities, thousands of candidates of both sexes boasting of their connections to the reform movement were elected to municipal councils in cities, towns, and villages throughout the country, including the greatest prize: Tehran City Hall. There they would enjoy greater freedom of action than at the national level; it would be a simple matter to demonstrate to the population what they were capable of. Managing a city of twelve million would be an undreamed-of opportunity to demonstrate their competence, to learn lessons that could be applied at the national political level. But all the fine campaign slogans rapidly degenerated into an orgy of backbiting. Members of the Tehran City Council, one of whom was the politically challenged Ebrahim Asqarzadeh—one of the student leaders of the U.S. Embassy takeover—seemed to spend all their time fighting off influence-peddling scandals and accusations of corruption. Meanwhile, the citizens watched a sorry spectacle from which they would quickly draw their own conclusions. The sitting mayor, Morteza Alviri, a close Khatami ally and follower of Ayatollah Montazeri, was dismissed for having attempted to put the municipal house in order. His replacement was a straw man who was to open the door to back-room deals, payoffs by the construction industry mafia, and the godfathers who exercised street-level control in the capital's posh northern districts where land speculation was rampant.

All the while, the population of Greater Tehran was grappling with soaring inflation, critical air-pollution levels, and growing insecurity. It was soon to lose its last, stubborn illusions. During the 2002 municipal elections, Tehran's voters stayed home. Only 12 percent of those eligible to vote took the trouble to cast their ballots. The conservative faction swept the reformists aside, and marched into city hall. It was a shot fired across the reformists' bow, a warning that could not have been more clear. It also had a name: Mahmoud Ahmadinejad, a modest, bearded school-teacher who had fought in the Iraq war and was now promising to clean up the mess. The reform movement had lost much of its credibility. It could not afford, in the hard-fought battle being waged against the conservatives at the national level, to put itself so clumsily in jeopardy.

Who was to blame for their failure, the reformists themselves, or the campaign of repression organized by the conservative regime? That was the question we asked Ali Arabmazar.

A graduate of an American university before returning to Iran during the revolution, Mr. Arabmazar's career profile matches that of many of his compatriots in the forty-to-fifty age bracket. Since his return, he has held a succession of key government positions, before returning to Shahid Beheshti University to teach economics. In his three-year tenure as deputy minister of economics, he almost single-handedly devised a national income tax system. It was an ambitious program; Iran had never before taxed income. Oil revenues had not only been used to fill state coffers, but to line the pockets of oil industry executives, most of whom enjoyed excellent mullah connections. There had been little to choose between monarchical and "revolutionary" economic policy.

Appointed by the reform government, Ali Arabmazar soon found himself unable to apply the program he had drawn up. In frustration, he tendered his resignation.

We had hoped for a detailed response to our question. We were not to be disappointed.

"Iranian society has set up its own rules for differentiating itself from other Muslim communities. Behind these rules are two primary concepts: the nation, which selects the president, and the *umma*—the community of believers—that chooses the Supreme Guide.

"When the president and the Guide are on the same side, there's no problem. Everything goes well. But when they disagree, as they do today, things start to break down. If you want to set up a religious society, an Islamic republic, you've got to follow the rules, and these rules cannot go against religious regulations. The revolution laid down what those rules should be.

"Iranians followed the rules, just like they've followed their leaders over the centuries. Just like they've followed their religion. It wasn't so long ago that the leaders of the Communist Party would spend the entire night discussing the existence or non-existence of God. The meeting would end, and they would turn off the lights, wishing one another: 'May God protect us.'

"Religion is deeply rooted in our society. Outside Iran, people say that the people are fed up, that the revolution is over, but come the anniversary of the revolution, you'll find ten million Iranians in the street.

"In 1997, to everyone's surprise, Mohammad Khatami was elected. The reformist strategists hoped they would get two million votes. They were more astonished than anyone else.

"There was such a dearth of political personalities that people voted for them. But they weren't ready to govern. The whole thing was a terrible misunderstanding. Not voting for the established politicians did not mean that a majority of electors had turned their backs on the revolution, or on revolutionary ideas."

But they had clearly voted for reform, we interjected.

"They voted for change. But they had no idea what kind of change it would be. Most of all, they were voting against Rafsanjani. He'd made a grave error. Here's a man who was a prominent political personality, but who committed a serious political fault. He behaved like Mossadeq in the 1950s, when the CIA staged its *coup d'état*. Instead of turning to the people, he sought help from the American ambassador. That was the end of him.

"Imam Khomeini had an enormous advantage. He knew the people. For example: when the U.S.S.R. left Afghanistan, they asked Khamene'i, who was president of the Islamic Republic at the time, 'Let us get out, don't interfere, and in return we'll give you long-range missiles.' Khamene'i went to the Guide, insisted that we needed the missiles. Khomeini told him, 'We cannot cooperate with a non-Muslim nation against the Muslims.' What he did was to correct the nation in the name of the *umma*. Conclusion: don't make decisions you can't explain and share the responsibility for in front of the people. No one from the reformists today has come forward to take responsibility before the people. No one.

"Khatami wasn't ready to become president. First, he didn't have a party to speak of; second, what kind of 'Islamic republic' were they talking about? The reformists who joined forces with him didn't have a political program. So when he suddenly became president, he couldn't even form a government. He just wasted his time, without any clear idea of what he was doing. People finally understood the situation, and decided they didn't want any more.

"True, for his first government, he had plenty of excuses. It was the first time, he wasn't ready; the opposition was strong, and he was facing a hostile parliament. But for his second term, he had a parliamentary majority on his side, and the support of twenty-eight million voters. And still, he did nothing, because he couldn't do anything. His government was deeply divided; it was dominated by cultural personalities more than by the statesmen he needed so badly. Mr. Khatami wanted everything; he had the parliament, the executive. He wanted the judiciary too! Why did he need to have it all? Because he had no clear vision of what he should do!

"During his first term, since he himself was a cultural figure, he chose people like himself. He knew nothing about the economy, yet it was the main issue. For any government, there are two determinant requirements: political line and economic action. People want to eat, to have a roof over their heads, to have a job. They want their demands to be fulfilled, and they are waiting to see what you will do for them.

"The problem with the reformists is that the reforms they wanted to bring in were primarily political. People won't accept that unless you've satisfied their basic needs beforehand. If I can feed my family, if it's easy to see a doctor, if I have enough money to get by, then I can understand why I should vote for the mayor, or for freedom of speech. But if I've got to rush from one end of town to the other day in, day out, in order to earn enough to survive, I'm not really interested in hearing about politics;

what people need to know is where they are going to get their daily bread. Inflation right now is running at 20 percent, and it will be worse next year. But wages have only gone up 6 percent.

"The masses couldn't care less what the reformists have to say. They're debating among themselves, people like Hajjarian and his group, or Kadivar and others like him. They've managed to create a kind of puzzle, but they haven't been able to build up a solid image. Khatami allowed all kinds of people into his government; he even kept the Rafsanjani team. The very same people kept on working for Rafsanjani, and not for the sitting president! They couldn't give a damn about what Khatami said. Let me give you an example: the oil minister is a Rafsanjani man. And in the same ministry, Rafsanjani's son holds down a key position. That's why the people who voted for Khatami couldn't understand what he was trying to do.

"What's more, no one ever gave us a clear definition of reform. Frankly speaking, people wanted a change; they needed a change, wherever it came from. They were sure it would be better than what they had. It was a choice between the best and the worst. Outside of Iran too, people were expecting a reform that never materialized, because Khatami never had his own political agenda. He launched the dialogue of civilizations and made some speeches about it. Then he introduced press freedom because a lot of his supporters came from the journalistic field, and were demanding freedom of the press. He responded to their demands, and many things happened, some quite successful. But he couldn't capitalize on it. When you win points, you have to be able to capitalize on it politically. But Khatami's Achilles' heel is the economy. That was his greatest obstacle, and he wasn't able to overcome it. He didn't have a plan; he just let things drift. When people saw this happening, this lack of concern, this lack of direction, they began to ask themselves, Who's running the country?

"The first consequence was the municipal elections in Tehran, and across the country. They showed his party the door; the 'new right' conservatives were the winners. And ever since, they've been scoring points by repairing the damage done by the former municipal administration, and by getting a handle on issues like the fight against poverty and drug addiction, and assistance for street children. This is how the new conservative right will bring about reforms, moving slowly and steadily; in the same way, they'll be attempting to enter into people's hearts and minds.

"So, you ask, why didn't reform catch on? Because there was no leadership, and to make reforms work, to move from ideas to words and from words to deeds, you've got to have leadership."

What are we to make of the conservatives? Why did they react so violently? Why did the Supreme Guide support them? Why is he more of a partisan than an arbiter? They paralyzed the reform movement, they stifled freedom of expression, and they used violence against the students, against any form of dissidence.

"People voted for the reformists. They knew all that. One of the main political figures of the Khatami government was Mohajerani.[44] As it happens, this guy was one of Rafsanjani's strongest allies even before he became president of Iran. But during the last two years of his presidency, the people rejected Rafsanjani. He had been a key figure during and after the revolution. But during the last two years of his term, he'd begun to believe that he was carrying history on his shoulders. That he himself had become 'History.' That brought back bad memories of the shah, who wanted to create that kind of image. Rafsanjani became Pharaoh, the only man who could rule the world. It went to his head: he began to inaugurate industrial complexes that hadn't even been built yet. He wanted to transform himself into the 'prince of construction.' But he'd lost the confidence of the population; he was finished.

"In Iran, to stay in power, you need sincerity. People said, 'He's beginning to look like the shah all over again.' He was walking on clouds, and his pal Mohajerani wanted to change the constitution to give him even more power. That's the kind of person Khatami chose as minister. Abdi and Ganji protested, and look what happened to them."

Today, is there a "third way" between the reformists and the conservatives?

"There is a kind of popular force that hasn't made it into parliament. Society is waiting, watching, with its eyes wide open. Anything can happen. If Iranians can find someone to represent them, they will vote for him. If not, they'll go to the polls but cast blank ballots. Religious law obliges everyone to vote; but this religious obligation does not mean you must vote for someone in particular. Several smaller groups in society are attempting to come together, but they don't represent a concrete political

---

44. Ataollah Mohajerani served as minister of culture in the first Khatami government. A member of the Kargozaran, "The Builders," affiliated with former president Rafsanjani, he was forced to resign after accusations of being "too liberal" by the regime.

force. The right and the left both did their best to win the municipal elections; they'll be facing off in the parliamentary elections. If one or the other wins enough seats, and if they know how to go about it, this parliament is likely to function more smoothly than the last one. One thing is certain though: the people need new personalities, new faces. As for the students, they don't constitute a truly representative political force. They're young, without experience; they're attempting to put some distance between themselves and Khatami."

What about foreign pressure, from the United States, for example? What is the impact of internal factors, such as the underground economy, on the immediate future of Iranian society?

"No one can put pressure on Iran from outside, whether positive or negative. Alexander the Great described Iranian soldiers as dogs: always fighting among themselves, until you attacked them, and they united against the outside enemy. Then they go back to fighting again.

"At home, the clandestine economy is a reality, and a powerful one. And it's intimately connected with the rise of corruption. People, usually very rich people close to the power centers, make money here and invest it abroad. The black economy employs 30 percent of all workers. You'll find mafias in the steel industry, the food industry, and elsewhere.

"There are plenty of ways to increase your wealth. For example, I can go to Dubai, borrow money at 2 percent, bring it here, and invest it at 18 percent, guaranteed by the state. The Iranian economy is unbalanced, and the national debt is huge. It's a terrible situation for a country that has made a revolution that promised justice and social ethics. Unfortunately, high-ranking political figures are deeply involved in the corruption.

"What kind of services can you expect to get from ministries, municipalities, police forces, from the courts, when corruption is rife in all of them? Khatami never said a word about it, and yet he could have exposed the whole thing.

"It's easy to see that the people who are holding jobs in these government services are living far beyond their means, and above all, beyond their wages: they're the living proof of corruption, and everybody knows it! Public funds are not being put to good use in our country today. It's clear that the next big political issue will be the economy."

God or the Republic

MORE CONTROVERSIAL THAN THE PHILOSOPHER Abdolkarim Soroush, more trenchant in his criticism of the regime, more radical in his positions, Seyyed Javad Tabatabaï rejects outright the religious system established in Iran in 1980. By refuting the legitimacy of the Supreme Guide and the arbitrary quality of his rulings, he has drawn dead aim on its heart. Dismissed from his position at Tehran University, he is forbidden to teach in his own country. Today, while a caste of regime insiders enjoys the finer things in life as it squabbles over the remains of the revolution, he resides in exile, in France. There was an ironic twist to our encounter: we met Mr. Tabatabaï in the research center where he is a short-term visiting scholar—a center that occupies what was formerly the luxury villa of a drug lord close to the former regime, whose garden wall overlooks one of the shah's palaces, today a cultural center.

Javad Tabatabaï is a graduate of Tehran University's faculty of religious sciences; he went on to study at the Sorbonne, where he wrote his doctoral thesis on Hegel. In several works dealing with political philosophy and Iranian history, he has crafted an original perspective on relations between Iran and the West. During the pre-revolutionary years, as a young conservative intellectual, he became a member of the circle of Professor Ahmad Fardid, who was to introduce him to philosophical inquiry into the relation between politics and religion—the subject that was to become the starting point of his research, and the driving force behind the philosophical stance he has come to espouse today.

In the Islamic regime, the subject is as sensitive as it is subversive. Tabatabaï had begun to swim in treacherous waters, where he was to encounter philosophical figures like Daryush Shayegan, who called directly into question the legitimacy and the functionality of the linkage between politics and religion, between God and the republic. Rigor, lucidity, and frankness may be the most excellent of intellectual qualities, but they were to provide scant protection from the intolerance of Iran's Islamic regime, where there is precious little room for criticism, and none at all for controversy when they impinge on the power—and the very nature—of the regime. The alternatives are few, and simple: exile, silence, and ultimately, death. Forbidden from returning under the presidency of Hashemi Rafsanjani, Javad Tabatabaï has returned to Tehran several times after the election of Mohammad Khatami for short stays as the guest of pro-reform intellectuals.

Tall, slender, eyes flashing, gesticulating enthusiastically, he brings a breath of fresh air to a culture where thinking aloud is far from a foregone conclusion. With assurance, he has applied the conceptual tools of the West to a thorough grasp of Islamic culture to throw the political and social aberrations of Islamic fundamentalism into sharp relief. As a committed intellectual, he calls for a mobilization of the human conscience, for a sharing of knowledge between East and West, the better to reject confrontation and to exorcise fear and intolerance.

"It's not because Islam is not perfect and complete as a religion that it cannot be reformed," he says, to open the discussion.

"On the one hand, you have Islamic tradition; on the other, the tradition of Islamic thought. The two are quite distinct. In the Arab countries, there is a living tradition of thought devoted to religion, to Islam. But it doesn't have the same density as the tradition you find in this country.

"On this particular point, a substantial effort is needed to deconstruct the tradition, and eventually to derive some basic principles for reform, that is to say, to bring Islam, as Kant said, within the limits of Reason. It's not an easy job, especially in Iran."

Is that because of the Islamic tradition itself?

"We must be clear about what we mean by tradition. Here, in Iran, it's not understood. We have the Sunnite tradition in its limited definition, i.e., the words and deeds of the Prophet. But the term 'tradition' has another, broader meaning, the Persian equivalent of the sociological tradition: how people act, the study of human behavior. In Christianity, tradition is the Church itself, the living magisterium of the Church. In this sense, there is also a kind of tradition in Iran, which no one has truly succeeded in analyzing up until now. In my opinion, this is the heart of the problem. In reality, what we have is twelve hundred years of a tradition of thought on the revealed text, and on tradition in its limited definition."

But what does this tradition mean; how are we to understand it from within?

"Within three centuries, it had become hardened, ossified. It exists, but it is not a living body of thought, and for this reason it acts as an obstacle to thought, it prevents us from escaping from its inherent limits. On this level, we have problems; serious theological problems in particular."

You say that tradition is not alive, but if we compare Iran with Saudi Arabia, Syria, or other Arab countries, we would surely find that interpretation of tradition is alive and well in Iran.

"Just before the Constitutional Movement, there were attempts to do something, and, from outside that tradition, there were efforts to reform society; there was a will to change the way things were done. Western ideas had begun to circulate among Westernized intellectuals. At that moment, and even up to the present day, there has been a kind of transmission of Western knowledge. That is what shook tradition out of its rigidity.

"Of course there is a movement of ideas in this country, but tradition remains deeply imbedded in people's minds. Today, this tradition has the power to prevent an unblocking of critical thought. This has led to a tug-of-war between modernity and tradition. If Iran has remained the most advanced, in comparison with most Muslim countries, it is thanks to this critical movement. The road forward has been blocked, but there has also been movement. In Saudi Arabia, the roadblocks are still in place; in the other Muslim countries, social demands have come to the fore. Here, both are happening at once.

"Even in Qom, when you talk to young mullahs, you get the impression that things are happening. It's very difficult, but at the same time, as Galileo said, 'It moves.'"

But don't the two threaten to cancel each other out?

"Yes, and it's been going on for ten or fifteen years now.

"Seven years ago, I was in Tehran, for the annual book fair. In chatting with students, I had a strong impression that something was afoot. There was a movement underway, and today it's gaining momentum, especially among young people. It is still in the minority, but for all its difficulties, and in spite of everyday emergencies, it's a vital minority, trying its best.

"So, I said to myself, almost as a joke, Perhaps Iran will be the first Muslim country to become a true country. A country, as we say 'France'—we don't say the Christian world. Which is not yet the case in the Islamic world: you're a Muslim before you are a Moroccan or an Algerian, before you are a citizen.

"It was the first time I felt so strongly that the main demand, particularly among young people, was to be a man or a woman first, an Iranian citizen. Period. I have the impression that we've reached this point, that Iran will be the first country to emerge from the Islamic world."

Isn't that a paradox? Couldn't we argue that its emergence will have been the work of official Islam?

"That's the ruse of reason! The ruling elite, the clergy, cannot have understood, but we have a presentiment."

They've refused to use the tools that would allow them to understand?

"Exactly! They should study their history; they should get some grasp of the history of ideas, about what's going on in the world. In that light, it's easy to understand that the Islamic Republic has actually worked against Islam. While practicing Islam, it will have turned against Islam! I think this is what's happened today. Many people understand it, even in the clergy. Something must be done. Islam has been destroyed; yes, it's already happened. These matters are always unconscious; it's impossible to determine consciously the movement of history. It's impossible to say, As of tomorrow, you will all become practicing Muslims. Sure, you can say it, but that's not how it's done!"

The clergy has the power to wield dogma, but it has no critical evaluation of history. Couldn't we term that a "sin against reason"? And wouldn't that explain, at least partly, young people's aspirations for a democratic state?

"Most people in Iran want democracy, even if they don't really know what democracy is, and what its consequences can be. It's clear that there is no 'third way.' Before, there was the illusion of socialism. No longer. Either we're a liberal democracy, or a dictatorship, an Islamic one, like we are today."

So, reform has failed?

"Yes. When a crisis arises, you can attempt to use your wits, to understand why. Then you can attempt to solve the problem. But you can also turn your back on the crisis and say, 'There's nothing to it, we'll fix everything, stage some kind of *coup d'état*, some kind of violent action, to cover up the crisis.' That's what they're doing now, and that's what they've been doing all along.

"I was expelled from the university because of my long-time efforts to explain that we were overlooking certain concepts. You can't live and manage yourself in the modern world without understanding what is going on around you. And to understand, you've got to accept that there are certain key concepts.

"One of them is the concept of the general interest. It's a subject I've written a lot about. I've demonstrated that the concept of the general interest does not exist in Shi'ism. I've even written a book on the transmission of Greek political philosophy in Islam. In it, I examined, step by step, how these concepts evolved. The general interest is the criterion for distinguishing between good regimes and bad. I tried to show that the Greek philosophical texts were translated and reworked by the philosophers of Islam, and that the concept of the general interest did not survive the transition; it has been eliminated. They re-read and revised the *Nicomedian Ethics*[45] in exactly that way."

But don't we find the concept, concealed and reworked, in the principle that is central to the power structure of the Islamic Republic, the *Velayat-e faqih*?

"We do indeed. In fact, it's become the foundation of state power. When we translate *Velayat-e faqih* into real terms, it reads exactly like a theory of state organization. In the same way, people here have not been able to 'digest' the concept of crisis, to follow it from its medical definition to its acceptance as a political term. Today, 'crisis' has become a political concept that can be applied to the social and economic fields. But in Iran, the concept is unknown; here, we have an equivalent in Farsi for the word 'crisis' translated from French and English—but it's only an equivalent, and not an evolution of meaning within the concept itself.

"Which explains why, in the eyes of the Iranian regime, a 'crisis' is a kind of illness, a sickness that dare not speak its name, that must be hushed up. Let us talk about other things … until death do us part! Now, that's brilliant, isn't it!

"Not long ago I participated in the writing of a book called *A Soul for Europe*. I was asked to answer the question: 'What is your vision of European identity, seen from the outside?' The subject was the inability of civilizations to understand one another. What are the obstacles to understanding? My first response was: 'You speak of crises. We never do. So, how can we speak of reform? That would amount to admitting that something is not working; that it should be changed.'

"Here, we cannot say that something is not working, that Islam is not advancing, that it does not have an answer to the crisis. We cannot say such a thing. So what does that make reform? Empty words! We say, 'We must reform! Islam is advancing!' Well, it's a lot of hot air, talk, and no action. Take the case of President Khatami. I've coined a phrase to describe what we're seeing, what I call 'the slither.'

---

45. One of Aristotle's major philosophical works.

"Why 'the slither'? Because we've adopted concepts imported from the West: crisis, reform, democracy, and so on. But since we don't know what we're talking about, what do we end up doing? When we cannot grasp the Western concept, we invent equivalents. This is how an expression like 'human rights' becomes 'Islamic human rights,' 'democracy' becomes 'Islamic democracy,' and so on. At every turn, we slither and slide. Democracy is my destination, but since I don't know how to drive, I slither to the other side of the road and end up heading in the wrong direction."

In Tehran, and in most places in Iran, the reality of driving an automobile appears to be based on Mr. Tabatabaï's model. Slithering is one of the rules of the road, as accepted as it is widespread. For the foreign visitor such widely accepted indicators as street signs, red lights, stop signs, and one-way streets are meant to be respected; for the locals they are open invitations to slithering, sliding, and avoiding. The idea expresses, with sharp irony, the conceptual and practical difficulties of the reform movement, and the underlying reasons for President Khatami's hesitation waltz with democracy.

"What did the president do? When he took office, in 1997, he used the words 'civil society.' Well and good. But at the Conference of Islamic States in January 2000, he said, 'You will understand, you who are the heads of state of the Muslim countries, that civil society is simply that of Medina.'

"Why did he say such a thing? The word *civil* can be translated into Farsi as *madani*—which means "pertaining to the city," "relative to the city"—but here, the reference is to the city of Medina, as founded by the Prophet. Medina was not really a city, but an extended mosque built up around the Prophet.

"What the president really meant was: 'Civil society is the Medina of the Prophet.' Suddenly, we'd leaped several centuries back in time. That's what I mean by slithering: a conscious, willed act. If you wish to understand this country as it is today, to pin down the chatter and the hot air of Muslims in the West, in Canada, the U.S., and Europe, you must analyze this counterfeiting of concepts, and analyze the slithering. They're disconnected from reality; they do not understand. Slithering and sliding makes it possible for them to live, and Westerners fall into the trap. Just listen to what's being said about the veil, the oval of the woman's face, the refusal of objectification. Look, do you think it's really necessary to go to all that trouble just to go to the mosque, without being objectified?"

Is it possible to say that religion has been taken over by politics, that politics has transformed religion into its instrument?

"That is certainly what has happened today. Politics has made religion its instrument. That wasn't the original intention. In Iran, over the last few decades, people have had the illusion that Islam could be reactivated as an integral religion, as a vehicle for reforming society, for changing the way things are done. In order to get rid of a corrupt monarchy, they 'ideologized' religion. The idea was invented three or four decades before the revolution. It was our own slithering and sliding that created the illusion. At the time, Marxism was all the rage. No one dared question the concept of class struggle. Shariati, who was one of the theoretical philosophers of the revolution, had been a Marxist before becoming an Islamist. Marxism is struggle, he said, and in the Qur'an it's the same— everything begins with the two sons of Adam, Abel and Cain, and continues right up to the Prophet. Shariati invented an extraordinary Islamic existentialism, because everybody in the Latin Quarter in Paris was an existentialist."

Weren't Shariati's ideas widely accepted? Didn't they fuel a political trend during the revolution?

"Yes, there was a cumulative effect, dating from his public lectures in Tehran. When the revolution broke out, Marxists and Islamists agreed that the existing structure had to be destroyed.

"Writing about the French men of letters just prior to the French Revolution, Tocqueville wrote, 'They invented in literature an imaginary society in which everything went marvelously.' In books, there are never any problems; in Iran, prior to the revolution, the intellectuals, and primarily the French-speaking intellectuals, did the same thing. But in real societies there are always problems. For Tocqueville, 'imaginary society has taken power over real society.' We can apply the formula to the Islamic Revolution."

Do you mean that it took place outside of real society?

"Yes. It worked badly, but it worked. Our intellectuals were victims of their own inventions. We had fundamentalists against Marxists, people who tried to make a synthesis of Marxism and Islam, and so on."

Where do Khomeini's followers fit into your schema?

"I believe they were a part of that movement. They had the same illusions, but they knew the clergy, and they were more conservative than the more recent movements, more dynamic too. Most of them were also latecomers."

And now, what do you foresee?

"I believe I'm a bit pessimistic. They are going to continue to hold society back until the young people revolt. People are not going to vote. If they do go, it will be because every effort has been made to get them out; in such an event, they will spoil their ballots. The result will be a conservative parliament without real legitimacy, with about 15 percent of eligible voters. They will be able to make a few reforms: some of them are more clever than the reformists."

Appearances Can Be Deceiving

TWENTY-FIVE YEARS AFTER THE REVOLUTION, the political and religious principles that guided it to power have been turned upside down.

Homeless children wandering the streets, widespread drug addiction, flagrant and flourishing prostitution are only a few of the most visible symptoms of the bankruptcy of what claims to be a religious state. Everything that the regime forbids is available providing one is prepared to pay the price ... or has the right connections. Prohibition has generated a lucrative parallel market; corruption thrives at all levels of society: what the Iranians call "mullah connections" are enough to sidestep laws and regulations. The regime's great families have developed their own networks of favoritism; the *aqazadeh*—the daddy's boys of the establishment—move effortlessly into key positions in the business world.

Iran's constitution defines the country as a state of law, possessing a parliamentary system. It also has one outstanding particularity: above the state structure stands a second level of power, based on divine inspiration. Real power lies at this second level; from it emanates control of the forces of repression, the Friday prayer preachers' network, and the state electronic media. It draws its legitimacy from the institution of the *Velayat-e faqih*, which attributes to the Supreme Guide full responsibility for managing the affairs of the believers in expectation of the reappearance of the Imam of the Age, the Twelfth Imam of Shi'ite tradition. The office of the *Velayat-e faqih*, in turn, can only be held by a "just, virtuous doctor of dogma, well informed of the evolution of the day, courageous, efficient and capable, and who must be accepted as Guide by the majority of the people."[46] The position itself was made to measure by and for Imam Khomeini, who discharged his duties with his legendary determination and charisma from 1979 until his death ten years later.

---

46. Constitution of the Islamic Republic of Iran, 15.

Ten years after being approved by 98.2 percent of eligible voters, the constitution was amended during the presidency of Hashemi Rafsanjani. The Iranian parliament, with a strong conservative majority, modified Article 5 to give the Supreme Guide absolute power. This legislative sleight-of-hand had become a necessity. No one, especially Mr. Khamene'i, possessed Imam Khomeini's standing among ordinary Iranians.

The shift in status was anything but a divine decision; it was brought about by an all-too-human, political intervention by the parliament. Some forward-looking commentators cautioned that if the voice of the people were conflated with the voice of God, the people might well assume God-like prerogatives one day, and vote to abolish the religious state altogether.

Without admitting it openly, this was the ultimate aim of the reform process set in motion by Said Hajjarian, and endorsed by Mohammad Khatami. In their eyes, the only reform possible would necessitate a modification of the constitution to limit or nullify outright the absolute power of the Guide, which would have meant a challenge to the basic tenets of the principle of *Velayat-e faqih* itself.

The death of Imam Khomeini in the bitter aftermath of the Iran-Iraq war and the Iran-Contra scandal had cast a pall over the religious-political alliance. Two months after the Imam's funeral the Council of Guardians appointed Ali Khamene'i, a former president of the Islamic Republic, as Supreme Guide. Curiously, Mr. Khamene'i did not even have ayatollah status, and unlike his predecessor, he was not a *marja*, i.e., "a source of emulation" for his followers. More surprising still, he had neither compiled nor published a book of religious edicts, the normal procedure by which Shi'a jurists make known their judgments and religious views in order to expand their circle of disciples.

Mr. Khamene'i's appointment created a certain malaise. Some clerics, religious intellectuals, and traditionalists who had accepted Khomeini's preeminence questioned his successor's competence. In fact, Shi'ite religious scholars had never unanimously accepted the doctrine of *Velayat-e faqih* in the first place. It owed much if not most of its force and prestige to the extraordinary personality of Ruhollah Khomeini, who had become the theory of the revolution, and the incarnation of the doctrine he had created.

Shortly after his death, dissident voices raised sharp questions about the arbitrary origins of the Guide's absolute power. Among them was a young cleric, Hojjatoleslam Mohsen Kadivar, who would soon emerge as

A billboard in downtown Tehran, showing Supreme Guide Ali Khamene'i (left) and Ayatollah Khomeini (right) flanking a young militiaman. (*Salam Iran*, courtesy of InformAction Films)

Iran's most radical and incisive critic of the institution of the rule of the jurist-consult.

For the hard-core of conservative clergymen who wield political power in Iran, the threat was serious and was taken as such. One does not idly call into question the *Velayat-e faqih*. Meddling with the image of the Guide can be dangerous. Anyone who dares to express doubts about the ideological underpinnings of the regime puts not only his freedom in danger, but also his head.

In 1999, Mohsen Kadivar was arrested and accused of plotting against state security. He was brought before the Special Clerical Tribunal—a court whose existence has no constitutional legitimacy—tried, and condemned to eighteen months in prison.[47]

Our first meeting had taken place in New York, in the corridors of Columbia University, where he had been invited as a guest lecturer. Our initial contact had been warm, and our exchange a stimulating one. A man with an easy laugh, Mohsen Kadivar expertly melds a sophisticated intellect with a keen sense of humor; his hearty laughter was invitation

47. Farhad Khosrokhavar, *Postrevolutionary Iran and the New Social Movements, in Twenty Years of Islamic Revolution* (Syracuse: Syracuse University Press, 2002), 12.

enough to meet again. A few months later, in Tehran, he opened wide the door of his office to us with that same laugh.

In New York, he was dressed in a well-cut jacket over a white turtleneck. In Tehran, he greeted us in the brown robe of a hojjatoleslam, the white turban atop his head accentuating his salt-and-pepper beard.

But whatever the dress, and whatever the place, we were talking to the same person: a man of religion caught up in action, a militant intellectual, a man who had received fresh death threats the previous day. But the threats in no way diminished the mutual pleasure of our meeting.

Mohsen Kadivar's presence—bantering, now serious, now joking— brought life and light to the dreary walls of his office on the sixth floor of a run-down building overlooking the north-south freeway not far from Vanak Square. The decor could best be described as Spartan: a packed bookcase, a meeting table illuminated by the afternoon sun, a steaming teapot. He seemed to radiate the urge to speak, the desire to break through the clouds of defeatism and indifference that shrouded his country. And the need to exorcise the genuine threats that hung over his head.

"You know, the situation in my country is sensitive; I must be cautious. A month ago, after I gave a speech at the Hosseiniyeh-e Ershad where I discussed the serial murders of intellectuals committed by secret police agents a few years ago, I received death threats. If this keeps up, I'll soon be on the death list. Besides, the Islamic Court has already warned me, 'If you keep it up, you'll find yourself in prison again.'"

We knew it all too well. Akbar Ganji, whom we'd met four years before, was still being held in Evin Prison.

"I've already demonstrated to my satisfaction that the real rules of the political game in Iran belong to the Supreme Guide. He is the author and the lead actor in the tragedy that's being played out here. What you see is not society expressing itself; the power structure does not derive its legitimacy from society. At most, 10 to 15 percent of the population supports the conservative regime.

"When I state these facts in public, I get more threats. Last week, they called my home three times and spoke with my son, to threaten me. We recorded the voice. I called the intelligence services and told them, 'Listen to this voice; it belongs to one of your people. If anything happens to me, you'll be responsible.'

"The same thing happened to Hajjarian. There was nothing he could do to head off the attempt on his life, but he knew it was coming.

"When I heard he'd been targeted by an assassin, I was in prison. I think it was the worst day of my life. I cried and cried, because where I was, there was nothing I could do. He was my best friend, and I didn't even know whether he was alive or dead. I sat there, holding the Qur'an, and prayed for hours on end. That was all I could do for him. When I was released, I hurried to visit him in hospital; he wasn't fully conscious. I called his name, but he didn't answer. Maybe he heard me, but he couldn't speak. Back in 1981, the Mujahedin tried to kill him, but he got away from them.

"Now look at him. He's alive, but that's all. He can barely walk, he needs three people to look after him, around the clock. He can't feel any pain. There's not much he can do; he needs a lot of sleep, and physiotherapy every day. He's ruined. Finished, at age forty-nine. His body just doesn't respond any more."

(We had met Said Hajjarian a few days earlier. Mr. Kadivar's description was no exaggeration.)

"He is the man who personified reform in Iran. That's why they wanted to eliminate him. He's not only a superb theoretician, but also a great strategist. The reform movement has plenty of theoreticians. What it lacked was a strategist. He was the only one. He knew the regime, the system itself. After all, he used to be part of it. From the revolution, he came over to the opposition against the conservatives. He's not the only one. In the decade after the revolution, plenty of top-flight people left the system, people from the security agencies, the Revolutionary Guards, members of the revolutionary apparatus, like Mr. Khatami himself. They quit because they couldn't accept what was going on. Today there are still some dissenters in the Revolutionary Guards, but the regime is doing everything it can to flush them out and eliminate them one way or another before they can escape. That was what happened to Ayatollah Montazeri, whom you call Trotsky to Khomeini's Lenin!"

Tell us about the life and career of a young scholar who could have had a comfortable career in the academic or clerical world, but who decided to break with the power elite at considerable danger to himself.

"I was eighteen when the revolution broke out, in my freshman year at Shiraz University. I was studying engineering. Then I changed over to sociology. After the revolution, then the 'cultural revolution'—which was more like an anti-cultural revolution—I decided to focus on Islamic studies, so I enrolled in the Islamic curriculum. I went on to study philosophy, where I took my Ph.D. Then I continued my studies at the Qom seminary."

For the second time in our conversation, he let drop a name that Iranians avoided mentioning in public, but whose defiant spirit seemed to have made its way into his words.

"One of my masters was Ayatollah Montazeri. In fact, many of the masters I studied under were men of high intellectual achievement. So, when I criticize the nature of religious power today, I know what I'm talking about; I'm sure of my facts, and 'they' can't trip me up. I've written three books on the *Velayat-e faqih*. I think I know just about all there is to know about it.

"I've done time in prison. The first few months were the worst. They held me for eighteen months altogether, but compared with Mandela's twenty-eight years, it was nothing! I was jailed on three charges; the most serious was political: I accused the Supreme Guide of having ordered the serial killing of four writers, they said. I told the judges that I'd only stated that Islam forbids murder, unless it is authorized by a *fatwa* from the highest religious authority in the land. I went on to say that I'd never accused the Supreme Guide of murder. They told me, 'But that's what you were thinking.' 'If that's so,' I answered, 'how are you going to prove it?'

"They said, 'We don't need proof. You're going to prison.'

"So, when I received death threats after my speech on the serial murders, I thought back to what I'd said two years ago, on the 'authorization to kill,' and I understood how right I had been. But this time, I'm the one they're talking about. I think I'll tell them that.

"You know, in Iran there are two prisons, the little one and the big one. When I was released from the little one, the one called Evin [he gestures toward the north-west, in the general direction of Evin Prison], I stepped directly into the big one, which is Iran itself; the whole country."

He burst out laughing. We parted company with an agreement to meet the following week, to take up the question of the role and power of the Guide, and to delve deeply into the connection between religion and politics.

There was much to look forward to: by identifying the fault lines that crisscross its very structure, Mohsen Kadivar has developed a finely wrought analysis of the failure of the Islamic Republic. He asks hard questions; provides sharp answers: how to loosen the vice grip of the *Velayat-e faqih* on Iran's political and spiritual life? What role does religious jurisprudence—*fiqh*—play in the affairs of state? What room is there for a secularist outlook, as opposed to the dominant religious one, in Iranian society?

"We can define three kinds of secular thought: the first is radical; the second, moderate; the third, minimal. By 'radical' I mean totally expelling religion from life, and leaving only the profane. The aim of the moderate version is to remove religion from the public sphere, but not from private life. The third version draws a distinction between the religious institution and the state; in this model, the clergy, or men of religion, would have no special rights.

"These three concepts are currently competing in Islamic political thought. The first one has no followers in Iran. But the second and third both have their supporters.

"The third, which highlights the distinction between state and religion, is widely accepted in Islamic society. Expelling religion altogether might be admissible in the Western world, under the influence of Christianity. But in the Muslim world, it's an option that won't get much backing.

"If we look closely at the third model, we will see that to create policies in the religious field, Islamic rules and regulations can be used and adopted. But society as a whole should be managed on the basis of human experience and reason.

"How policy is devised and formulated in the public domain will ultimately depend on the nature of the society itself: is it Islamic or not? So, if we apply the third model, we will have a democratic society; but it will also be a society that takes both Islamic rules and the popular will into account."

This was just the beginning. Mr. Kadivar now led us into an explanation as thought-provoking as it was complex. Seated across the table from us was a man from within the beating heart of the system; a man intimately familiar with its mechanisms, and able to pinpoint its weaknesses and contradictions.

"Look closely at the third model. If we separate religion from politics, there will be no official position for the clergy, no place for religious jurists. They would enjoy no special status, no privileges. Their eventual participation in public affairs would depend on each one's personal capacities. When I talk about this model—the separation of politics and religion—I mean the separation of mosque and state, of seminary and state, of all religious institutions and the state—but not the separation of religion and the state.

"It's like the difference between Church and state, except that in Islam we don't have exactly the same situation. You mustn't confuse church and mosque. In Iran, it's the *Velayat-e faqih* that is opposed to the third model. But this concept is a mixture of religion and politics. According to this theory of management by the jurist-consult, the Supreme Guide takes all the important decisions for society. As the person responsible for applying and respecting the regulations that he himself has formulated, he stands at the summit.

"In this case, the separation of the religious institution from the state, and the theory of *Velayat-e faqih*, are diametrically opposed. When we come to the separation of religion and politics, the civil society, which is made up of believers, is responsible for religious matters, not state authority, or any other power."

So, Iran has been innovating!

"It certainly has! According to the theory of *Velayat-e faqih*, the Supreme Guide alone is responsible for supervising and applying all regulations. There's a great difference between the two theories. According to the first one, the people themselves observe religious regulations freely and voluntarily; under the second, the political authority assumes responsibility, and can enforce obedience of the regulations. But the idea is to convince people, not to compel them by the use of force and power; we always have to distinguish between authority and force.

"What the religious intellectuals wanted to see materialize was the first theory. But after the victory of the revolution, the theory of the jurist-consult carried the day. The first prime minister, Dr. Mehdi Bazargan, and Ayatollah Taleqani were in favor of the separation of the religious institution and the state. But Ayatollah Khomeini favored the second.

"What I am telling you today has never before been explained, never before clarified to society as a whole. A fundamental question like this has never been debated."

Are we to conclude that if there hasn't been a debate, it's because no one wants one?

"The question isn't really quite ripe. First, we should answer a prior question: how to practice Islam in our society? This experience, these twenty-five years of Islamic Republic have been immensely meaningful for us as religious intellectuals. Without the experience, it would have been impossible for us to postulate the necessity of the third model.

"For a quarter-century now, our society has had as its slogan: 'Our religion is quite precisely our political outlook, and our political outlook is exactly our religion.'"

Let's carry the discussion a bit further. Is the theory of *Velayat-e faqih* based on Shi'a jurisprudence, or does it derive from the arbitrary judgment of the authorities?

"To tell you the truth, the *Velayat-e faqih* is more Iranian than Islamic. In fact, it is an Islamized version of the theory of the Iranian monarchy. You can see that theory being worked out in the *Shahnameh*,[48] for instance. And when I say Iranian theory of monarchy, I mean the theory as it is expressed in the *Shahnameh*, and not in Iranian society. In Ferdowsi's epic, the king must be just; he must have charisma, which he obtains from God.

"What I am going to tell you is based on my ten years of study on this subject. The *Velayat-e faqih* is made up of four components: first, what I just told you, which we can call the ancient Iranian monarchy theory. It is not the monarchy in a real society, but an idealized realm. I don't want to suggest that it could be compared with the Qajars or the Pahlavis."

So, it's an idealized realm?

"Yes, but it can be a real one as well, if we're to believe some of our contemporary thinkers. For example, Javad Tabataba¨i defends the theory for Iran today. Furthermore, he's a Hegelian, so he interprets the theory in the light of Hegelian thought.

"This theory has deep roots in ancient Asia, not only in Iran but also in Japan, China, and Egypt. I believe it is the theory of ancient Asia and Africa. But it reached its greatest heights in Iran.

"The second theory is that of the kingdom of the philosophers, which you will certainly recognize as being that of Plato, who is quite close to Iran's *Velayat-e faqih*. The latter means the rule of the jurist-consult, for Plato, the rule of the philosopher-king. The only difference is the specific competence of the king; nothing else."

Our expedition into the history of ideas was certainly leading us into uncharted territory.

"The third theory is that of the superior human being, founded by Ibn al-Arabi.[49] Such a being must lead society; through his agency, relations may be established between human beings and God. It represents the most advanced form of mysticism. You're familiar with Meister

48. See footnote 50.

49. Born in Andalusia in 1165, Muhyi al Din ibn al-Arabi was one of the great Islamic mystical thinkers. After spending several years in Mecca, where he resided close to the Kaa'ba, he retired to Damascus, where he died in 1240, and where his tomb can be visited today.

Eckhardt? Well, Ibn al-Arabi is the equivalent in the Muslim world of Meister Eckhardt in medieval Europe. They share the belief that the man who must lead other men in society is distinguished by his great qualities in every field. He is the perfect being—God's successor on earth. God's vice-regent, if you will.

"Before he studied *fiqh*, Ayatollah Khomeini studied and taught mysticism. In fact, he was more an expert in mysticism than in Islamic jurisprudence. The *Velayat-e faqih* derives much more from mystic thought than from the traditional legal curriculum. You won't find its terminology in Islamic jurisprudence, but in mysticism, in the absolute authority conferred on the perfect being. This is exactly what Ibn al-Arabi argues, but in the mystical sense, not the political or the juridical sense. So, Khomeini found his terminology in mysticism, and slipped it into the fields of politics and Islamic law.

"It's an extraordinary combination. I don't mean to suggest that it's a good combination, but it certainly is extraordinary, and it has produced extraordinary results."

By combining Islamic mysticism with Shi'a jurisprudence, Imam Khomeini was to release explosive energies. Its first victim—but not the only one—was the imperial regime of the shah, swept away in the tumult and the shouting of a revolution propelled by a powerful centrifugal force.

But there was also a fourth component, continued Mohsen Kadivar, warming to the subject: one which originated in the Shi'a theory of the Imams.

"*Imam* is the Arabic term for the person who leads the public prayers in Islam. But according to Shi'a beliefs, the twelve successors of the Prophet Muhammed's family are also known as *Imams*. These twelve are innocent—free of all sin—and possess divine knowledge. So, the theory of *Velayat-e faqih* appropriates the authority of the innocent Imams with regard to the *velayat*—that is to say, the administration of society—minus their innocence. The prestige of the innocent Imams is invoked in order to justify the exercise of political authority by the Imam in our day. Ayatollah Khomeini was absolutely clear on that point: the authority of the *faqih*, the jurist-consult, is the authority of the innocent Imams applied to the governance of society. In Shi'ism, we do believe in the special rights of the Imams in spiritual matters; but that is not what he is talking about."

We knew, from our own reading, that the spiritual preeminence of the Twelve Imams, only one of whom—Ali—wielded true state power, was based on the family connection with the Prophet.[50] Nowhere in the Qur'an, the revealed text of Islam, is this lineage mentioned. It would only be developed later, over the centuries, taking shape around the Shi'a "Holy Family": Fatima, her father Muhammad, her husband Ali, and their two sons, Hassan and Hossein. The succession of the Twelve Imams, the last of whom, the Mahdi—the Lord of Days—will return to earth to establish the reign of universal justice, is derived from their descendents.

Shi'ism grew up around the "followers of Ali," those who believed him to be the Prophet's legitimate heir. Over time, it would emerge as a place of refuge for two types of discontented partisans: political and mystic. Mohsen Kadivar has grasped—in his brilliant analysis—that at the precise moment of the Islamic Revolution, both political and mystical trends of thought were to identify with Imam Khomeini, and to be absorbed into and concentrated in one sole figure.

"Ayatollah Khomeini simply reinforced the notion that, for the Shi'ites, the Twelve Imams are the source of spiritual and political authority. By his lights, society needs a political authority. He does not even claim the spiritual authority of the innocent Imams. Which means that today, whether or not the Imam has the spiritual competence or authority is of no concern; what matters to the clerics in power is that he provides them with all the latitude they need to do whatever they want in the public sphere."

This is precisely, writes Yann Richard, Ayatollah Khomeini's great innovation in comparison with those who, in the eighteenth century, created the concept of *Velayat-e faqih*, and particularly with Sheikh Morteza Ansari, perhaps the outstanding Shi'a theoretician of the age. For Ansari, the jurist-consult (*faqih*) may exercise three functions: the promulgation of religious opinions (*fatwa*) dealing with problems submitted by the faithful, the arbitration of conflicts between individuals, and the administration of goods and individuals. But for this same Ansari, only the Prophet and the Imams possessed full powers in the temporal and spiritual spheres. The *faqih* can mete out punishments and respond to the necessities created by new circumstances; in other words, he can assume the administration of spiritual affairs while awaiting the return of the Twelfth Imam. His power was limited, and his stature in the community had no connection with politics, as we understand the word today.[51]

50. See Yann Richard, *L'Islam chiite*.
51. Ibid., 108–09.

Khomeini was well aware of all of this. Moreover, he had instinctively grasped what he might be able to accomplish with the mobilizing energy released by the combination of the political and the spiritual. As prime mover behind the insurrection of June 1963, he was able to demonstrate conclusively that the awakening of religious feelings could provide a powerful antidote to the unbridled Westernization then being carried out by the shah's regime.

In 1971 Khomeini published in book form the lectures in Islamic law he had delivered in the holy city of Najaf, in Iraq, where he was then residing in exile. The collected articles, entitled *Islamic Government*, were not widely distributed at the time. But they clearly enunciated the concept of *Velayat-e faqih*, in precisely the form that it would take after the revolution. By the end of the decade, what was an immense doctrinal innovation could draw upon the charisma of Ayatollah Khomeini, who had been transformed into a figure of heroic proportions. Now it was Mohsen Kadivar's turn to deconstruct the mechanism, to display its component parts for all to see, and to reveal the theory's hidden face.

"For the religious members of the clerical party, the legitimacy of the theory comes from God. But that is their claim, which I don't accept.

"In other words, the *Velayat-e faqih* can be described as 'the shah with a supplement of knowledge of religious jurisprudence.' It's clear that what we see is nothing but the way the dominant clerics think society should be governed. Or to put it more bluntly, what we see is despotism."

And now, a short historical digression.

When, at the beginning of the sixteenth century, the founder of the Safavid Dynasty, Shah Ismail, conquered the city of Tabriz and proclaimed Shi'ism the official religion of the state he had just created, he could find not a single theologian in the city. Perhaps because of their Azeri origins, the Safavids had already begun to seek for ways to set themselves apart from their hostile kinsmen, the Ottomans, whose expanding empire had begun to nibble at their lands. Inspired by the Sufi orders that had broken with the strict Sunnis of Istanbul, the newly founded dynasty began to import not only textbooks of Shi'ite jurisprudence, but also religious scholars to explain them from the Jabal Amil, a little-known corner of Lebanon where Shi'ism had sent down its first roots.

During the glorious years of the Safavid Dynasty, particularly under Shah Abbas, the builder of its capital Isfahan, the religious hierarchy established by the king functioned first and foremost as an intermediary, only gradually to emerge as a counterweight to royal power. Between the fall of Iran's first Shi'ite dynasty in 1722, and the rise of the Qajars, founded at the end of the eighteenth century, the roles had become inverted: the power of the *ulama* had come to exceed that of the kings.

And when, in 1828, the disastrous Treaty of Turkmanchai brought the war between Iran and Russia to an end, bringing with it the loss of Iran's Caucasian provinces, the shah badly needed the support of the religious hierarchy.

"So, the religious establishment designated the king as its representative in the war. The shah became the representative of the *faqih*, and not vice versa, as had been the case during the years of Safavid rule. This meant that the shah's legitimacy derived from the *ulama*. If they agreed, the faithful could obey him. If not, the shah forfeited his legitimacy. This was as far as the theory of *Velayat-e faqih* went at the time. It revealed the considerable power of the *ulama*, and the weakness of the shahs. What is clear is that the theory does not derive from religion, but from somewhere else. Still, under the Qajars, the clerics didn't want to assume a political role. They limited themselves to permitting the kings to act or not act, depending on the circumstances.

"Then came Ayatollah Khomeini and the revolution. Now the clerics said to themselves, 'If we truly have this kind of authority, why should we allow the king to rule? We'll run the society ourselves.' Before him, no one had ever made such a claim; no one had even imagined it. All at once, we had a leader who had no intermediaries. In Qajar days, the clerics managed through the agency of the shah. But under Khomeini, they administered the country themselves, without any middle man, so to speak!"

Throughout the Pahlavi era, which was initiated by the *coup d'état* of February 21, 1921, administration by the religious hierarchy was not an option. Reza Khan, who would proclaim himself shah in 1925, intended to drag Iran kicking and screaming into the modern age, following the example of his Turkish counterpart Mustafa Kemal Atatürk. Two authorities were one too many. Lacking the inclination to take on the heavy-fisted shah, the clergy withdrew into silence. The idea of *Velayat-e faqih* was shelved until further notice. This became particularly apparent when the son of Reza Shah, Mohammad-Reza Pahlavi, attempted to revive the glory of the ancient Persian Empire by crowning himself at Persepolis. Could he have imagined that his religious "successors" would not only follow his example, but eventually out-do him?

"The shah exiled Ayatollah Khomeini to Iraq. The clergy had no opportunity to show its feelings, or to make its power felt. We might say that the *Velayat-e faqih* has two faces: one is potential, the other, real. The clerics may have the potential to take charge of society, but in real terms, they may not be able to do so. This was the case during the shah's era. But as soon as they could realize the potential, which they did with the revolution, they seized power.

"You can see the difference between Khomeini and Khamene'i. The first was a 'source of emulation.' But not Khamene'i; he is not what we call a 'grand ayatollah' at all. Khomeini was, but Khamene'i is only a *hojjatoleslam*, that is, someone at the third level of the Shi'a religious hierarchy: grand ayatollah, ayatollah, hojjatoleslam."

How can someone like him become Supreme Guide?

"The Council of Experts ruled that he was competent. It's a reality, and there's nothing virtual about it. And if we continue to move in this direction, it may well be that the next one will be less than a hojjatoleslam—only someone who can guarantee the continuity of power.

"As you can see, it's Islamic monarchy! Give them credit: they're honest about it. It doesn't matter, they say. It's an *Islamic* monarchy. It's not a bad thing at all; you're the ones who think it's bad. Democracy comes from the West, from the devil. That's the way they think. One century ago, a scholar proved that monarchy was preferable to a constitutional state, that it was closer to Islam."

Indeed. Almost exactly one century ago, this scholar, Sheikh Fazlollah Nouri, was an active participant in the often-bloody struggle against the constitutionalists who wanted to establish a parliamentary regime in Iran. He, and others, fought the movement that threatened the throne of Mohammad-Ali Shah. The sheikh's most telling argument was that a constitution would weaken religion, the role of the clergy, and as a result, clerical interests.

At first, the shah gave ground to the constitutionalist forces. On November 9, 1907, he signed Iran's first constitution. A month later, with British and Russian assistance, and with the complicity of Sheikh Nouri, Mohammad-Ali Shah attempted a *coup d'état* that met with stiff resistance from the Majlis deputies, and eventually failed.

In June 1908 the shah tried again. This time he successfully overthrew the constitutional regime and governed from then on by royal decree. But he had underestimated the energy and the strength of the democratic forces, which also enjoyed the decisive support of the *ulama* of Najaf, in Iraq. The democrats could boast double legitimacy: constitutional and Islamic. Great Power support for the shah began to weaken; as he became increasingly isolated his own power began to erode. On May 10, 1909, he was finally forced to reinstate the constitution, then fled into exile in Russia. Sheikh Nouri refused to leave the country and was "summarily tried by a revolutionary tribunal: his execution by hanging in a public square in front of a large crowd took place on July 31, 1909, only widening the gap between the constitutionalists and the clergy."[52]

"You know, one of Tehran's main expressways is named for Sheikh Nouri. The regime has given the name of the greatest enemy of democracy to the most important highway in the capital. At the same time, the name of the greatest constitutional authority has not even been assigned to an alley, let alone a street. Neither Khorassani nor Naïni are honored here. Khorassani[53] was the leading *marja* of the day. Thanks to him, Mohammad-Ali Shah was overthrown. But you won't find his name anywhere, not even on a dead-end alley. The same holds true for Naïni, the second-ranking constitutionalist cleric.

"Nouri was executed by the constitutional government for defending the monarchy. So, the state perpetuates Fazlollah Nouri's memory, but not Khorassani's, or Naïni's."[54]

In 1989, Ayatollah Hossein-Ali Montazeri, one of Iran's five living grand ayatollahs and designated successor to Imam Khomeini, was abruptly dismissed. Every revolution, concludes Mohsen Kadivar, has its charismatic personality; his successor inherits all the problems. But the case of Ayatollah Montazeri is complicated by the fact that not only has he moved away from the theory of *Velayat-e faqih*, but also from many of the practices of the regime.

In July 1988, soon after Iran had accepted UN Security Council Resolution 598 that brought the Iran-Iraq war to an end, Montazeri lashed out at the arguments the authorities had used to justify the war:

---

52. *L'Iran au XXe siècle*, 39–43. [My translation. —FR]

53. Even though Mohammad Kazem Khorassani had openly called for a constitution, he agreed with Sheikh Fazlollah Nouri's demand that it contain a clause against heresy, the idea being to block a foreign model of justice that was considered incompatible with Shi'ite tradition. On this question, see Roy Mottadeh, *The Mantle of the Prophet: Religion and Politics in Iran* (New York: Pantheon, 1985).

54. In 1909, Mirza-Hossein Naïni provided theological justification for Muslims to participate in parliamentary democracy, comparing the mullahs who favored collaboration with the absolutist Mohammad-Ali Shah with the murderers of Imam Hossein at Karbala. In 1955, Ayatollah Taleqani republished Naïni's treatise on the theological justification for parliamentary constitutionalism. See Yann Richard, *L'Islam chiite*, 136–37, 217.

the empty slogans, the lies, the death and destruction. A few days later, he violently spoke out again, denouncing the liquidation of several thousand members of the MKO by the power elite. From that moment on, his days as successor were numbered. A decade later, he was to excoriate the current Guide for his lavish life style.

But is Montazeri's position on the *Velayat-e faqih* as sharply articulated as his outbursts against Khomeini and Khamene'i?

"Two weeks ago I asked him several questions. By the way, you should be aware that the theory of *Velayat-e faqih* was inscribed in the constitution while he was president of the Council of Experts. His contribution was considerable. So, I asked him, 'Did you have the same understanding of the concept then as you do today?' His answer: 'No, I was dazzled by Ayatollah Khomeini.' We must also add that he was Khomeini's greatest student; he sincerely believed in him. Even today, he believes in him, within a religious framework. At the time, he believed Khomeini could help Islam, that he was ideally placed to help his religion.

"What is the difference between Khomeini and Montazeri, in theoretical terms? They both believe in the *Velayat-e faqih*, but with slight differences. Montazeri believes the people must elect the Guide; for him, the *Velayat-e faqih* must be an elective position, and not one designated by God. So, according to him, the person who guides society must be a religious scholar, but he must be elected.

"When Khomeini wrote his treatise on Islamic law, he totally dismissed the question of elections. In some later speeches, he seemed to admit that they might be possible; he never denied the possibility of elections. Even today, a certain amount of ambiguity persists.

"The reformists have tried to interpret Khomeini as favoring an elective *Velayat-e faqih*. But the conservatives' answer is no. So, what you have is a case of both sides claiming Khomeini, but in total opposition to one another: election or divine appointment. Which gives us two versions of the *Velayat-e faqih*, the first elective and limited, that of Montazeri, and the second, absolute and unelected, that of Khomeini.

"But if we want a democratic, Islamic state, we cannot accept that an institution like the *Velayat-e faqih* regulate our society. The Islamic state can easily exist without either the *Velayat-e faqih* or Supreme Guide.

"The regime won't forgive me for bringing all this to light. I am the first to demonstrate that there is no connection between Islamic rules and regulations, an Islamic state, Islam as a religion, and the *Velayat-e faqih*. We can be believers without being obliged to believe in the power of the Guide."

Mohsen Kadivar pulled a newspaper from his briefcase, opened it on the table in front of us, and with an ironic grin pointed to the impact of his statements in the regime's semi-official press.

"This is *Resala'at*, one of the three main conservative newspapers, along with *Kayhan*. Today's editorial is devoted to me. It quotes three of my books, emphasizing that I don't believe in the power of the Guide.

"The clergymen close to the regime are furious at me. I argue, in general terms, that the *Velayat-e faqih* has no basis in the Qur'an, or in the Sunna, the Prophetic tradition. I go on to add, It's a creation of your imagination, of your own mind, and not the creation of God. Their position is: 'If you obey God, you must obey us.'

"My answer to them is no. We obey God, the Holy Qur'an, the Prophetic tradition, but we will not obey you as successors of God, the Prophet, or the Innocent Imams."

What's their answer?

"The answer for people who hold the same position as I do is prison. Aqajari is in jail right now; I've been warned. Mohsen Rahami is behind bars, with Shirin Ebadi acting as his lawyer. This newspaper wants parliament to reject the candidacies of these malefactors who don't believe in the *Velayat-e faqih*.

"They're frightened—frightened of any discussion. Four years ago, I was invited to visit the Council of Experts' archives to discuss the issue. All I was permitted to do was write down my opinion. I had no opportunity to speak, and certainly not to speak in public.

"What can we do? Well, we can publish, because print runs for books in Iran are very low, two to three thousand copies at most. My books are quite popular; they've been reprinted five times. But the total circulation of my books doesn't exceed twenty thousand copies. They can accept such arguments in print; expressing them in public is much more dangerous.

"If they're reported in a newspaper, that paper will be closed. So, I prefer to write, and to say nothing. If I say so much as a word on that subject, that will be the end of me."

The regime seems to be marking time. How can it sustain itself without the support of the majority and in the face of radical criticism of its fundamental precepts?

"By force, by the application of power; not by democratic means. The regime can get by with the appearance of elections, but it could not survive a true, fair, and open vote. The *Velayat-e faqih* cannot coexist with democracy. Democracy requires that if a citizen wishes to criticize the way power is exercised, he can still be elected to parliament. For them, the answer is no. It's our red line, they say. If someone criticizes the Guide, that person cannot sit in parliament. He lacks the necessary qualifications.

"Dante wrote his *Divine Comedy*, but what's going on in this country is no divine comedy! Our comedy is tragic. Still, I'm quite happy with the experience of the last twenty-five years. You know, the other Islamic countries have not had our experience, and bin Laden tops the public opinion polls just about everywhere. In Iraq and in Egypt, he's seen as a hero. Syria too. Not in Iran. His support is extremely limited. For me, that is a victory. The Iranian people have learned a lesson from the unlimited power of the jurist-consult, not the other Muslim countries.

"The Iranians say, 'We don't need another bin Laden here; if you would like one, we can export one to you.'"

When you get right down to it, do the conservatives understand how much Iranian society has changed, whether they like it or not?

"I think they understand perfectly. They know that the majority disagrees with them. So they need the forces of repression even more than before; the Revolutionary Guards and the Basijis are much more visible than ever. They are hiding behind the armed forces. With only about 15 percent support in the country as a whole, the regime has to keep the military and the judiciary on its side. It is doing exactly this, and of course, it controls oil revenues."

It was time to go.

As we departed Mohsen Kadivar's office we understood just how deceiving appearances could be.

Body Language

EVERY YEAR, IN EARLY FEBRUARY, Iran celebrates the anniversary of the 1979 revolution. *Shah raft, Imam amad*, read the newspaper headlines of the day: "The Shah is gone, the Imam has come."

The official commemoration is preceded by three weeks of intense cultural activity: the *Fajr* Festival, the "festival of dawn." It's show time, Tehran style. Throughout the city, concert halls, theaters, public parks, and even sidewalks are all but taken over by Iranian and foreign actors and musicians. The festival, which operates as a display window for the regime, provides visitors and residents with an excellent opportunity to take the pulse of Iran's artistic life, and particularly of the theater. It is also a rare occasion—perhaps for only one night—for Iranians to see what is happening on the stages of the world.

Filmgoers can make the acquaintance of works by Iranian filmmakers who are far more visible outside their country than on domestic screens; there is also a selection of foreign films, which are rarely encountered in Iranian motion-picture theaters. The festival doubles as an informal meeting place for much of Iran's artistic community, and for young people in search of new ideas—as well as functioning as an informal barometer pointing to trends in what can be said, seen, and shown ... and not.

It was here, in the febrile, hectic festival atmosphere, that we met Pari Saberi, a stage director who belongs to filmmaker Abbas Kiarostami's generation, and doyenne of the contemporary Iranian theater. A well-known stage personality under the monarchy, she spent several years in the artistic wilderness before returning to the fold, in the late 1980s, in the Islamic Republic. Pari Saberi's singular conception of the theater draws its style and originality from her unlikely professional life.

That evening the festival was presenting her most recent work, a "play in music and dance." The subtitle was more than enough to pique our curiosity. Baldly stated, the combination of music and dance was in itself a none-too-subtle form of provocation in a country where the representation of the human body, and of the female body in particular, is a sensitive political, ideological, and religious issue. Music, dance, the relationship between the two sexes on stage, the female voice—women's solo voices must not be heard in Iran—are among the most crucial issues that theater in the Islamic Republic has been faced with over the last twenty-five years. As we took our seats in the crowded auditorium of Tehran's City Theatre, we had no idea what to expect.

We did have ample reason to be wary. On state television, the image of women is a depressing one. Her place is in the kitchen, with her children, moving back and forth between housekeeping chores and maternity. Love stories are endless tales of tribulation; the rare "happy endings" are presented as a release rather than the assumption of responsibility. Women's movements have challenged the devastating effects of a stereotyped representation so far removed from Iranian feminine social and political consciousness—and reality. But the retrograde vision finds reinforcement in both custom and tradition, and is supported by the country's religious regulations.

There exists, in public life, a clear-cut dividing line between the sexes. In private this line is constantly being crossed, but in public it looms over all social relations. Not only dress but also behavior function as markers of discrimination. Imagine for a moment a spacious park, where a bicycle path winds pleasantly through the trees. But for women, the path is off limits. The only bicycle path available to them is a short circular track hidden behind a stockade, like an Indian village, far from prying masculine eyes. One-third of the seats in the rear of city buses are reserved for women, the remaining two-thirds for men; taxis, minibuses, and the Tehran metro are not sex-segregated however. Crowding six or seven people into a Paykan for a trip across town transforms mixed-sex transportation into necessity, if not inevitability. There is a strong possibility that a woman will end up half-seated on a man's knees—or vice versa—or squeezed up against him when an extra passenger pries him or herself into the car. But outside of everyday prohibitions, the expression of desire and the interplay of mutual attraction continue to seek out their own innumerable, often unmentionable paths through the thicket of the proscribed, eventually to find expression, for the body has its reasons.

These thoughts—and images—were going through our minds as Pari Saberi's play began. The musicians filed onto the stage, a group of traditional instrumentalists stage right, modern instruments stage left. They began to play, each group answering the other, their sounds progressively mingling. Then a reciter strode onto the stage, followed by the actors who would dance, sing, and speak. Already it was clear that the evening ahead was far removed indeed from state television. The women's chorus was the dominant voice, accompanied by male voices humming like a *basso continuo*. Then, soaring above the chorus, a woman's voice rang out in response to the male solo. All at once it was hard for us to distinguish emotional and aesthetic response from pure astonishment. Staging a play that features music and dance in a country where women are not allowed to dance in public demands more than a little daring, especially when the dancers project the kind of expressive power and physical presence we saw unfolding on the stage in front of us. Dress regulations—bolstered by custom and tradition—stipulate that women should wear dark, loose-fitting clothes that do not reveal the shape of their bodies. Pari Saberi had contrived to respect the letter of the law, while every movement of her actresses and dancers flouted it openly. Their costumes, their tunics, and their veils were bright and colorful, the fabrics light and filmy enough to reveal the black bodysuits beneath them, revealing and concealing their silhouette in an interplay of light and shadow.

Without ostentation, her audacious staging had pushed back the limits of what may be represented. Now only the beauty of the play—its text and its music—commanded our attention as it unfolded in a crescendo of intensity, driven forward by the tragic tale it told and by the imperative of speaking of the past in the present. Not a whisper of protest could be heard; not a hint of the ever-threatening flying squads of the guardians of public morality. Pari Saberi had won her wager: the pulsing of desire, the erotic tension that was palpable on stage gently mocked the self-righteous censors in a flurry of whirling veils and scarves.

The play, entitled *The Sacrifice of Siavosh*, is an adaptation of the *Shahnameh* (The Book of Kings). The epic, by Iran's national poet Ferdowsi, relates the founding myths of Iran before the Arab conquest. Alongside Ha'afez, the poet of Shiraz and author of the *Divan*, Ferdowsi belongs to Iran's cultural pantheon, venerated for the quality of his poetry, and for its spiritual and political qualities; revered as the Dante of Iran, the man who single-handedly created the modern Persian language. A devout Muslim and an ardent nationalist, he set out to "purify" the national idiom of its Arabic words and expressions.

Pari Saberi has built her play upon excerpts of the poem that relate the sacrifice of Siavosh and, indirectly, of the death of the poet. For

Ferdowsi's fate proved to be almost as tragic as that of his hero. After devoting more than ten years of his life to the composition of his masterpiece, Ferdowsi undertook the long and harrowing journey to the court of Sultan Mahmoud, at Ghazna, in today's Afghanistan, at the beginning of the second millennium of the Christian era. The sultan was a cruel man, and a Sunni fundamentalist before the fact. Ferdowsi had come to present his work, a necessary precaution in order to survive in a world where poets had to stifle their pride to please the powerful. The sultan failed to appreciate the work that the ageing poet recited that day before a throng of courtiers and fellow poets. Ferdowsi was to spend some time at court, where he could admire the sultan's extraordinary collection of miniatures, before being dispatched with a pittance. A few months later, the sultan changed his mind. A royal caravan laden with gifts and gold coins arrived at the gates of Tus, the poet's home town, just as Ferdowsi's funeral procession was winding its way toward his last resting place.

Siavosh, the figure around whom the play turns, is the embodiment of nobility, the incarnation of perfection, purity of soul, and courage. He resists all temptations, and abjures the amorous advances of the wife of his father, the king. Bravely he joins a military expedition, where he concludes an alliance with his father's defeated enemies. Finally, betrayed, denied by his followers and family, he is decapitated, the innocent victim of human hatred.[55]

It is this timeless tale that Pari Saberi has brought to the stage: a tragedy that resonates through Iranian history and culture. The martyrdom of Siavosh evokes the torments of Imam Hossein in the desert at Karbala. In the *Shahnameh* the prince, who knows that his death is near, becomes a symbol of the struggle between good and evil, between justice and injustice, a recurring theme in Shi'a martyrology:

> Little time indeed will pass before the pitiless, suspicious king will put me cruelly to death despite my innocence.... Thus has God inscribed upon the firmament, and all that He sows bears fruit as He ordains....

Then, in a nightmarish dream, Siavosh witnesses his death, which he describes to his wife:

55. See Yann Richard, *L'Islam chiite*, 132.

Then they will cut off this innocent head, and my heart's blood will be its diadem, and I shall be given neither bier nor tomb, nor shroud, and none among the throng will weep over me; I shall be laid beneath the earth like a stranger, head severed from body by sword.[56]

When Siavosh dies—the culminating moment of the tragedy—the eight young women of the chorus drop to their knees and rhythmically strike their breasts in movements that recall the solemn ritual of Ashura, as their torsos sway from side to side in the ultimate expression of the pain of the soul.

* * *

After the performance, we make our way backstage to meet Pari Saberi in her dressing room, where she is surrounded by a group of young actors and actresses, their faces flushed with the pleasure of their performance. There are no stars here; the young actor who plays the male lead is also an assistant stage-manager. His job is to coordinate the daily rehearsals where the players hone their body language to a sharp edge, both for the dances and the combat scenes that are played out in the stylized manner of a dance sequence. Each of the dancers, we learn, has been trained on the job, in response to the play's specific need for disciplined, controlled action. In real life, the statuesque lead dancer teaches aerobic gymnastics in a women's health club.

Pari Saberi is an old theater hand. Trained in France in the 1960s, she began her career in Iran under the shah. She worked as a translator, and adapted and staged works from the Western theatrical repertoire popular with Iranian theater-goers of the day: Chekhov, Pirandello, Sartre, Ionesco.

"My main concern was staging. That's how I learned my trade. I worked on stage sets, I performed, and I translated European dramatists. By translating, I learned how to write for the theater.

"After the revolution, I experienced a period of silence. Theater had been reduced to a bare minimum. For a few years, there was very little in the way of cultural activity. I used those years to think hard: what was I lacking in theater? I was neither happy nor satisfied with what I had

---

56. Ferdowsi, *Le Livre des Rois*, trans. J. Mohl, Paris, 1842 (reprinted 1976), vol. 2, 347, 391, quoted in Yann Richard, *L'Islam chiite*, 133 [My translation. —FR].

been doing; I felt as though I had been missing something. But I couldn't figure out what it was.

"I had a sense that my country's culture, that my own roots, were pursuing me, but I could never give a positive response because I was under the impression that we had no theater of our own. We were so under the spell of Western theater that we couldn't imagine creating a theater for ourselves.

"I was dividing my time between Paris and Los Angeles back then; I would always find myself among fellow Iranians, for evenings of poetry and music. It was then that my eyes were opened to Iranian culture. I couldn't work here, of course, because there was no theater. It was a time of thought and meditation. The more I thought about it, the more clearly I saw that poetry is the mirror of the Iranian soul. Poetry contains everything Iranian.

"Every nation has its own particular form of expression: the novel and painting for the French, music for the Germans. For the Iranians, poetry is where the emotional power lies. And when I began to study the great poems of our tradition more closely, I understood their great dramatic power. They were not the kind of poem you read in bed, like any other book. No! So, Iranian poetry became my reason for living! I began to write plays based on poems, and on the lives of poets as well. Of course I was apprehensive, because the theater-going public in Iran was accustomed to seeing translations of foreign plays. People were convinced there was no such thing as Iranian theater, so I had no idea whether they would accept what I had to offer.

"I staged my first play here in Tehran, fifteen years ago, at the end of the 1980s, based on a text by one of our great poets. The public response was excellent. In fact, it was love at first sight between us! Not for theater people, or for the critics. What I was doing didn't conform to existing standards. For them it wasn't theater; to this day they're still convinced it isn't theater. Either they look down on my plays, or they dismiss them scornfully. But I've kept at it, and this play, *Siavosh*, is my seventh. Up to now, each one has been an unbelievable success.

"The theater has come back to life in Iran. Some theater people are still traditionalists, following the lead of foreigners, the Brechts, the Ionescos, and others. Each period demands freedom of expression in its own terms. As for me, I got started without too many difficulties. I hadn't been entirely pushed aside by the people who took our place after the revolution. These were the same people who, before, may have looked upon us with admiration or jealousy, and who considered us usurpers. Afterward, they attempted to eliminate us, but once things calmed down a bit, they came to recognize the worth of the people who had worked under the shah's regime. People began to understand that a filmmaker like Kiarostami was not a product of the revolution, and that his career spans more than forty years. Slowly but surely they realized that we were capable of doing good work, that we had something to offer; finally, they opened the doors to us.

"Personally speaking, I've had no difficulty in presenting the pieces I wanted. Today, I only work on subjects that touch our culture directly. And when I say culture, I am not talking about something that belongs to me, but to all Iranians.

"Take *Siavosh*. It tells a story that resonates in every Iranian. The same is true for my newest work, about Rumi, which we'll be performing soon in Paris.[57] It evokes the amorous encounter between a young man and poetry, which in itself reflects the Iranian collective spirit. For the last fifteen years, my work has been moving in this direction, focused on contemporary and ancient poetry and culture. It's Iran's subconscious, and modern and ancient poetry are intimately connected because they both embody the same values. Like Shakespeare, where you touch the depths of the human soul."

Your work depends heavily on actors, on the physical quality of their bodies, of their relations. Do you feel restricted by the limitations you have to work under?

"There's no problem with the actors and actresses not being able to touch. You can create an amorous relation between a man and woman without them even having to touch. In fact, their relation will be stronger if they do not. You need only to create a situation, and the audience can easily grasp it. The simple presence of bodies creates an erotic reality. You can't obstruct the expression of the relation between a man and a woman. That would be like saying the force of creation doesn't exist."

That's not what one sees in the soap operas broadcast on state television.

"Of course not. In those programs, all the prohibitions are respected, but there's not a sliver of emotion in the relationships they show. You

---

57. The reference is to Mawlana Jalaludin, known as Rumi, author of the *Mathnawi*, one of the masterworks of Islamic mysticism, who is claimed by both Iranians and Turks. In 1244, in the marketplace of Konya, he encountered and fell under the amorous and spiritual influence of a certain Shams Tabrizi. Rumi's entire poetic corpus is dedicated to seeking his lost connection with Shams.

have to create a sense of intensity, of presence. Even if body contact were permitted, I'm not sure I would actually show things. I like to make the spectator's imagination work; but I also attempt to create a maximum number of situations of attraction between a man and a woman.

"Of course touching on stage is forbidden, just like appearing in public unveiled. But, as you know, there are veils ... and veils. You can solve the problem aesthetically, and the veil becomes a costume; it is no longer the obligatory head-covering. The trick is to transform it into a mystery, into a source of enchantment.

"Each morning all the actors are hard at work, preparing the evening's performance. They rehearse every single movement. Preparation of the body is essential in the kind of theater I do. We work on the relation between bodies, on what the body should express."

But doesn't that create a tension between the rules of social behavior and dress in the Islamic Republic?

"If you respect the rules imposed by Islamic law, women's hair cannot be seen, men and women may not touch one another, and, of course, anything that might resemble pornography is forbidden.

"But those things aside, you can be quite free. For example, people say that you can't use color; I, for one, use a lot of color, the women in my plays are very well dressed, they sing, they dance; I experiment with the way cloth folds and drapes, and the way bodies move. There are no bare breasts on display, I grant you. But, you know, beauty is more than nudity. Concealed nudity is often more attractive.

"So far, I've had no problems with censorship, either in my choice of subjects or in my productions. Touch wood! I've never had any problem with the kind of plays I write and direct. But I don't know how far I can go. I even managed to play Ha'afez at the poet's tomb, in Shiraz."

Your play, Siavosh, can be read in a very contemporary light, can't it?

"Yes. With sincerity and emotion, you can touch the spectator. I'm a bit of a mystic myself; I believe we are all from the same common stock. If someone is struck by adversity, everyone is moved. Just look at the Bam earthquake and all the solidarity. Sure, people go back to their egocentric selves afterward. But the theater can remind them of that solidarity. My play Siavosh is a cry of revolt against injustice, against abuse and force, against everything that goes against basic values. That's what the play is about. Siavosh dies a victim, but at the exact spot where he shed his blood, at the place where he sacrificed his life for the happiness of humanity, a tree has taken root and will grow, a tree of abundance."

Isn't that one of the recurring themes in the *Tazieh*?[58]

"The *Tazieh* is one of the main influences on my work. It's a theatrical form from the past that uses the most modern of means. In *Siavosh* the reciter, whose vocal power is extraordinary, is from a real-life *Tazieh* troupe.

"We developed the staging of the play as the musicians were creating the music, right on stage. You could say that the entire production, including the dances, the songs, the male and female voices, is constructed from the music up."

Does politics have any role in your work?

"Politics doesn't interest me. I don't belong to any party. Of course artists have a political sensibility; we live in this society. But today, what I am looking for is sincerity. My causes are those of justice and freedom, the same as for all other human beings. And I use all the means that I have in the theater to say so. I stage my plays without hypocrisy. People accept it, and that's fine with me. Until now, they accept it.

"People keep telling me, 'You can't stage plays like that in Iran.' Yes I can, I answer, just like that. I can't say that anybody is censoring me.

"It's true that I put men beside women in my plays. These women sing, they express themselves. And that helps stir up society. I know it. It even helps stir up the most fundamentalist people. They come to see the play, they like what they've seen, and they slowly change the way they see the world.

"That's how women fight. And everywhere you go in the world, you'll have women to contend with!"

---

58. *Tazieh*: a stylized, dramatized representation of the martyrdom of Imam Hossein, performed during the month of Moharram, either in the street or in the *hosseiniyeh*.

The Winds of Fate

"I LEFT MYSELF TO THE WINDS OF FATE," says Mehdi Jafari[59] as we settle back into our armchairs in his office at his economic research institute in Niavaran, the prosperous northern suburb of the capital. After eight years abroad, he has come back to Iran to take up a position as an economic analyst: a job rather like walking a tightrope between observation and policy-making, between the devil and the deep blue sea, between the reformist government and the ultra-conservatives of the regime.

He is also an old friend; our conversation quickly takes up a dialogue begun years ago. As usual, he is keen to talk, to bring us up to date. For like him we have also been carried this far by the same winds of fate.

Since his return, Mehdi Jafari has witnessed at first hand the shifts and undercurrents working their way through the depths of Iranian society. We have arrived on the eve of an election of which he already knows the outcome. For him, the failure of the reform process is a foregone conclusion. We are anxious to hear more about the causes, the nature, and the consequences of that failure. Was it the regime's intimidation of civil society? The intellectuals who were physically attacked and driven into exile for challenging its premises, the students who were beaten and thrown into jail; the death threats, the newspaper closings, the women harassed, not to mention the violent deaths of dissidents—hadn't all that created a climate of fear and intimidation?

"Here, if you want to fight the system, you should know which way you are heading.

"Whoever challenges power has to accept the consequences. Here, it's prison, and even death: a case of over-punishment. But today, compared with the previous regime, society is more open in spite of the price we have to pay, which is far too high. But that's how life goes in this part of the world."

59. Not his real name.

Call him lucid, cynical, a fatalist: Mehdi Jafari is as hard to pin down as the winds of fate. Does he simply want to provoke us, or set our Western attitudes straight; could he be suggesting that our way of seeing the world and our analytical tools are of little use to us in Iran? To say we're disconcerted is putting it mildly. He looks at us for an instant, smiles, and takes up where he left off.

"Here, intellectuals should be aware of where they're heading. Here, life is harder, the struggle is harder. That's why freedom is so expensive. We're not fighting for ourselves, but for the generations to come. Still, in Iran, belonging to the opposition is not only a matter of costs; there can also be some benefits. Some people expect too much of society. If I were to give them a word of advice, it would be: 'If I were you, I wouldn't go so far.'"

We have already heard the same words of caution from the mouths of reformist "fellow travelers." Some of them believe that the audacity of Iran's militant intellectuals in confronting the regime and their excessive confidence may well be brave and dangerous, but could have a negative impact in the long term. The attitude is counter-productive, they argue. It needlessly heightens conservative reactions, and may even win them more followers.

"Some intellectuals, whom I won't name, have taken an opportunistic approach. They observed that the religious authorities were in decline; they could see which way things were moving. So they began to criticize; they began to adjust their behavior. It was easy to speak out against the power structure."

We interject a question: Did they ever believe for an instant that it was possible to change the regime from within, by infiltrating it, if you like?

"Don't be naive! None of us had any experience in confronting power. Our only experience of tyranny came from our pre-revolutionary understanding, which was heavily tinged with Marxism. Many also fought the old regime from their understanding of Islam, but most were influenced by the conventional, dominant ideology, which was Marxism."

But for those who invoked Islam, wasn't the path clear?

"The Qur'an is very explicit: you must fight against tyranny. All Muslims are called to fight on behalf of the oppressed. Many of the young revolutionaries believed that Islam had an impact on their fight. There was a strong influence from militant Islamic movements like the Muslim Brotherhood in Egypt. Plus, Iran had its own tradition of holy violence and assassination in the name of God. And finally, Marxism, as an ideology of struggle, definitely influenced our fight against tyranny."

What Mehdi Jafari is telling us is that the political horizon of the young militants who actually fought the Islamic Revolution was limited to a reading of the Qur'an, the writings of Imam Ali, and Marxism. But it had all taken place in a new and unpredicted political context.

"As the New World Order was emerging, we didn't know what was going on. There was a techno-scientific revolution; it had an impact on the world power structure, and ultimately led to the collapse of the U.S.S.R. These were the forces that were emerging as we won power on the basis of our naive understanding. We were convinced that it wasn't so difficult to run the country."

Was it enough to apply the precepts of Islam to change and improve society, to show a prototype of a better world?

"We still think that Islam has such a capacity. Islam was created not by men but by God, and can be spread among all nations and all races. There is a common ground between all three monotheistic religions. All of them are basically the same, and all of them have the same message, that of humanity."

The Islamic Revolution was the only religious revolution of the twentieth century. But it is also a part of the heritage of the Russian, Chinese, and Cuban revolutions. It was a great moment of hope. But today, it has become one of the great disenchantments of the last century. Marxism could not rescue the first three; Islam could not ensure the success of the Iranian experience: neither Marx, nor Khomeini, when all is said and done. For both, the century proved to be a rude awakening. What went wrong with the Iranian Revolution, between the naive intentions of the revolutionaries and the dismal reality of the regime today? It's the same question that could be asked of Fidel Castro. Was the Guide naïve; was he unaware of the world around him, or neither? What are we really talking about? Is it a case of decline, or of failure?

"The message of the revolution was frightening to the West. And in Iran, the new managers had to confront crises, particularly the imposed war with Iraq, which shaped future developments.

"Neo-liberal thought was emerging in the West, especially in the United States and Great Britain, the two countries that supported Saddam Hussein against Iran, which became the topic of a new label that power holders in the West could exploit. They tried to make Iran into a new threat for the entire region and the rest of the world. They had to weaken Iran, by every possible means.

"Inside Iran, the leadership wasn't innocent. Above all, it didn't understand the consequences of its slogans. If we'd had then the experience we have today, we could have predicted the consequences of the kind of extreme positions they took. In fact, the slogans of the revolution, even then, were obsolete. They simply didn't take into account the changing realities in the West. Were we really going to change the whole world system? When the world system is consolidating itself and is challenged by an emerging force, we all know what it will do.

"The Iranian Revolution should have adapted to modern times, but it didn't; it failed to learn from history. The various political parties and factions must accept part of the responsibility for our failure. The left saw Iran as part of the Soviet Bloc. But the overwhelming majority of Iranians couldn't accept that; they wanted to be free from both the West and the East.

"The People's Mujahedin had an enormous responsibility. Their violent actions pushed society into extreme positions.

"The U.S. Embassy events were a reaction to the domestic situation. The Muslim students who took it over wanted to show that they weren't any less revolutionary than the leftists. This was one of the most important reasons for what they did. It was as if they wanted to say, 'We can bear arms and fight imperialism just as well as you can!'

"At the same time, the leadership opened up new war fronts, in violation of the practice of Prophet Muhammed. Due to our lack of experience, we were facing the whole world. We had public support in the Arab societies, but that support could not express itself. Maybe among Africans, too, but they couldn't help us. And all the while, the world system was changing, but we didn't notice it, so we ended up organizing them against ourselves!

"Yes, Imam Khomeini was a great personality. He was a nationalist, and an internationalist, but he had poor advisors. And he was certainly not infallible. He dismissed from the circles of power people like Ayatollah Taleqani, who was opposed to any form of tyranny. Taleqani was the one who used to say, 'A small king lurks in each one of us, and wants to become a great king.' In his last years, the rush for power had begun; all of society was the loser when he died."

But to understand the decline and failure of the revolution, shouldn't we examine processes, and not the lives of two or three individuals?

"That's right. We have to study the role of the Zionists, who worked against us; neo-liberalism saw 'us' as working against its interests. We have to admit that our leadership was inexperienced; we are suffering from a long tradition of tyranny that has spoiled many parts of our culture. Today, we are living with the impact of the war, and yet we are facing new enemies. In short, we're demoralized."

How can you encourage a regime that dismisses and threatens freedom of expression, shuts down newspapers, and monopolizes public television?

"The first thing we have to do is analyze the structures of power. No matter where we live, the media have an adverse effect on us, whether it's in the form of subtle manipulation or of a stick.

"Here, the power structure does not feel secure. Due to its failures, and to its decline in popularity, it has become more conservative, less tolerant. And if they feel weakened or threatened, they will become even more conservative."

The tradition of intolerance is well established in Iran, we note; whatever embryonic liberties may have existed after the revolution were quickly stifled. Mr. Jafari responds that even in the United States, today, professors have lost their jobs and journalists have been threatened because of their opinions. True. But we also remind him that they were not sent off to prison, were not tortured and that they are still alive. In Iran, the regime is a good deal more expeditive.

"True! In Iran many can criticize the regime, but they face danger in doing so. This kind of opposition turns them into power seekers. The game is spoiled; it becomes a contest, to see who will chop off whose hand."

Is he trying to persuade us that no matter which way we turn, thirst for power is the motivating factor in Iran? Isn't there a risk of cutting corners, of justifying a particular state of affairs by attributing it to history, and to a despotic tradition? Perhaps it's too simple to abandon one's self to the winds of fate, as though the violence that accompanies the outcry for freedom were a foregone conclusion?

"Iran has gone through several stages of development in a short time. The first years after the revolution gave the image of a dynamic, fruitful society, but also of a highly unstable one. Then came the war. That was when the extreme left betrayed the nation, and gave justification to those with a totalitarian mentality to capture power.

"During that same period, the 'left' faction in power was systematically pushed aside, but continued to plan for power. Imam Khomeini tried to establish a balance. The so-called 'cultural revolution' was part of this struggle, which showed the weakness of our political structure.

"Controlling the universities was not easy. Once freedom of expression and the right to form political parties had been lost, only the students could carry on these functions, to whatever possible extent. So, the campuses became the only places where a variety of political ideas could be expressed."

But was the "cultural revolution" anything more than a bloody purge carried out by a regime that wanted to exclude any form of opposition or criticism? And didn't the war also strengthen its hand?

"Look, the authorities wanted a pretext for closing the universities. After all, the students had changed the previous regime, and they could do it again. It was a period of consolidating power."

And didn't the regime take advantage of the Iraqi invasion and the war to expand its domination? Wasn't it for certain people an ideal excuse to grab a larger share of power, then total power?

"We can say that they succeeded. And with the demise of the Imam in 1989, an entirely new power discourse emerged. Before, social justice had been the main theme. Now, protection of capital became the primary concern."

It appears to us that the heads of the regime haven't changed all that much, despite the change in discourses.

"You can't be a hero of both. When he became president, with a constitution rewritten for him, Hashemi Rafsanjani wanted to present a neo-liberal image—'we are changing'—and to reduce hostility in society. But he used contradictory tactics and tools.

"His 'new' tools seriously undermined social capital. They were also meant to show that Iran could deflect hostility at the international level. For eight years, the UN was 'the law of the jungle,' now, all of a sudden, we're 'good guys'!"

It's clear to us that social justice has not been achieved. Why is that?

"The new discourse required new men, not the same ones that have been there from the beginning. Their credibility in the eyes of the revolutionaries and of Muslim youth is dead. When they adopted the new discourse, they lost the support of this key segment of the population.

"New slogans have replaced the old slogans. There is security for capital but not for citizens. This is why they're in the position they are today. Once they'd lost popular support, which they definitely have, it was inevitable that they would become more rigid and fearful.

"Today they must live with other world powers; they must have dealings with foreigners. But in the process, they've become more and more alien to their own people. Such is the nature of dictatorship. What we have now is a stock exchange, not a cultural exchange. The gap between the authorities and the population is growing wider and deeper, and the equation between power and legitimacy has become an unequal one.

"Today, the power structure would like to make use of Mr. Khatami's proposals. Relations between Iran and the United States will be re-established, but by a conservative government. But society as a whole will be the loser. Because they don't know anything, they will sell out the country to the United States. They will lose even more legitimacy, and they will fall.

"In the final analysis, what we have is a confusion between free markets and freedom."

The rain that has been falling since early morning has finally ended. From the heights of Niavaran, we can see the lights of Tehran sparkling far below. As we leave Mehdi Jafari's office, his last words echo in our ears. What if modern Iran's dilemma is also our own?

The Philosopher and the Future

HIGH NOON, at the corner of Revolution Avenue and Palestine Street. Crowds throng the streets from dawn to dusk and beyond in this district of office buildings, small businesses, shops, and even a university. Our destination is the seventh floor of a dust-caked, nondescript building where we have an appointment at the Institute for the Study of the Future, one of the think tanks created several years ago in the wake of Mohammad Khatami's election as president. We are far indeed from the former imperial villas of north Tehran that now house a spectrum of pro-government—and pro-regime—institutes, and from the subdued atmosphere of their conference rooms. Here, amid the teeming sidewalks below us, the "Study of the Future" has set up shop in the beating heart of today's Iran, with its relentless rhythm, its choking pollution, with all the overflowing energy of a vibrant, almost terrifying new world. Ali Paya is expecting us in an office reduced to the barest essentials: beige-toned walls and unmatched furniture. Tea is already waiting for us on a rickety oak table laden with stacks of books and papers. With a generous smile, he invites us to take a seat in front of the window.

Ali Paya holds a doctor's degree in philosophy, and belongs to that slender fringe of the Iranian intelligentsia that has taken upon itself the task of laying the theoretical foundations for a peaceful and thoroughgoing transformation of the innermost structure of the state. Their aim is to breathe new life into the Islamic Republic, to reshape the self-image of Iranian society, and to conceive a new relationship with authority. But there is no guarantee whatsoever that the vision held up by Ali Paya and his colleagues at the Institute will coincide with the aspirations of Iranians at a critical phase in their country's social and political evolution.

The group he directs is made up of intellectuals and researchers trained both in the West and in Iran. Each boasts a solid background in traditional thought, and an intimate familiarity with contemporary trends in economics and the social sciences. Far from the prying eyes of day-to-day politics, the Institute sees itself as creating the conceptual tools that will allow Iran to free itself from the clerical caste and set up a modern state. Its Western members have gained their experience through years of study abroad, particularly in Europe, Canada, and the United States. The ultimate intention is to create an original social model, one that can respond to the aspirations of Iran's young people without betraying the ideals of the revolution, and of the country that the revolution has created.

In his mid-forties, fluent in English, Ali Paya identifies himself as one of his country's intellectual "sentinels" stationed in the West for a part of the year, while teaching and directing research projects in Iran for the remainder. The danger of being absorbed by one culture at the expense of the other, of losing touch with the fast-evolving realities of Iranian society, is a common occupational hazard.

"I've been teaching in both Iran and Great Britain since 1995. My training is in the analytical philosophical tradition, but continental philosophy has always been strong in Iran; we were exposed to it early on.

"Philosophy has deep roots in Iranian civilization. When Imam Ghazali,[60] an eminent Muslim jurist of the fourth century of the Islamic calendar (eleventh century of the Christian era), issued a *fatwa* declaring that all philosophers were blasphemers, he made it impossible for philosophy to survive in the Sunni tradition. But in Iran, philosophical schools developed and engendered a distinct Persian philosophy."

The distinction is a crucial one, Ali Paya insists. The specific nature of the Iranian experience derives in part from the recognition of a distinct Persian philosophical tradition.

"This had a civilizing effect on the social psyche of the Iranians, who are, by their nature, non-aggressive. For instance, you need only compare what happened during the Islamic Revolution with all the so-called regime changes that have taken place throughout the region. Ours was the least violent.

---

60. Abu-Hamid al-Ghazali, born in Tus, in eastern Iran in 1058, saw himself as the defender of tradition and demolisher of "innovation." Though he agreed that there was much truth in the works of the Greek philosophers, he asserted that all that contradicted the teachings of Islam should be considered as belonging to disbelief. His principal adversaries were the Muslim Neoplatonists, notably al-Farabi and Ibn Sina (Avicenna). His polemical masterwork, *Tahafut al-Falasifa* (The Breakdown of the Philosophers), reaffirmed Sunni hostility toward philosophical rationalism. Ghazali was also, as a result of his profound religiosity, the forerunner of several Sufi orders. His work integrates the "external" framework of the observance of religious rules and the "internal" quality of the mystical experience. For further reading, see Malise Ruthven, *Islam in the World* (New York: Oxford University Press, 1984), 237–42.

"You can see this same love for philosophy in the way Iranians view power. In the Shi'a tradition, all temporal authority is illegitimate if it has not been appointed by one of the authentic Imams. In the absence of the Twelfth Imam, temporal authority can only be tolerated, never approved. This philosophical tradition, along with Shi'a teachings, has given Iranians a particular consciousness. They are skeptical about power, and at the same time, they strive to manage the affairs of state in the most effective way possible."

For many philosophers, he argues, the question of the legitimacy of those who govern is a capital one. To avoid clashes and conflicts between the public interest and the ruling classes, which in Iran have historically been non-clerical, they have spent much time and effort devising the best way to connect the two.

"When I was young, I was fascinated by the idea of a completely legitimate system of government, headed by a member of the clergy directly appointed by God's representative, thus establishing a continuity from on high to far below. But over time, we learned how to inquire more deeply into these sensitive questions. We began to doubt, to call the system itself into question.

"When you encounter a system of thought, there are several different ways to evaluate it critically. You can concentrate on its fundamental premises, you can scrutinize its internal connections to determine if the system is coherent, or you can examine the products of that system, its practical aspects, what you can obtain from it."

After close critical analysis, philosophers have come to the conclusion that the system as practiced in Iran today is indefensible, on all three counts. Moreover, Mr. Paya adds, there is no evidence in the history of Shi'ism to support the existence of such a regime.

"We need another model, one that is more appropriate to our needs, and more efficient. Mr. Khatami's election was a sort of miracle. He created a new breathing space, an opportunity to develop new talents that could approach these questions from another perspective. New ideas have appeared, and won a following: democracy, human rights, the rule of law, women's rights.

"It was the beginning of a period of intense intellectual activity. Researchers and scholars began to develop new models. If we examine what has been produced since the earliest days of the revolution, we can observe a progression from strict adherence to the teachings and an extremely literal interpretation of the texts, to a more rational, liberal interpretation of the Islamic faith."

Before the revolution, the religious intellectual movement had been powerfully influenced by ideology. Ideology, for them, had been their most precious possession, something to be protected at all costs, with total obedience. Hadn't the price been too great?

"Indeed it had. When you blindly follow an ideology, you abandon your status as an intellectual.

"But after the revolution the situation reversed itself. The values and norms of the middle class became the model. Having rid themselves of the ideologies of the 1970s, intellectuals began to evolve toward a more critical position.

"We can divide intellectual currents in Iran into four main trends: the leftists, the non-religious intellectuals, the religious intellectuals, and the nationalists. When I say 'intellectuals,' I mean those who possess a modern conception of the world, as opposed to the traditionalists, whom I exclude from this breakdown. Between the four groups there exists a continuity of ideas: you can find secularist intellectuals, in the sense that they do not believe in religion, and you can find, at the same time, nationalists and religious believers. Some left-wing intellectuals share religious concerns, others do not. It's a situation that has created a new definition of secularism in Iran.

"For me, 'secular' means rationality, rationalism. I don't see any conflict between having secularist positions and religious feelings. Others define secularism as being anti-religious. But most religious intellectuals accept the idea that secularism does not exclude religious feelings.

"The religious intellectuals who accept this definition believe that it represents the only way to deal with the reality of religion. When we examine the role of reason with regard to religion, we understand that reason must be free to question revelation; reason must make the final determination. They have raised a crucial question concerning the very nature of revelation: is it truly the Word of God? What does 'being religious' mean? What choices does it involve? My answer is clear, and I've expressed it and defended it repeatedly: our only guide is our reason."

That brings us to today's situation, which is one of great uncertainty. What kind of philosophical work remains to be done, given the state of religion in Iran, and the divisions it has produced between tradition and the modern world? Isn't religion itself part of the "fear of the wave"?

"Well, in our society there are groups that we can call, a bit simplistically, 'hard-liners.' They're not ready to budge even a centimeter. Just between us, I'm not certain that they really believe their own arguments. They seem to be much more interested in power than in tradition, piety, or the love of God, even if there are some true believers among them. They are the strongest opponents of any kind of change. They are even ready to turn back the clock. Between them and us are a large number of the undecided, people with doubts, people who are hesitant about which direction to follow. A significant part of our youth is in this situation today. This is one of our main concerns. The younger generation is beset by doubt; it doesn't know which way to turn.

"But training an elite is the most pressing task. We are living in a state of what I term 'epistemological confusion.' Iranian philosophers are not really philosophers in the classical sense of the word; after all, a philosopher is someone who lets reason take them where it will. But here, our philosophers draw red lines for themselves, lines they refuse to cross. When they do, they are delimiting the uses and aims of philosophy, and seriously reducing the exercise of critical thought."

You seem to be fighting on several fronts simultaneously. In your own camp, you must deal with epistemological confusion and mysticism. The analysis of ideas and the development of reason in harmony with tradition are not just the task of philosophy, but also of social and political action. If this isn't done, confusion and violence may take over in a way that philosophers never intended. But if you do, there is the danger that you will suffer from the same violence as the philosophers when they come to grips with society, with politics. How do you explain your approach in these turbulent times?

"Have you heard of Neurath's boat?[61] It's the story of sailors on the high seas caught in a storm, with no safe haven in sight. They must repair their boat as they sail on. That's what we're doing. We must stay on course, repair the damage, while fighting on several fronts, and in stormy conditions.

"Still, there are situations that we can turn to our advantage. They may appear to be threats, but they can be excellent opportunities. For example, the great waves of globalization and the pressure from outside are having a powerful impact on our society. Even the ultra-conservatives have come to the conclusion that change is inevitable. The pressure is so strong that they cannot just sit still and do nothing. They must make adjustments. They don't have any choice in the matter.

---

61. Otto Neurath, Austrian sociologist and "anti-philosopher."

"One of the greatest achievements of President Khatami and his intellectual entourage was to force those people to change their discourse. They managed to oblige them to use the concepts, terms, and ideas of modern thought. To such an extent that today they accept words like 'public sphere,' 'human rights,' 'rule of law', 'democracy' ... "

Is it possible that the arch-conservatives use the terms and concepts of their opponents all the better to criticize them and, ultimately, to wring their necks?

"That's exactly what they're attempting to do. They have their own philosophers, who keep them supplied with theories; some of them are even my friends, my colleagues. For example, let's look at the notion of democracy: in Persian, we've developed a translation: *mardomsalari-ye dini*. Which means roughly 'democracy': *mardom* means *demos*; *salari*, *-cracy*. But to that they've added *ye dini*, which makes it 'religious or Islamic democracy.' So the real meaning now refers to the idea of a power, of a government, of a state whose legitimacy comes not from the people, but from God."

Does that mean that the reformists, after seven years in government, have failed, that they accomplished too little, that they won't be able to do anything more before they lose power?

"At first glance, I would say you are right. The reformists have not produced tangible results that can clearly indicate the progress achieved. But if you look more closely, you can see that Mr. Khatami, with his reform project, has achieved a number of significant breakthroughs. He has created a new way of seeing Iranian society; he has transformed the mindset of an entire generation. Even the ultra-conservatives have not been able to escape this cycle of change. It's true, the reformists couldn't keep their promise of instituting social justice, of fighting economic corruption, of restraining the domineering behavior of the power structure; but they did succeed, up to a certain point, in helping people understand that they have rights, that they are no longer the subjects of the ruling elite; that they are citizens. Before then, citizenship didn't exist; it's a very recent achievement.

"Today, the ultra-conservatives have realized that the *demos*, the public, has a considerable, and unrealized power that can be actualized, that must be made use of. We observe that there is a healthy tendency toward the creation of NGOs, of local assemblies through which civil society can exercise its power."

Time has come for us to take leave of Ali Paya, and to plunge once more back into the tumult of the streets: a time for summing up—and for some last questions.

We have the impression that the reformist intellectuals have successfully opened up a critical dialogue on the very nature of power. Bearing in mind the authoritarian nature of the regime, the limitations they face are real enough, and there is always the possibility of coercive action. Criticizing can be dangerous. Could we imagine that, in a situation where the way forward is blocked, that reforms cannot go ahead, that the smallest spark could touch off a conflagration?

"What you suggest is a possibility, but it seems unlikely at this time. The armed forces are in control of the situation. Because of economic hardship, people are more concerned about surviving than about changing the regime. Uncertainty has made people more cautious, and less prepared to accept the consequences of radical action."

How far can dissidence, be it religious or political—or both—hope to go?

"Political dissidence isn't tolerated, but the voices of more and more intellectuals are being heard. Ganji the journalist is in prison because he stepped over the line. He named names, but if he had expressed his views abstractly, they might have been tolerated. Even in the religious establishment divisions are beginning to show. On the one side are those with a more pragmatic outlook, and on the other, the traditionalists. We see a new generation of clerics who are quite close to the religious intellectuals. They are attempting to change outlooks from within, and to convert their colleagues to a greater degree of openness. The highest ranks of the establishment are becoming more and more isolated, frozen in their hyper-conservative positions.

"A substantial number of ayatollahs support the reformists, explicitly or implicitly. This is good news for them, and bad news for the ultra-conservatives. But, as you know, the clergy is always quick to tell which way the wind is blowing, and it can adapt rapidly to shifts in the situation. What the ultra-conservatives absolutely do not want is for the reform movement to take the credit for any positive changes.

"Mr. Khatami has said that ideas like personal freedom, respect for human rights, equality of opportunity, and social justice are more important than seizing power, or hanging on to power. He wanted society as a whole to realize this.

"But unfortunately, in Iran, we have a long tradition of despotism. It will take us a long time to transform our despotic behavior toward women, children, and friends. We also have the bad habit of waiting for a hero to rescue us. Mr. Khatami and the reform movement have tried to tell the people: You are the hero.

"There's a story from the work of Attar, our great mystical poet, the story of the Symorgh.[62] The reformists have been attempting to convince the people that they are the Symorgh: 'In your multitude, you are the hero.' You need no one else. Perhaps as a result, the people ferociously opposed Mr. Rafsanjani, who was behaving in a dangerous manner, and putting the Republic at risk. The reformists attempted to stop him. Today, we tell the people, Our system is a republican one. Up until now, the conservatives have put the accent on the Islamic side. Now, the important thing is the republican side. We must find ways of persuading people to participate in public affairs, to become involved. In the Iranian context, it's a vital message."

If you succeed, the reform movement in Iran could become a model for other social-democratic regimes, especially in the Islamic world. Not to mention in the West!

Ali Paya bursts into laughter before answering.

"I'm a lot more modest. But I see what you're getting at. Yes, it could happen, providing Iranian intellectuals take themselves much more seriously, providing they establish a true presence on the international scene. But first, we must win the battle inside our own country, and it's not a simple matter.

"We must establish a true front, bringing together all the movements, we must be aware of the reality of our base, and evaluate our relationship with the power structure. Just like any boxer, you have to know your real weight before you step into the ring."

---

62. Farid od Din Attar, one of the great Iranian mystical poets of the thirteenth century, C.E. His masterwork, *Nantiq ut-Tayr* (The Assembly of the Birds) relates the perilous journey of a flock of birds seeking the Symorgh, the fabulous bird that they wish to crown as their king. Only thirty of them survive the voyage. When they come before the Symorgh, they see themselves in him: they are the Symorgh, and the Symorgh is thirty birds. (*Symorgh* in Farsi means "thirty birds.")

"Too Late"

FEBRUARY 2004. As Iran's upcoming parliamentary elections drew nearer, the defeat of the reform movement seemed more and more certain.[63] Incumbent reformist candidates disqualified by the Council of Guardians had been occupying the Majlis for several weeks. The public response ranged from indifference—as if to certify that the populace had lost confidence in the representatives of the reform movement—to outright disavowal, turning a cold light on President Khatami's lack of combativeness. Several government ministers had earlier attempted to hand in their resignations, which were immediately rejected by the Supreme Guide. The occupation had been dragging on for weeks, finally all but disappearing from view. Would the elections be postponed? A compromise between President Khatami, the Guide, and the Council of Guardians finally produced an eleventh-hour agreement: for the greater good of the Islamic Republic, the elections would go ahead as scheduled. No delay would be tolerated. Supreme authority had spoken.

With only a few days to go before an election that was once again to redraw Iran's political map, the atmosphere of disillusionment had cast a pall not only over the regime, but also over those who had once believed—and still believed—that the power structure could be reformed and rebuilt from within.

By now it had become clear that the principal victim of the public awakening stimulated by the reform movement seven years ago was none other than the movement itself. The broad coalition that made reform its slogan had been under the illusion that the voters who had cast their ballots for its candidates in the 2000 Majlis elections, or for Mr. Khatami in 2001, were its "base."

63. In the February 20 Majlis elections, 50.6 percent of registered voters cast their ballots nationally, as against 28 percent in the capital. The seventh Majlis will enjoy a strong conservative majority, leaving the government of President Khatami to face a hostile chamber.

For us, the events unfolding in this drama were hardly surprising. A few days earlier, we had taken a taxi to the Majlis to meet Fatima Haqihajou, one of the most outspoken members of the reformist faction, and a leader of the group of eighty reform MPs who were occupying the white marble building known as the "House of the Nation" that overlooks Imam Khomeini Avenue, in the southwestern quadrant of downtown Tehran. The occupation, which was accompanied by a hunger strike, enjoyed wide coverage by the reform press and the parliamentary radio network; predictably, state television, under strict regime control, had breathed not a word. In a country where much of the audience has no illusions about the objectivity of information, this could have been a positive development. But the symbolic power of the action was tarnished by the publication, on the front page of a reform daily, of a photograph showing the self-proclaimed hunger strikers wolfing down kebabs in a nearby restaurant.

The parliament buildings are located in the heart of a high-security zone. Access roads are barred, and checkpoints are multiple. When we arrived at the first of them we were immediately directed to another, at the opposite end of the government complex. In fact, we were now being told to report to the main entrance, the place where we had hoped to see crowds of people mobilized in support of the hunger-striking MPs or, at minimum, groups of curious citizens. When we arrived, there was not a soul to be seen. Armed soldiers stood rather lackadaisically on guard. We entered, walked up to the press counter, and explained that we had an appointment with Ms. Haqihajou.

"Do you have a letter?"

We had no letter. But we did have our press cards, and had confirmed our meeting by telephone one-half hour earlier. It would have been easy for the desk clerk to call Ms. Haqihajou, the hunger-striking MP. After all, she was waiting for us inside the parliament building.

"If you don't have a letter, you can't go in."

We restated our case, "We do not have a letter, but Ms. Haqihajou is expecting us; call and see … "

"You must have a letter."

To assuage our bruised dignity, we decided not to withdraw immediately despite the absurdity of the situation. Forty-five minutes later, we concluded that we had demonstrated good faith and good will. Once more we attempted to convince the zealous desk clerk. No luck. We were wasting our time.

As we stepped out onto the sidewalk, we spotted a small gathering, and several police officers. We walked over, relieved to be able at last to witness some expression of popular support. False alarm: a push-cart had been knocked over by a speeding minibus.

Two days later, we met Said Hajjarian at the headquarters of the Iran Participation Front, the spearhead of the reform movement, on Sommayeh Street in the heart of downtown Tehran.

We had expected to find a supercharged atmosphere to match the hectic last days of a campaign that would decide the political fate of several members of the movement's leading faction. But the building was silent; the corridors and offices empty; not even the ring of a telephone could be heard, as if to underscore the urgency of the moment. The concierge led us up to the first floor, and into a small room that was probably used for meetings of the party leadership. Fluorescent ceiling lights cast a pallid glare over a handful of chairs and two faded sofas. There, Said Hajjarian awaited us, along with the physiotherapist who remained constantly at his side, guiding his every step, his every movement.

We had last met Mr. Hajjarian two years earlier, only a few months after the attack that had irrevocably damaged his brain and destroyed much of his mobility and his ability to speak. What could the man who had so powerfully represented the reform movement, who had become its symbol in his pain, his resistance, and his stubborn refusal to die, possibly be thinking today? After all, this was the same man who had told us then, "They wanted to kill me. They left me for dead. God gave me a second life, and I will devote it to the progress of my country."

Bearing in mind the political situation, we had imagined a man on the verge of depression. Everything that had happened had betrayed his predictions, had cast doubt upon the very meaning of his fight, which in turn had been his only reason for surviving. We were delighted to see one another. But we were reluctant to reveal our thoughts even though within a few seconds we had plunged back into the warmth and intimate tone of our first encounters.

Then, as though he had read our minds, Mr. Hajjarian burst into peals of laughter that echoed off the walls of the empty meeting room, while with a halting gesture, he traced a circle in the air.

"Do you see anybody? So here we are, the largest party in parliament; we make up two of the largest factions, we have a majority of ministers in the government, we are leading a hunger strike, we're in a critical situation, and there's not a soul here, right here in our headquarters!"

Between each sentence he paused to catch his breath. Said Hajjarian's intelligence, his sense of repartee, his penetrating insight may have escaped the would-be murderer's bullet, but he can only speak with the greatest difficulty. It was as if he were wrenching each word away from the silence, as if his entire paralyzed body were being mobilized behind each sentence to be enunciated, articulated, projected. We hardly dared to compare his painfully incomplete recovery with the political health of the movement whose strategist he had become. As we looked at him it seemed clear that the reformists would have to go back to their dynamic beginnings, to rediscover their ability to speak up, loud and clear.

"If we look at the last few years, we see a see-saw effect," he said, enunciating painfully. "We had some progress, and some setbacks. The student movement has regressed; in fact, it is almost demolished. The civic movement has also had its difficulties; not only have they not been successful, they have regressed. The municipal elections confirmed these trends. Now there is cynicism.

"Look, our MPs are 'on strike' for the last two weeks, members of Mr. Khatami's cabinet have resigned, and people are indifferent.

"In the last two years, we've realized how isolated we are; we have gone backwards politically. Possibly it is the calm before the storm. But we have to admit that people have gone back to their private lives; they have given up on politics. You get the impression today that the Iranians have 'privatized' themselves.

"What's hot these days? Family reunions; artistic performances. Take the example of Mohammad Shajarian, the popular traditional singer. Just a few days ago, he performed before a crowd of four thousand people. In a few weeks, he'll be singing in a sports center that will hold fifteen thousand; he's even talking about staging a show in a soccer stadium with a capacity of a hundred thousand! People are ready to pay to hear their favorite singer. But if Mr. Khatami wanted to address the nation, he couldn't attract that kind of crowd, even if it was free!

"Did you ever see anything like that, tens of thousands of people lining up to hear singers perform outdoors? One hundred thousand people!? I'm not talking about pop stars; I'm talking about traditional artists. And when I say traditional, I mean traditional."

In the West, a handful of traditional music groups might be able to draw crowds, but rarely. Except when national feelings are involved, as in the recent past in Québec. Then you might see it.

"In Iran, things aren't quite the same. Our neighbors are Iraq and Afghanistan. We are a third world country; it's almost unheard-of for one hundred thousand people to congregate in one place to listen to a concert by a traditional singer, no matter how respected he is. People are listening to their hearts. What they want is what their heart desires. They're not interested in anything else.

"The novel market is strong; the cinema, the theater. These things are hot these days. But for the reformist party, nothing, zero. Our party is the largest in Iran, and you can see for yourself what we have to show for it."

He paused to rest, then slowly gestured around him. "No one cares, is that it?" we asked. "No one can be bothered?"

He nodded agreement.

"People just don't care."

Then he burst into laughter.

"Look, I am a member of this party. But I would rather go listen to Shajarian in concert than sit through one of our meetings! Of course, I am a party member so I would attend out of a sense of discipline; I would not walk out of the meeting, especially since we are having elections in a few days. But I am telling you the truth; that is the way things are.

"When you build a house that's constantly being demolished, you end up losing your motivation; when you know it will be destroyed ten times over, you lose the will to rebuild, to reconstruct. For six years now, ever since Mr. Khatami's election, we've been building this house, and it has been ruined dozens of times, over and over again. What remains of your motivation?"

Is it because of the weakness of your strategy? Shouldn't you have known your opponents' strength? After all, you were close enough to them in the past. Did you underestimate them and their power?

"Do you mean, did we underestimate the right-wingers, the conservatives?"

Exactly.

"We may have been too proud of those twenty-two million votes cast for President Khatami. The right wing took advantage of that to rethink its strategy. It became stronger—and more violent. It used terror, it adapted its strategy to the situation. That's how and why we underestimated them. They carried out the serial murders. We certainly underestimated them on that score.

"Political succession in third world countries is absolutely different than in the developed countries. Take Clinton; when his term ended he left office and went back to private life. The same for Al Gore; he went back to his law firm. But here, in a third world country, it's different.

Politicians can't accept defeat; they become violent, they kill. Not like in your country.

"Peaceful succession is one of the indices of development. If you see it happening without violence, you can conclude that the country is truly developed. If not, then it belongs to the third world. That's our problem."

Isn't there another problem, directly related to the nature of the state? Considering the specific nature of the Islamic state, how can the reform movement ever hope to progress? Not only does the state have a monopoly on violence; it also has religion on its side.

"Religion is not what determines what happens at the highest level of the state. Religion and the state are on the same level. After the death of Imam Khomeini Iran has become like Tsarist Russia. Religion has become a component of the state bureaucracy. It is not a cooperative institution, but a coercive one."

But in order for the reform movement to grow, shouldn't this situation first of all be changed?

"Soroush, Kadivar, and Shabastari will see to that."

Fine. But they are working on two different levels: politics and rational truth. When you compare the state here with the Russian system, aren't you suggesting that it's dark on the outside and also rotten inside? If that's so, perhaps it might even collapse by itself. For all the violence and the tragedy, isn't there room for hope?

"We are reformists, not revolutionaries. That's why we don't want it to be rotten inside; we don't want it to collapse. We want to reform the system gradually, in a peaceful way. We've already had one revolution; we don't want another. Never again!"

But how will you convince the citizens to participate in public life?

"The public sphere is never empty. It may be occupied by an oligarchy, by a democracy, or by an autocracy, but it is never empty. Iran has a long history of struggle for democracy. Our constitutional revolution took place in 1906. The same revolution took place in Russia in 1905, and in Turkey in 1908. No other country in the region has this tradition. Iraq and Syria weren't even independent back then.

"But let's forget about the past and concentrate on the present. Look at the nationalization of Iran's oil industry. We were the first. Egypt followed suit when they nationalized the Suez Canal. Nasser himself admitted that he borrowed the Iranian approach. Or consider the revolution in Iran. The shah was a good friend of the United States; in fact, he was America's gendarme in the region. Twenty-five years ago Carter visited Iran, and hailed it as an 'island of stability.' The revolution broke out almost immediately after that, and in a few weeks the shah was gone.

"They accuse us of having links with al-Qaida. False. There have never been any such links. The public mobilization that brought President Khatami to power proves that we have a powerful social movement. In Iran, the people have been a key political actor for a long time. Today, we're seeing a return to the family, a kind of disillusionment with politics. But I'm convinced it's a short-term thing, that it won't last forever."

What can you do to reverse the trend toward the rejection of politics?

"Confidence. Only a return of confidence can do it. Over the last few years, the people have lost confidence in us, and in Khatami. People expected us to move more rapidly. We moved very slowly instead."

We could hear the telephone ringing in the office next door. No one answered.

"But if we'd moved quicker, we would have had to contend with violence. There would probably have been murders, and we would have had to face the consequences of another revolution. Reform, which is supposed to be an evolution, could have quickly turned into revolution. We didn't want to go down that road."

We've met many people, from the poorer segments of the population and from the middle classes, who have told us how frustrated they were with the slowness of reform, with the "evolution," as you put it. They said they were prepared to go into the streets peacefully if the president were to call on them. They simply wanted to say yes to the government, to support the president and to show the regime where they stood. It would have been a democratic way, and a convincing way, to demonstrate the cohesion of society around such a demand. Why did President Khatami sit on his hands? Some people even accused him of being "soft" on the mullahs!

"I know that's what we should have done. But the president could not have made the appeal without putting the entire country in jeopardy. The risk was that it would worsen the situation. We could have seen the kind of killings that blackened the early days of the revolution. Provocateurs would have infiltrated the crowd to smash the windows of banks, and attack the police to show how supporters of the reform movement behaved. That was the only reason for not calling a mass demonstration of public support during the last seven years."

If the entire government were to resign tomorrow, what would happen?

"Nothing will happen."

Is it too late?

"It's too late.

"Six years earlier, there might have been a popular outcry. Today, there will be nothing. You can see for yourselves: over the last two weeks, no one went to support the MPs who were hunger-striking. You saw for yourselves: there was no one in front of the parliament."

But what will the leaders of the reform movement do? Where will they go, which direction?

"We're going to prison."

Said Hajjarian's laughter was more brittle now; his eyes, in the silence that had fallen, mirrored his sadness and his alarm.

"It's too late," he whispered.

Then he fell silent. Breathing heavily as if to catch his breath, he slumped back onto the sofa. We were about to end the interview for fear of exhausting our host, when, in a soft voice, Hajjarian murmured, "When will you be back?"

"In a few months, we hope."

"We'll meet again, God willing."

He fell silent once more, his eyes fixed on us. Behind his broken voice, his abrupt, mechanical gestures, the motionless tilt of his head, we could still imagine how this once-powerful man, this once-brilliant orator, had been the instigator and the driving force of the reform movement. He had strived for an evolutionary process against a hardened regime, against a power elite determined to eliminate anything that might threaten its survival and its stranglehold on the wealth of the nation.

The reformists' battle had ended in defeat.

But the reform movement itself has had a powerful impact on Iranian society. The fear of the wave is much less acute than seven years before. And yet the road to be traveled will be long, winding, and full of pitfalls. The international situation, and above all the American thrust for power in the Middle East, will certainly shape events to come. When George W. Bush included Iran in the "Axis of Evil," his intention was to abolish any prospect of autonomous democratic development.

Four years ago, the "masters of darkness" of the conservative regime ordered Said Hajjarian shot down in broad daylight. They knew exactly what they were doing; they had neutralized perhaps the only man who could have given the disparate and divided reform movement the cohesion and strength of a party capable of governing, a party that could bring about what we might call "a quiet revolution."

The driver and the physiotherapist, in a ritual we had come to know, were ready to take Said Hajjarian home. One at each side, they grasped him under his arms to help him to his feet, holding fast to his elbows as he moved slowly forward. Then, turning his back on us, he walked through the door, a prisoner-for-life of the violence that he had hoped his country would avoid, with his hearty laugh as his sole weapon.

As he stepped out into the Tehran night his laugh echoed in the empty room. Had it been Said Hajjarian's way of telling us his secret hope?

Epilogue

IN JUNE 2005 THAT HOPE LAY SHATTERED. Mahmoud Ahmadinejad, a hard-line conservative candidate, had been elected president on a program of fighting poverty and rooting out corruption. The new head of government moved rapidly to match deeds to words. A member of Iran's revolutionary generation who had preached a return to revolutionary purity, Mr. Ahmadinejad fired dozens of career diplomats and dismissed a large number of high-ranking civil servants suspected of belonging to influential networks.

And, in a rhetorical flourish calculated to warm the heart of Iran's most obdurate fundamentalist factions, he quoted Imam Khomeini's admonition that the "Zionist regime should vanish from the pages of history," issuing a direct challenge to the United States as he did. Not stopping there, he raised doubts about the Holocaust, and lashed out at the way in which Europe had shifted its historical responsibility onto the shoulders of the Palestinians.

"Look here," he told the German periodical *Der Spiegel*, "my views are quite clear. We are saying that if the Holocaust occurred, then Europe must draw the consequences and that it is not Palestine that should pay the price for it. If it did not occur, then the Jews have to go back to where they came from."[64]

The president's tone was provocative; throughout the West his words were predictably labeled as antisemitic.

But there was more to Mr. Ahmadinejad's outbursts than met the eye. What seemed simplistic, even caricatural at first glance was in fact the result of cold political calculation rather than of deep personal conviction. His predecessor, President Khatami, had launched a dialogue of civilizations, a policy of openness to the "other"—up to and including even the United States. But the policy had failed when George W. Bush

---

64. Stefan Aust, Gerhard Spörl, and Dieter Bednarz, "We Are Determined," interview with Mahmoud Ahmadinejad, *Der Spiegel*, May 31, 2006.

included Iran in his "Axis of Evil." The picture would soon become clearer, along with American threats of "preventive war" to reassert control of Iran's petroleum resources.

Enter Mahmoud Ahmadinejad, declaring that Iran had nothing to gain from good behavior. Adopting another strategy, with the tacit support of the Supreme Guide, he began to exploit the rising anger against the West, and against the United States in particular, felt by significant sections of Iranian and Arabo-Muslim public opinion. It did not take long for his refusal to submit to the American and Israeli nuclear threat to win him friends.

Mr. Ahmadinejad is no neophyte in the corridors of power in Iran. Like his most radical reformist adversaries Said Hajjarian and Akbar Ganji, he made his way up through the ranks of the state security forces. Like them, he belongs to the revolutionary generation that was barely twenty years old when the shah fell, and which, today, has certified the failure of the Islamic Revolution they had so bitterly defended.

Though they may have agreed on the diagnosis, they disagreed on the remedy. For Said Hajjarian—as we had witnessed firsthand—democracy had to be brought to Iranian society through reform of its institutions and political culture. It was to be, implicitly, a return to the main thrust of 1979, the desire to throw off the heritage of the monarchy and break with the decades—centuries—of absolute power. For Mahmoud Ahmadinejad, the answer was a return to religious roots and to revolutionary purity. His message appeals to the non-Westernized elements in Iranian society, to those who have been left behind—and they are legion. His strategy is an authoritarian one, a return to what he sees as the cornerstone of the Islamic Revolution.

The election of the new president dealt the reformists a severe blow. In desperation, they called on their supporters to vote for the "lesser evil," in the person of Ali Akbar Hashemi Rafsanjani, in the second round run-off. But Iranians found it difficult, if not impossible, to put their trust in the controversial figure of the former president, a man who had spent the last twenty-five years in the upper echelons of the clergy-big business alliance, and who had been president for eight disastrous years. The electorate massively rejected Mr. Rafsanjani for a third time; the reform movement that supported him emerged further weakened, if not crushed.

Mr. Ahmadinejad's election has brought to the presidency a man of modest means and appearance, a non-cleric and devout Shi'ite whose success confirmed the emergence of the powerful movement he helped found, called the Abadgaran-e Iran-e Islami (Developers of Islamic Iran). Most often described as "right-wing," if not "extreme right-wing," the Abadgaran's program could be best described as populist and anticapitalist, with a clearly "left-wing" emphasis on social justice. During his victorious campaign, Mr. Ahmadinejad accused the religious caste of profiting from a system that has brought ruin to the people, lined the pockets of a new privileged class, and betrayed the social commitments of a revolution that had promised to promote the welfare of the dispossessed.[65]

The reformists gave voice to the hopes of the many Iranians who longed to enjoy political and individual freedoms; the Abadgaran's outlook can best be described as technocratic and religious. But while the Rafsanjani and Khatami governments applied elements of the structural adjustment programs promoted by the World Bank and the International Monetary Fund, the new president's strategists plan to offer the country's poorest citizens the opportunity to become shareholders in public enterprises.

The reformists spoke a language Western visitors could understand. The new president's men run the risk of being ill-understood, if not misunderstood in the West: a prospect about which they seem crashingly unconcerned. The reformists had committed themselves to govern in a spirit of respect for the constitution and the rule of law. The Developers of Islamic Iran have promised to return to square one; to make Islam, as they understand and interpret it, the governing principle of social and political life.

Mohammad Khatami, a philosopher in clergyman's robes, launched a dialogue of civilizations. Mahmoud Ahmadinejad, a man with a reputation for efficiency and self-effacement, tends to speak of the Mahdi, the Hidden Imam whose imminent return lies at the heart of Shi'a millennarist thought.[66]

Surprisingly, and for the first time in Iran, the vast majority of neo-conservatives are non-clerics; perhaps more surprisingly, they have openly criticized the clerical caste that has monopolized state power. Even the

65. William O. Beeman, "The Revolution Begins Anew in Iran," Agence Global, November 8, 2005.

66. Mr. Ahmadinejad's government accredits the tradition, and has identified the precise location of the Occultation, in a well close to the holy city of Qom. There, the local authorities have begun infrastructure works to promote pilgrimage and, perhaps, the reappearance of the last Imam.

legitimacy of the Supreme Guide has not escaped their anti-mullah broadsides. Far from sharing the political, religious, or moral authority of Imam Khomeini, Ali Khamene'i is widely perceived as the man who has allowed corruption and nepotism to fester. Under his rule, "Islamic" Iran had become the republic of fast-rial artists fattened on petrodollars.

The Iranian state, ostensibly guided by religion, today faces a multi-layered crisis: drug addiction, prostitution, influence peddling, urban violence, pollution, and inequality. The Ahmadinejad campaign implicitly asked the question: How could a regime that claimed Islamic credentials have tolerated such ills?

Mr. Khatami's only argument was the weapon of persuasion. Mahmoud Ahmadinejad can rely upon the Revolutionary Guards, and upon the Basiji militia, two redoubtable military and political forces that constitute a state within a state. He can also count on the weight of tradition transmitted by networks of influence in the country's mosques. The new president's support networks are far indeed from the urbane, Westernized, English-speaking upper-middle class neighborhoods of north Tehran.

In the long term, a return to purity may be hard to achieve, and even more difficult to force down Iranians' throats. Mr. Ahmadinejad, who campaigned hard against nepotism, appointed his brother to head up his political bureau. Many of his followers, connected with the Revolutionary Guards and lacking qualifications, have been appointed to sensitive, high-level positions. Yet another source of concern for those who voted for him may arise from his close ties with Ayatollah Taqi Mesbah-Yazdi, who is thought to covet the post of Guide.

The reformists suffered from a crucial weakness: they had no popular base. It was a fatal flaw that neither the personality of Mohammad Khatami nor the strategic brilliance of Said Hajjarian could overcome. Today's complex Iranian society is split down the middle; a gap has opened between promises and their fulfillment, between pious wish and policy. It is a gap that President Khatami may have intuited but could not act to bridge. His successor, with the backing of a majority of voters, as well as of the security forces, enjoys much greater real power to work toward his declared objectives: roll back poverty, rehabilitate social justice, eradicate corruption. Will he be able to do so? Does he truly wish to?

Behind the curtain, Iran may well find itself on the eve of a massive reappraisal of its governing system, carried out by that same system. The religious caste's days may be numbered. Since 2005, all indications point to a rocky road ahead for the Tehran regime.

Tehran, February 2004
Montréal, June 2006

Appendix

Persons Mentioned

Al-e Ahmad, Jalal (1923–1969): Nationalist ideologist; author of "West-Sickness."

Ali Ibn abi-Talib (d. 661): Fourth Caliph; First Imam; cousin of the Prophet, father of Imams Hassan and Hossein. Ali is the symbolic figurehead of Shi'a Islam. Shi'ites consider themselves to be the "the partisans of Ali," the rightful successor to Muhammed, and, in their eyes, unjustly deprived of the succession.

Al-Banna, Hassan: Born in Tanta, Egypt; assassinated in Cairo in 1949; founder of the Muslim Brotherhood, an organization that opposed the secularizing trend in the Muslim world and that led a fierce campaign of resistance against the British occupation.

Ebadi, Shirin: Judge under Shah Mohammad-Reza Pahlavi; won prominence as a lawyer and human rights advocate in the Islamic Republic. Winner of the 2003 Nobel Peace Prize.

Ebtekar, Massoumeh: Vice-president of the Islamic Republic and head of the Environment Department under the Khatami government. Editor of *Farzaneh*, an Islamic feminist publication. In 1979, at the age of eighteen, she participated in the capture of the United States Embassy in Tehran. As spokeswoman of the occupying students, she became widely known as "Mary" by the international media.

Erdogan, Recep Tayyip: Prime minister of Turkey and leader of the Justice and Development Party (AK Parti). Former mayor of Istanbul and moderate Islamist; was imprisoned following the 1997 "post-modern coup."

Fallahian, Ali: Interior minister in the government of President Hashemi Rafsanjani.

Ganji, Akbar: Investigative journalist, jailed for having publicly denounced Hashemi Rafsanjani. A former member of the Revolutionary Guard intelligence services, he became a pillar of the reform movement, and spent six years in prison.

Ha'afez (Shams od-Din Muhammad, d. 1391): The great mystic poet of Shiraz; his masterpiece, *The Divan*, is loved and recited by Iranians in all walks of life.

Hossein, Ibn Ali (620–680): Son of Ali, Fourth Caliph; died on the battlefield of Karbala in Iraq on the tenth day of Moharram (October 10, 680). His martyrdom would become one of the founding symbols of Shi'a Islam.

Ismail, Shah: Founder of the Safavid Dynasty; in 1501, created the first Shi'a state and instituted Shi'ism as the state religion.

Kadivar, Mohsen: Religious intellectual; ally of Said Hajjarian, Abdolkarim Soroush, and other reformist intellectuals; has produced a radical deconstruction of the *Velayat-e faqih*.

Karbaschi, Gholam-Hossein: Former Tehran mayor and ally of Hashemi Rafsanjani; fired and jailed in 1998, later released on order of Supreme Guide Ali Khamene'i.

Karoubi, Mehdi: Speaker of the sixth Majlis; suspected of involvement in the secret October Surprise negotiations with the United States Republican Party that in 1980 ended the occupation of the U.S. Embassy in Tehran.

Kazemi, Zahra: Canadian photographer and photojournalist of Iranian origin; died in Iranian intelligence service custody in 2003.

Kiarostami, Abbas: Filmmaker, best known for *A Taste of Cherry* (1997).

Khamene'i, Ali: Supreme Guide, former ally of Ayatollah Khomeini; third president of the Islamic Republic (1981–1989).

Khatami, Mohammad: Fifth president of the Islamic Republic (1997–2005).

Khoeiniha, Mousavi: Hojjatoleslam, publisher of *Salam* daily, counselor to the students following the capture of the U.S. Embassy in 1980–1981.

Khomeini, Ayatollah Ruhollah: Founder of the Islamic Republic; in the early 1960s, assumed leadership of the religious opposition to the imperial Pahlavi regime and its links with the United States and Israel. Exiled to Turkey after popular uprisings in 1963, he moved to Iraq, then to France. From his residence in Neauphle-le-Château outside Paris, he directed the final phases of the Islamic Revolution. Khomeini also perfected the doctrine of the *Velayat-e faqih*, under which the supreme jurist-consult (*vali*) wields power as a representative of the Holy Imams of Shi'a tradition. On his return to Iran, he was welcomed as the "Imam" and venerated by much of the population. More than ten million Iranians attended his funeral in 1989, at Behesht-e Zahra cemetery, where an immense mausoleum was later erected.

Makhmalbaf, Mohsen: Filmmaker, most recently of *Kandahar* (2002).

Montazeri, Hossein-Ali: Grand ayatollah currently under house arrest in Qom. Designated successor to Ayatollah Khomeini, he was dismissed in 1988 after condemning the execution of several thousand prisoners belonging to the MKO, and criticizing the Iran-Iraq war. Sharply critical of Ali Khamene'i's administrative methods, he has rejected the absolute power of the *Velayat-e faqih*, which he believes should be an elective office.

Mortazavi, Said: Revolutionary prosecutor, "hangman of the press"; suspected of direct involvement in the death of Ms. Zahra Kazemi.

Mossadeq, Mohammad: Prime minister under Shah Mohammad-Reza Pahlavi; piloted Iran's nationalization of its petroleum resources. Overthrown in a CIA-organized *coup d'etat* in 1953.

Nouri, Fazlollah: Anti-constitutionalist ayatollah, executed July 31, 1909.

Pahlavi, Shah Mohammad-Reza: Son of Reza Shah; replaced his pro-Nazi father in 1941 at British and American behest. Overthrown by the Islamic Revolution in 1979, he died of cancer in Egypt on July 27, 1980.

Rafsanjani, Ali Akbar Hashemi: Fourth president (1981–1989) of the Islamic Republic and one of the regime's leading figures. Under his presidency, economic liberalization and privatization programs were introduced.

Reza Khan: Founder of the Pahlavi Dynasty. Head of the Persian Cossack Brigade, he seized power in 1921 and declared himself Reza Shah in 1925, bringing to an end the Qajar Dynasty. Following the lead of Atatürk in Turkey, he sought to modernize Iran. Suspected of Nazi sympathies, he was replaced by his son Mohammad-Reza in 1941.

Shariati, Ali (1933–1977): Born into a clerical family, influenced by the nationalist struggles of the early 1950s; educated in the "Western" educational curriculum in Iran, and obtained his doctorate in France. Drawn to the anti-colonial struggle in Algeria, he became friends with Frantz Fanon ("The Wretched of the Earth"). On returning to Iran in 1964, he created the Hosseiniyeh-e Ershad, a religious institution from which he attacked the traditionalist clergy ("black Shi'ism") and propounded the model of "red Shi'ism" as embodied in the lives of Imams Hassan and Hossein. The police closed the hosseiniyeh in 1972. Imprisoned, then sent into exile, Shariati died in London in

1977, an event widely attributed to the SAVAK, the shah of Iran's secret police. In death, he went on to become one of the symbolic leaders of Iran's revolutionary youth; his influence was second only to that of Imam Khomeini.

Shariatmadari, Hossein: Editor-in-chief of *Kayhan*; official representative of the Supreme Guide. As a member of the anti-shah resistance, he was tortured. Under the Islamic regime, he assumed responsibility for the "interrogation" of dissident intellectuals.

Soroush, Abdolkarim: Dissident philosopher. Studied pharmacology and philosophy of history in England; returned to Iran prior to the Islamic Revolution, where he sharply criticized Marxism in the universities. Named to the Cultural Revolution Council, which coordinated purges of professors. Soon after, he resigned to join the opposition. Has become the inspiration of a generation devoted to the freedom of thought he argues for in his critical writings on the religious state and the interpretation of the sacred texts; since then, he has been frequently threatened with death, and forbidden from teaching. Dr. Soroush currently lives and teaches in exile.

Taleqani, Ayatollah Mahmoud: Leading figure in the struggle against the imperial regime; spent several years in prison, alongside young leftists. While respecting Ayatollah Khomeini, he did not share his ideas on state administration, and opposed the *Velayat-e faqih*. Died September 9, 1979.

Yazid Ibn Mu'awiyyah: Second Omayyed Caliph (680–683), son of Mu'awiyyah (661–680), ordered the killing of Imam Hossein; a figure of opprobrium among Shi'ites.

Selected Chronology

622	The Hegira (Hijra); the Prophet Muhammed emigrates from Mecca to Medina and establishes a state; the Islamic era begins.
637	Arabo-Islamic conquest of Iran; collapse of the Sassanid Empire.
680	Death of Imam Hossein at Karbala; Hossein goes on to become the symbol of Shi'ism.
1501	Establishment of the Safavid Dynasty; creation of a Shi'ite state in Iran.
1732	Fall of the Safavid Dynasty.
1794	Establishment of the Qajar Dynasty.
1906	Promulgation of the Constitution; beginning of the constitutional period.
1921	Reza Khan seizes power in a British-supported *coup d'état*; end of the constitutional period.
1924	End of the Qajar Dynasty.
1925	Reza Khan proclaims himself shah and establishes the Pahlavi Dynasty.
1941	Pro-German Reza Shah removed from power by the Allies, replaced by his son Mohammad-Reza.
1953	Anglo-American *coup d'état* against Prime Minister Mohammad Mossadeq; the shah becomes an absolute monarch; Iran, "gendarme of the Persian Gulf."
1963	The shah's "White Revolution" introduced over violent protests.
1963	Popular uprisings sweep Iran following the arrest of Ayatollah Khomeini.
1971	Mohammad-Reza Pahlavi crowns himself shah at Persepolis.
1970–80	Oil shocks.

1979	Capture of the American Embassy by a group of Muslim students; fall of the Provisional Government; the Shi'a clergy takes power.
1980	Military coup in Turkey.
1980 (April)	Tabas incident: an American mission to rescue the embassy hostages comes to grief in the desert.
1980 (July 9–10)	Nowjeh coup attempt fails.
1980 (July 22)	Assassination in Washington of Ali Akbar Tabatabaï, by David Theodore Belfield, alias Davud Salahuddin, who later becomes Hassan Abdulrahman in Iran.
1980 (September)	Iraqi invasion of Iran.
1980 (October)	Secret U.S.-Iran negotiations with the hostages as bargaining chips; the October Surprise breaks the impasse.
1981	Release of the hostages as Ronald Reagan is being inaugurated as president of the United States.
1986	Iran-Contra scandal in the United States: arms are exchanged for American hostages held in Lebanon.
1988	UN Resolution 598 ends the Iran-Iraq war. Ayatollah Montazeri relieved of his duties as "designated successor."
1989 (June)	Death of Ayatollah Khomeini.
1989 (July)	Ali Akbar Hashemi Rafsanjani elected president of the Islamic Republic.
1989 (August)	Ali Khamene'i appointed Supreme Guide by the Council of Experts.
1995 (January)	Russia resumes construction of the Bushehr nuclear plant.
1995 (April)	The United States decrees a total embargo against Iran, labeling it a "terrorist country."
1997	Election of Mohammad Khatami as president with 70 percent of votes cast: beginning of the reform movement; Mr. Khatami launches the "dialogue of civilizations."
1998	Serial killings of secularist intellectuals by Information Ministry operatives.

1999 (July)	Closure of *Salam* daily newspaper; anti-student repression; rioting in Tehran and in other Iranian cities.
2000 (February)	Election of the sixth Majlis, with a majority of reform candidates.
2000 (March)	Assassination attempt against Said Hajjarian.
2001	Re-election of Mohammad Khatami.
2002	George W. Bush includes Iran in the "Axis of Evil."
2003	Municipal elections; reformists defeated in Tehran.
2004	Election of the seventh Majlis, with a majority of conservative deputies.
2005	Election of Mahmoud Ahmadinejad as president, with 60 percent of votes cast.

About the Authors

Jean-Daniel Lafond

Jean-Daniel Lafond was born in France in 1944. In 1974 he chose voluntary exile in Canada where he has since pursued a distinguished career as a filmmaker and author. His films include *Les traces du rêve (Dreamtracks)*, 1985; *Le voyage au bout de la route (A Journey to the End of the Road)*, 1987; *Le visiteur d'un soir (The Man Who Came One Night)*, 1989; *La Manière Négre ou Aimé Césaire, chemin faisant (A State of Blackness: Aimé Césaire's Way)*, 1991; *Tropique Nord (Tropic North)*, 1994; *La liberté en colère (Angry Liberty)*, 1994; *Haïti dans tous nos rêves (Haiti in Our Dreams)*,1995; *L'Heure de Cuba (Last Call for Cuba)*, 1999; *Le temps des barbares (The Barbarian Files)*, 1999; *Salam Iran, une lettre persane (Salam Iran, a Persian Letter)*, 2002; *Le faiseur de théâtre (The Theatermaker)*, 2002; *Le cabinet du Docteur Ferron (The Cabinet of Doctor Ferron)*, 2003; and *Le fugitif (American Fugitive)*, 2006.

Alongside his films, he has created several original documentary radio series broadcast by France-Culture and Radio-Canada, and has published several books on the cinema.

Co-founder of Les Rencontres internationales du documentaire de Montréal, he was awarded the Prix Lumières in 1999. In 2005 he was named a Companion of the Order of Canada. He is married to Michaëlle Jean, Governor General of Canada.

Fred A. Reed

Fred A. Reed was born in California, in 1939, and moved to Canada in 1963. After several years of trade-union activity, he took up a career as a free-lance journalist, translator, and author. His reports from Iran, Turkey, Syria, and the Balkans were published in Montréal's two leading French-language dailies, *La Presse* and *Le Devoir*. He also produced several major radio documentaries for the CBC flagship program *Ideas*.

His first book, *Persian Postcards: Iran after Khomeini* was published in 1994; it was followed by *Salonica Terminus: Travels into the Balkan Nightmare* (1996), *Anatolia Junction: A Journey into Hidden Turkey* (1999), and *Takeover in Tehran: The Inside Story of the 1979 U.S. Embassy Capture* (2000), an as-told-to account by Massoumeh Ebtekar. His most recent book, *Shattered Images*, was published in 2003.

Fred A. Reed is a three-time winner of the Governor General's Literary Award for translation, twice for works by the late Thierry Hentsch. He is married to V. Ingeborg Brunner and lives in Montréal.